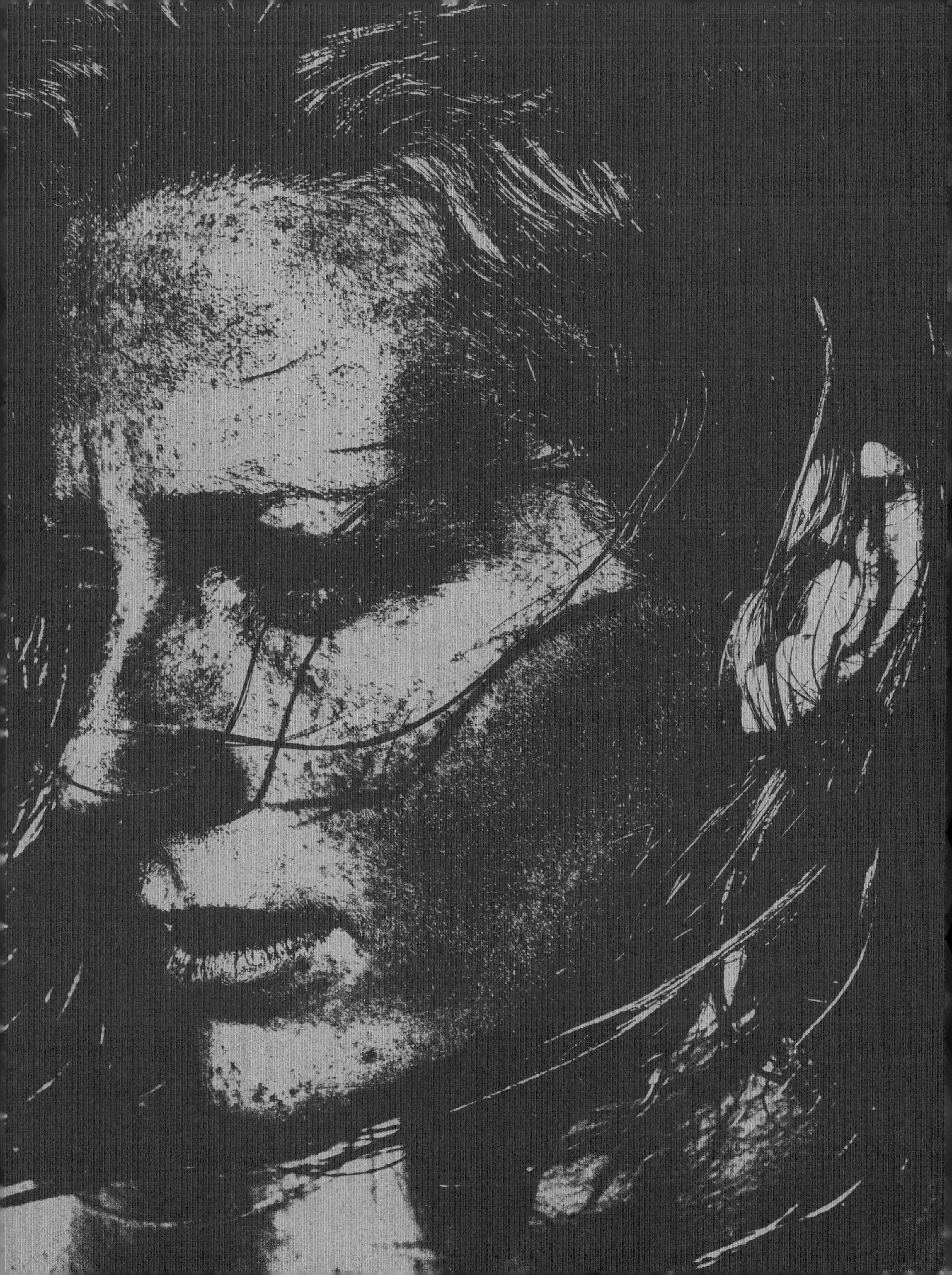

architecture + beauty

john balsom

GOST

Architecture and beauty

This project captures the architecture of public diving boards in New South Wales, Australia including Parramatta pool, Leichhardt pool and Lambton Swimming Centre near Newcastle.

Many diving platforms, built in the 1950s and 60s are deteriorating from the corrosion caused by salty sea air and are being dismantled for health and safety reasons—the crystallisation of salt within the board's porous structure can generate enough force to destroy surrounding material, causing the exterior to break down over time.

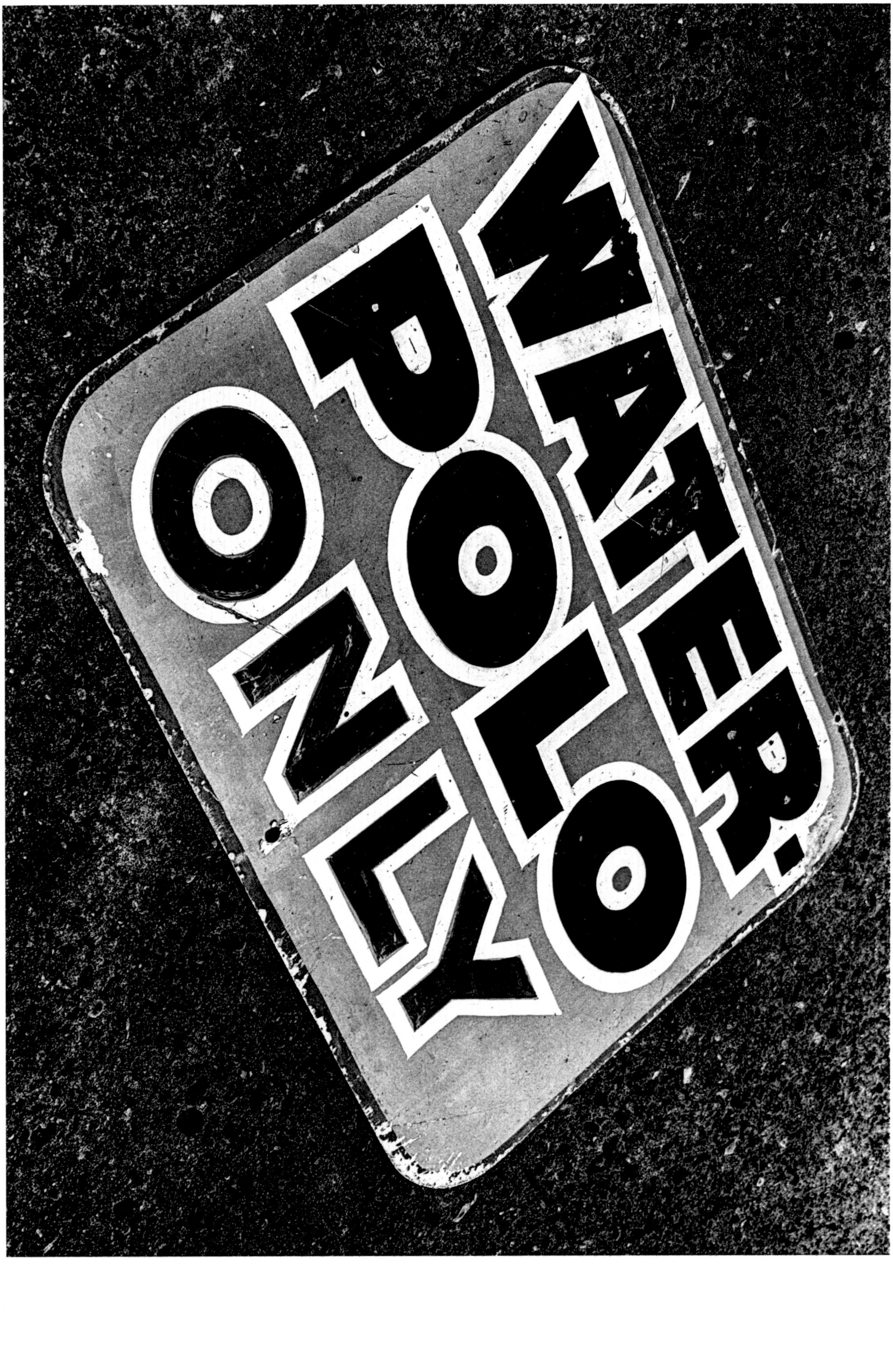
WATER
POLO
ONLY

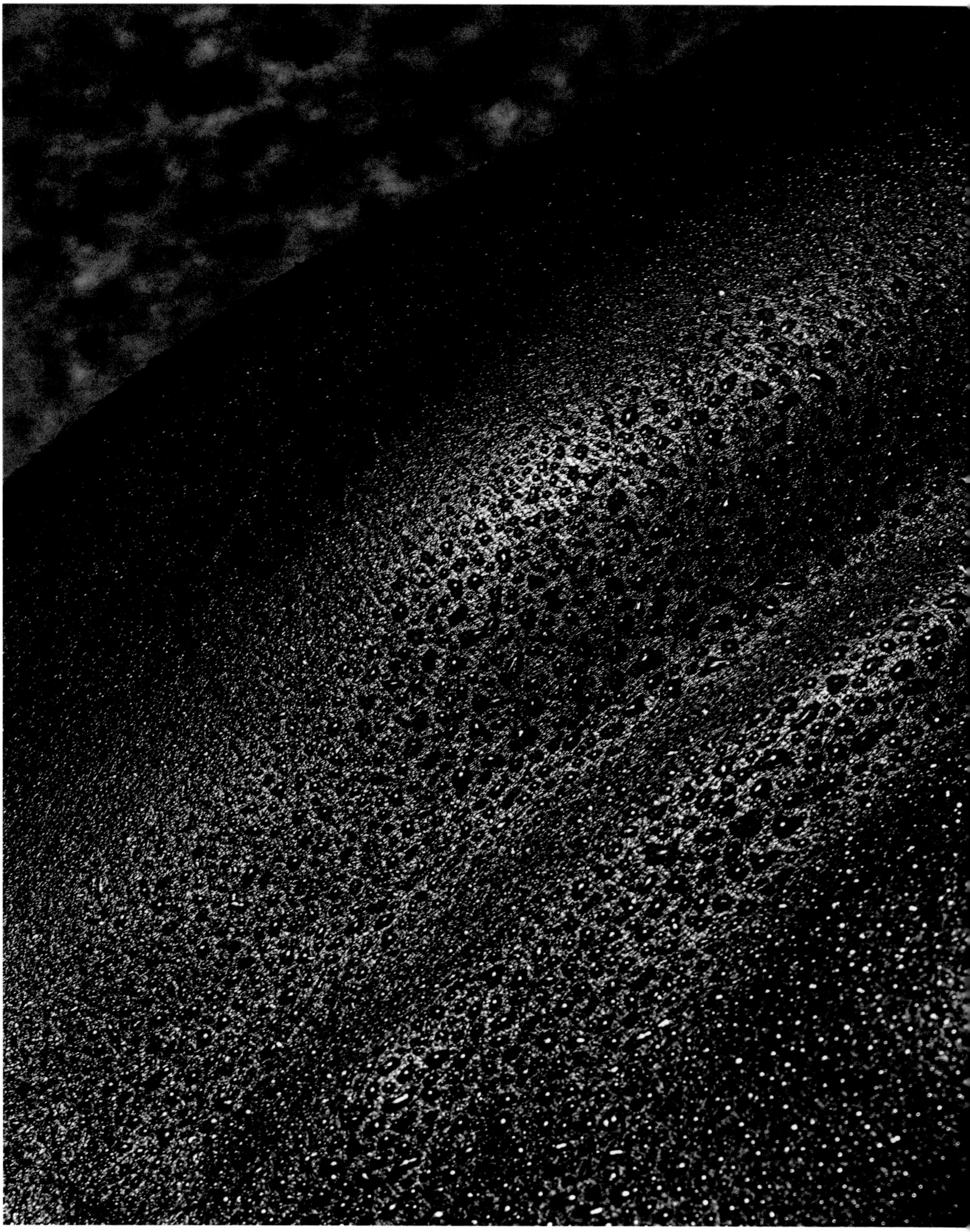

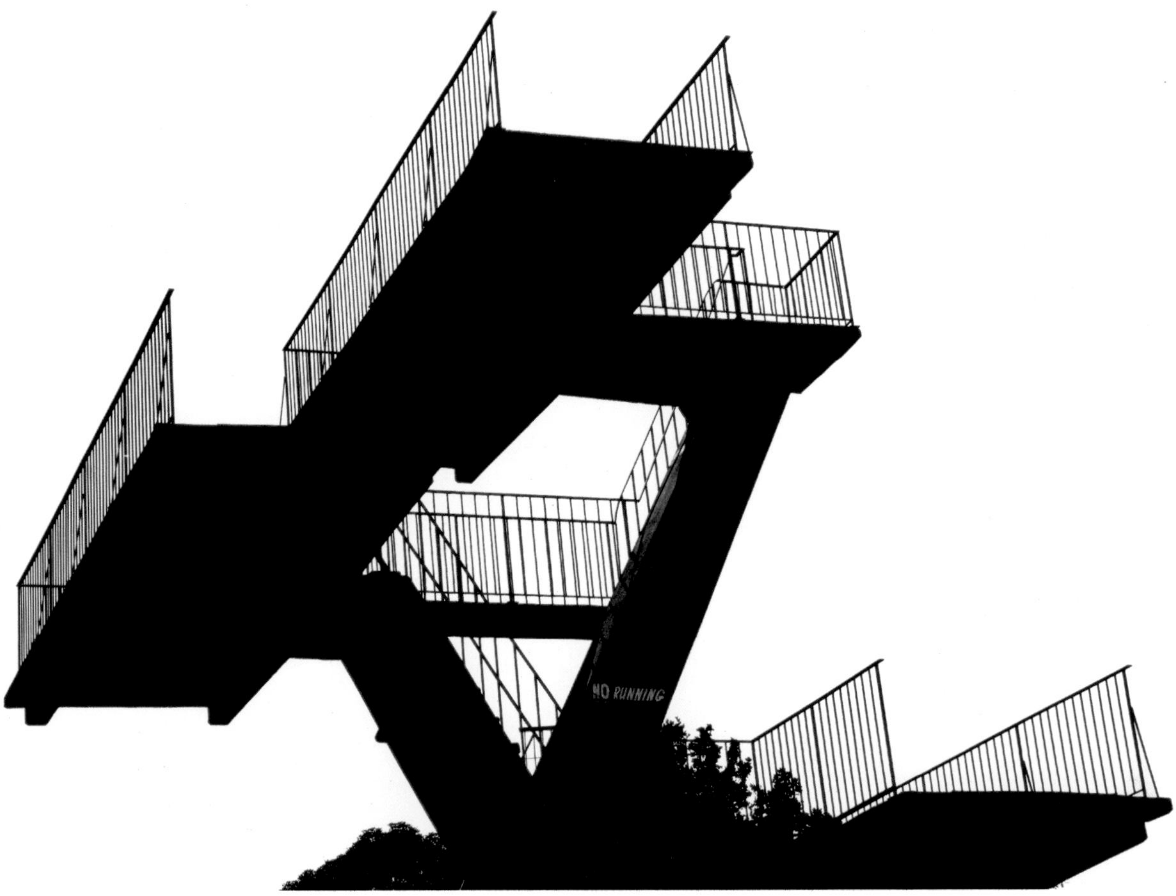
NO RUNNING

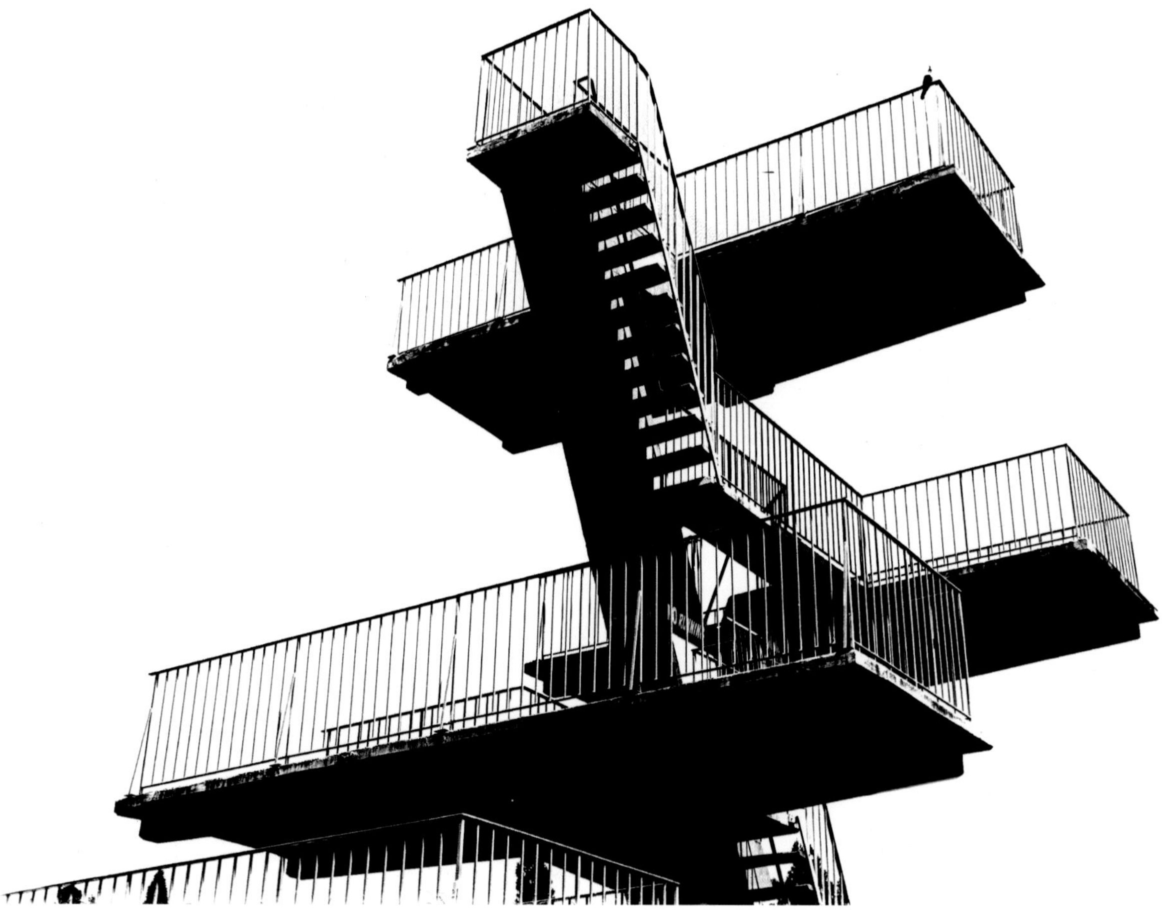

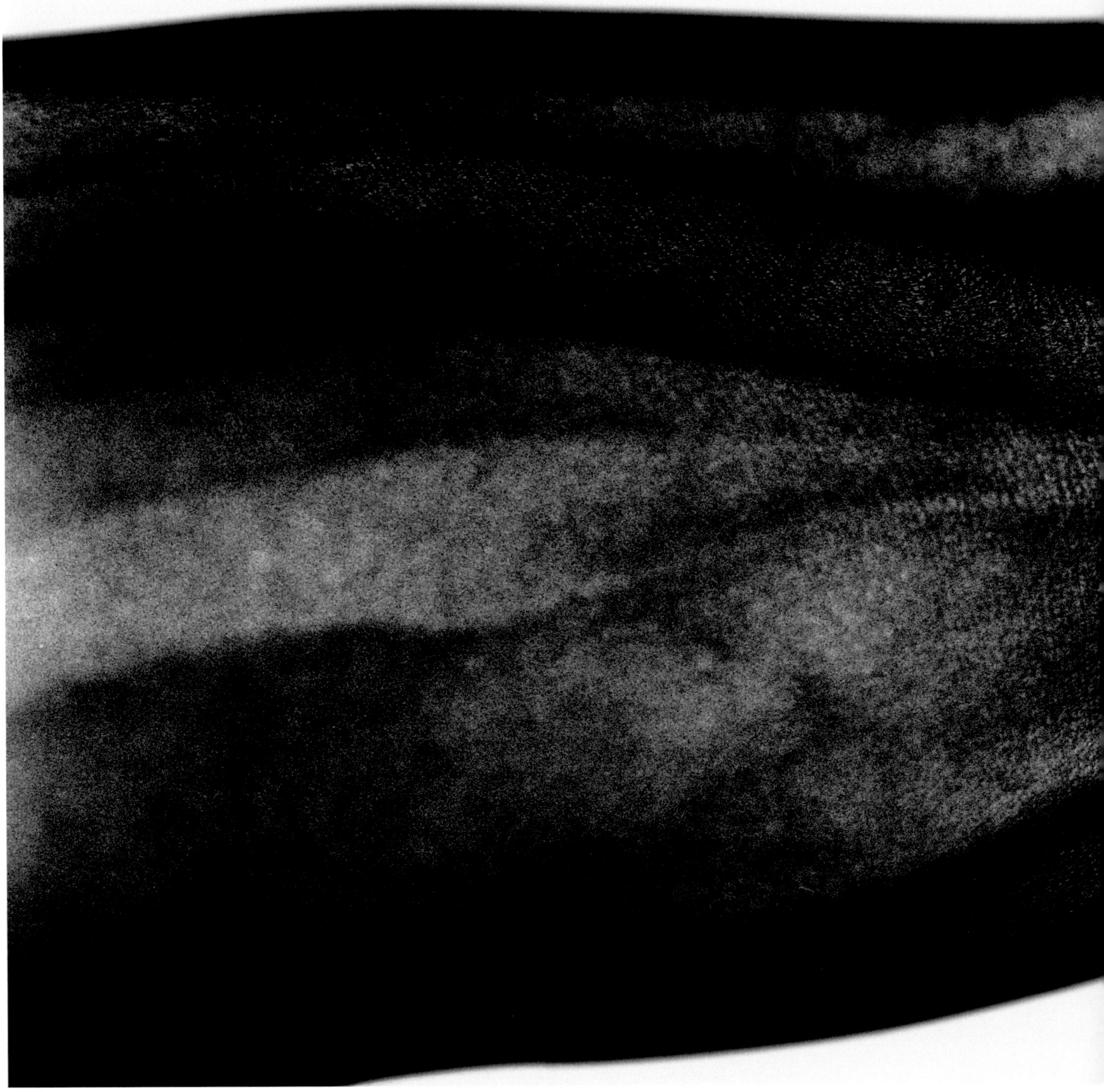

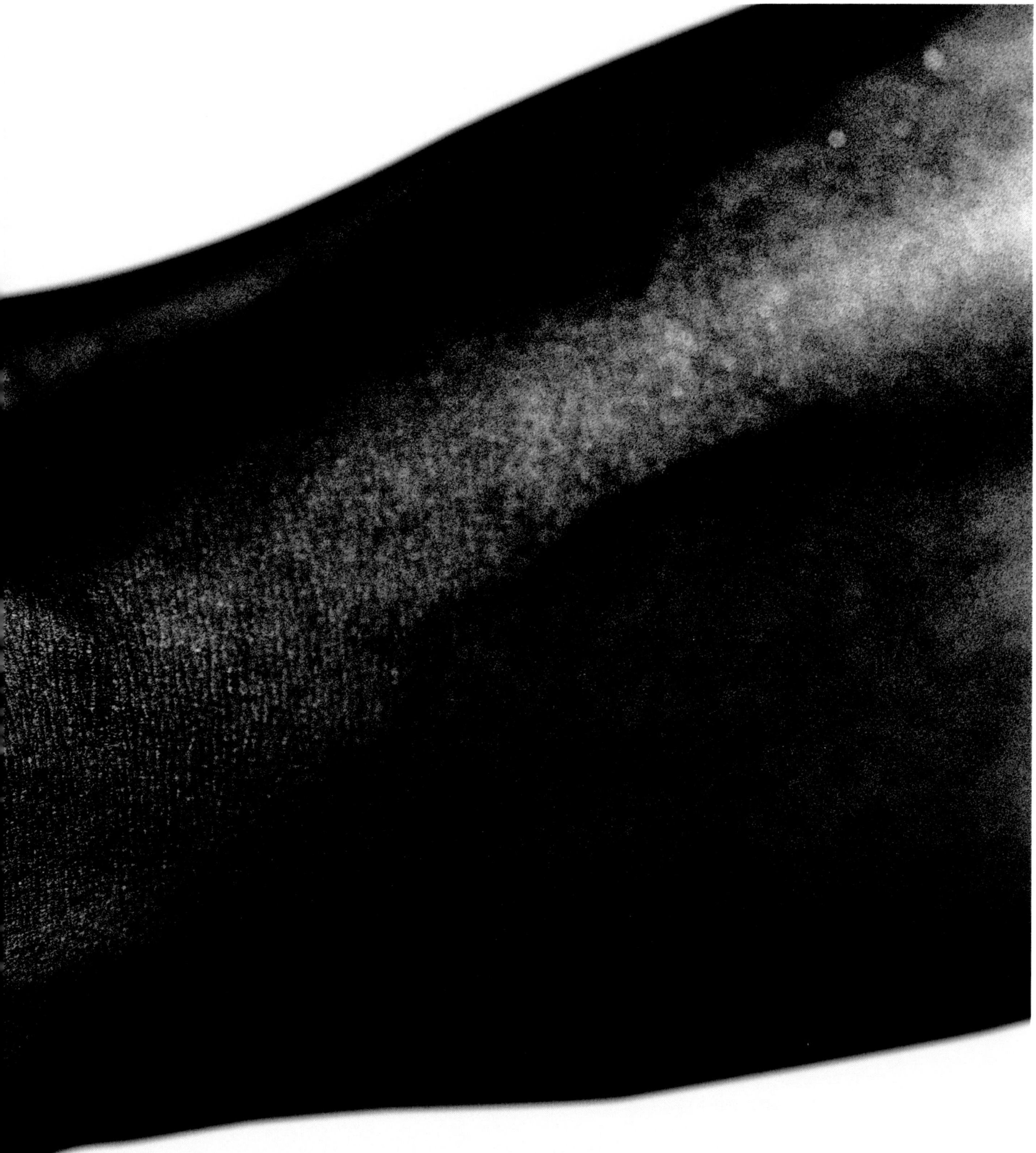

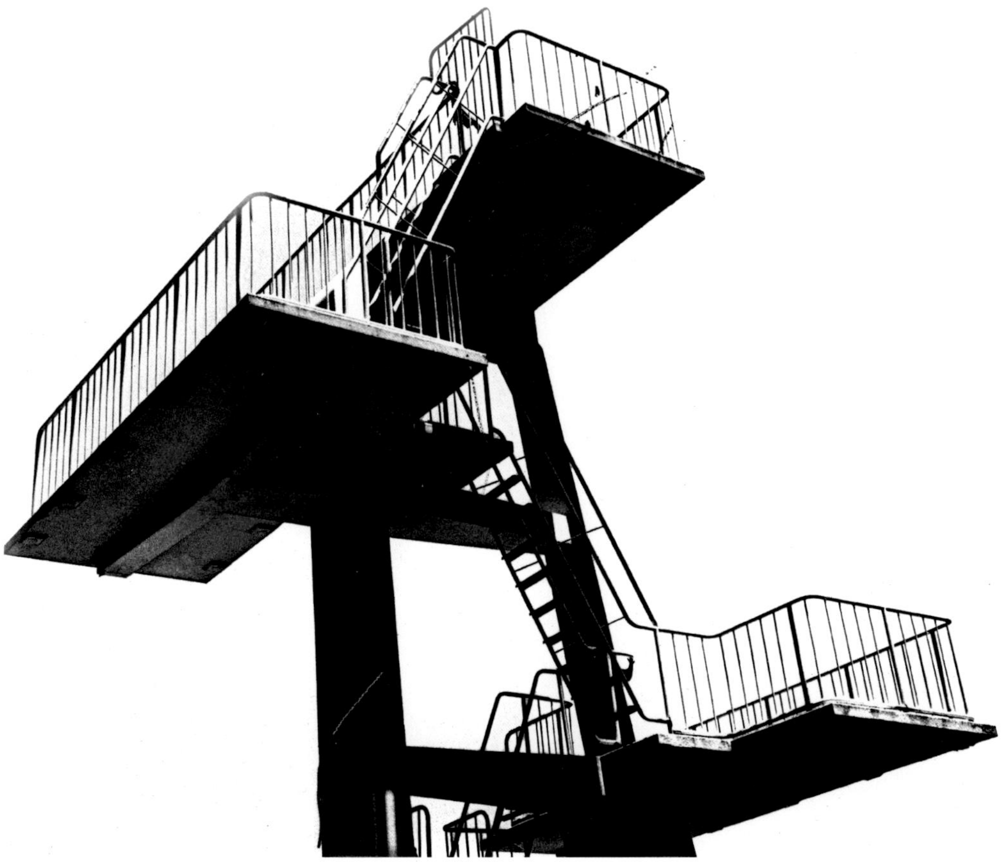

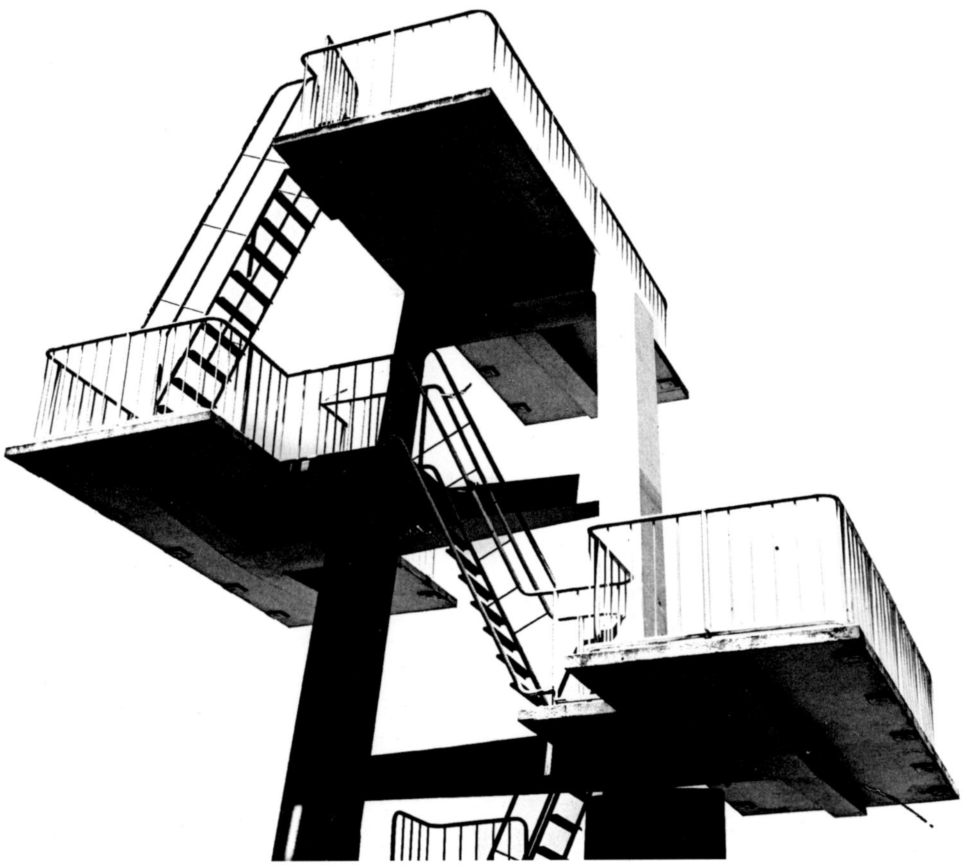

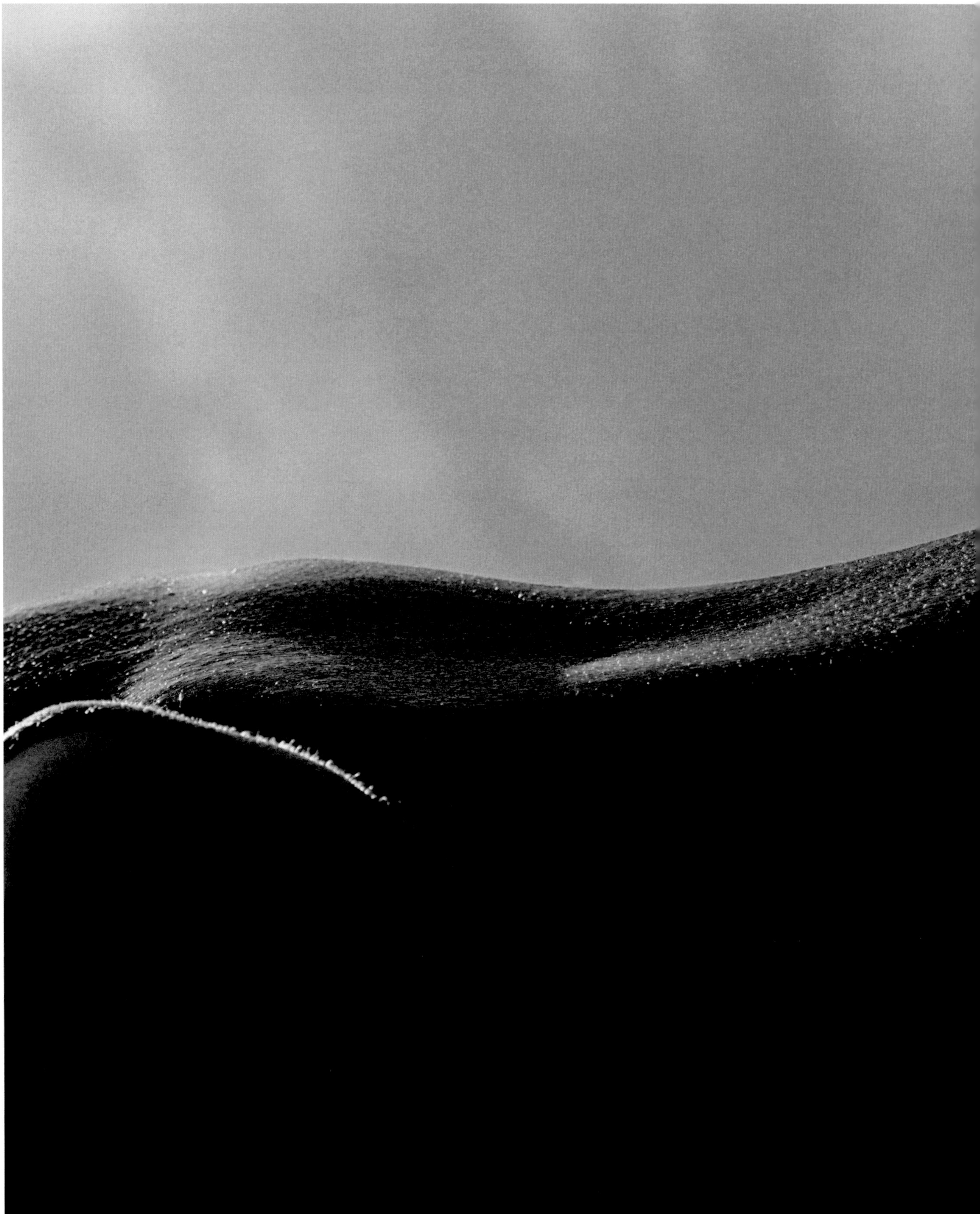

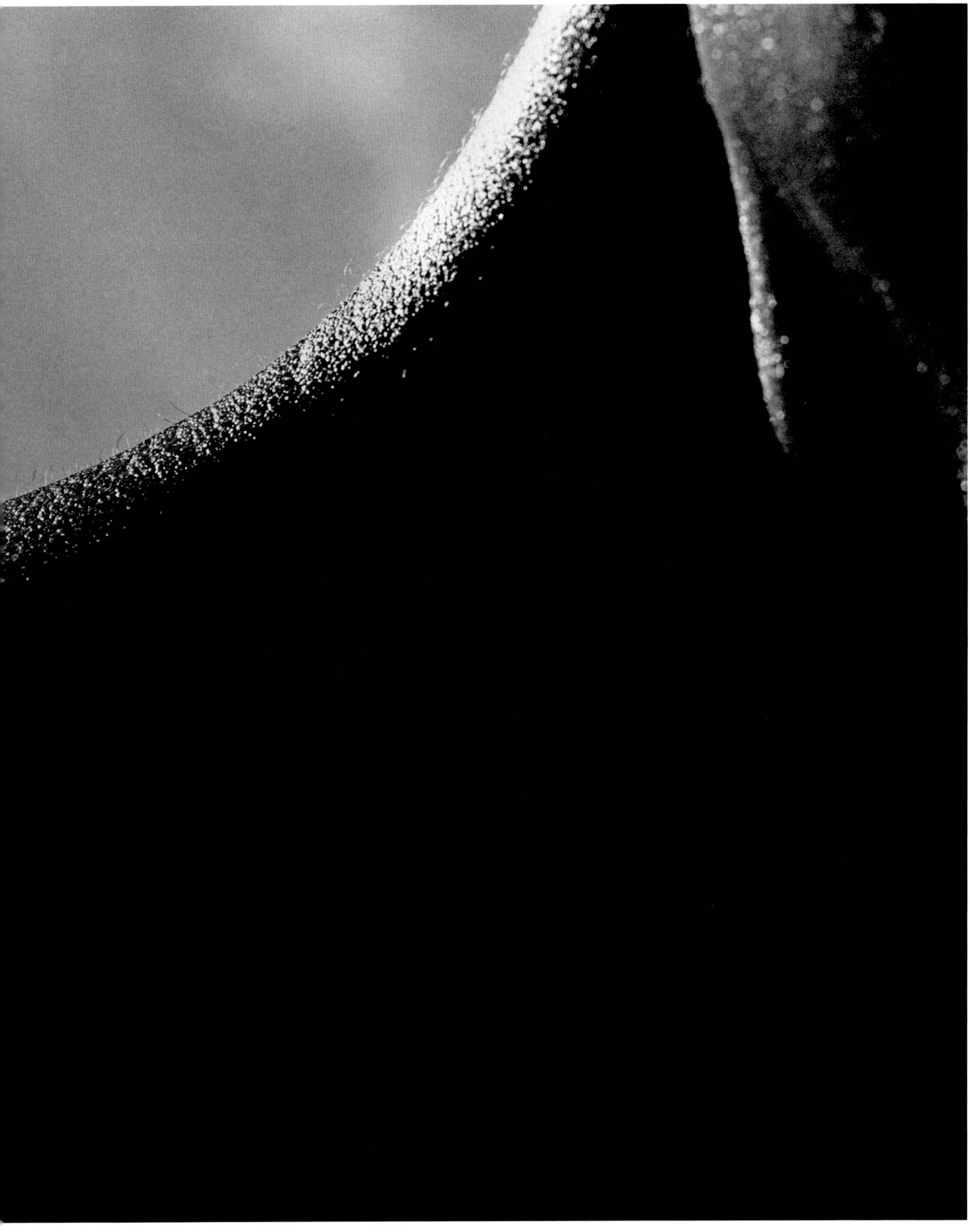

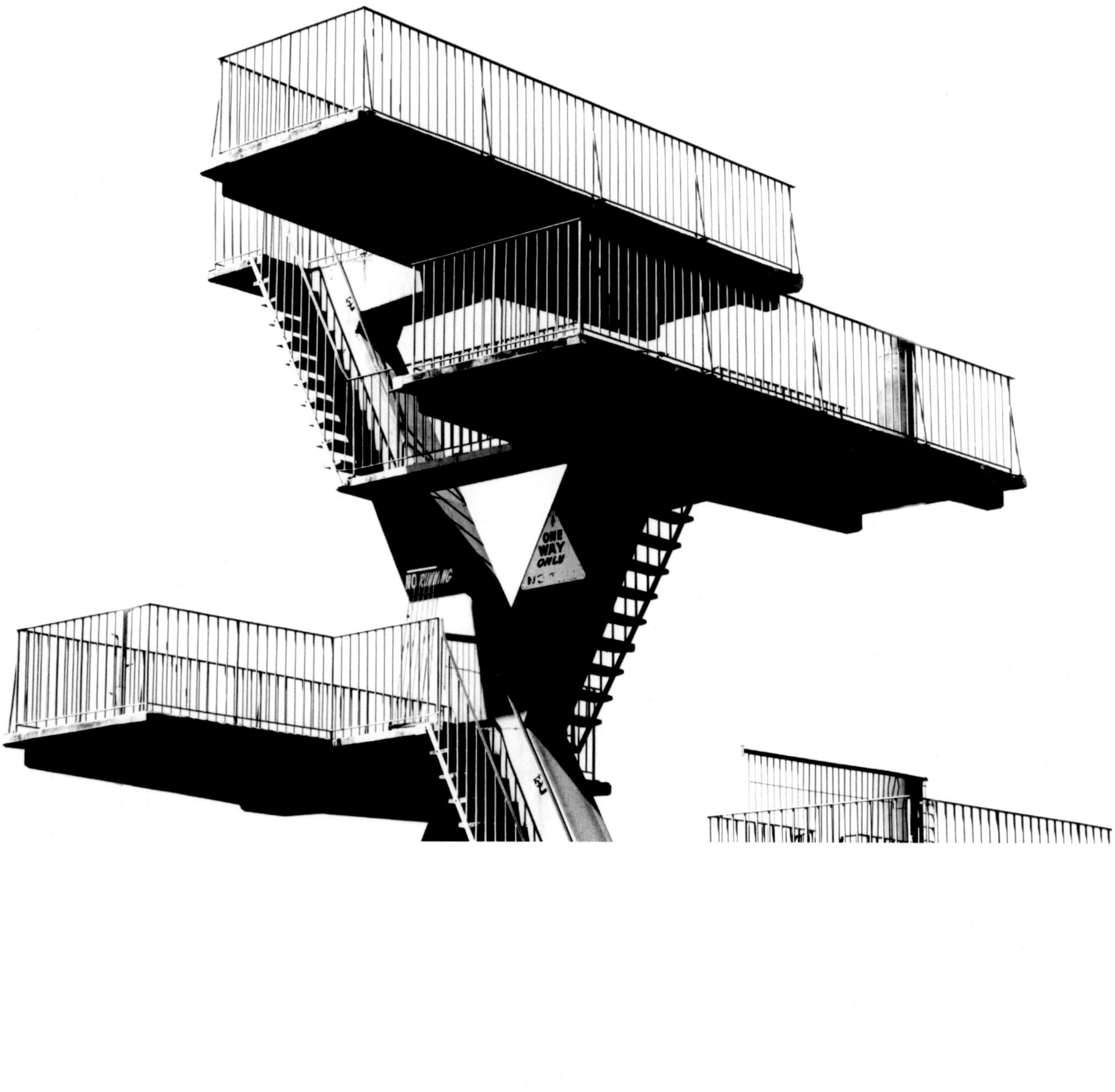
ONE
WAY
ONLY
NO RUNNING

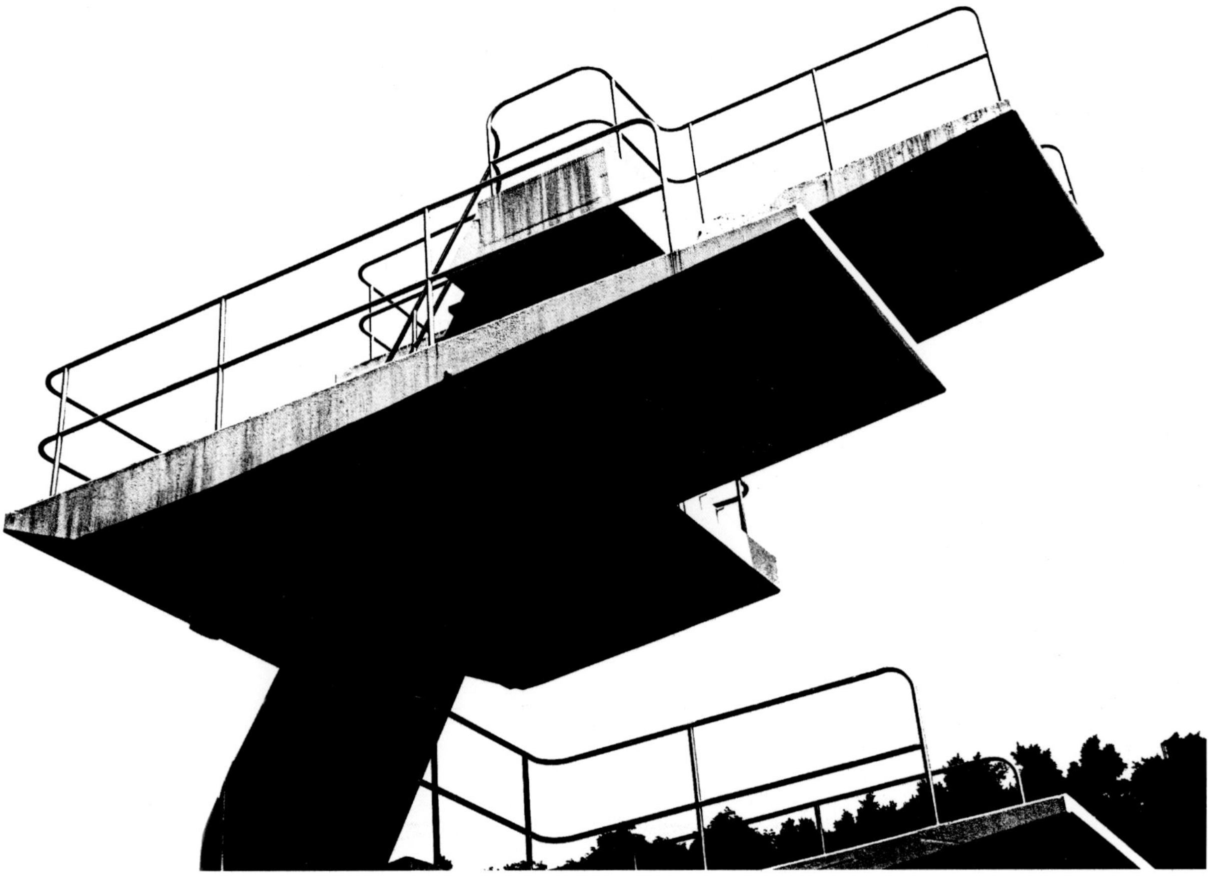

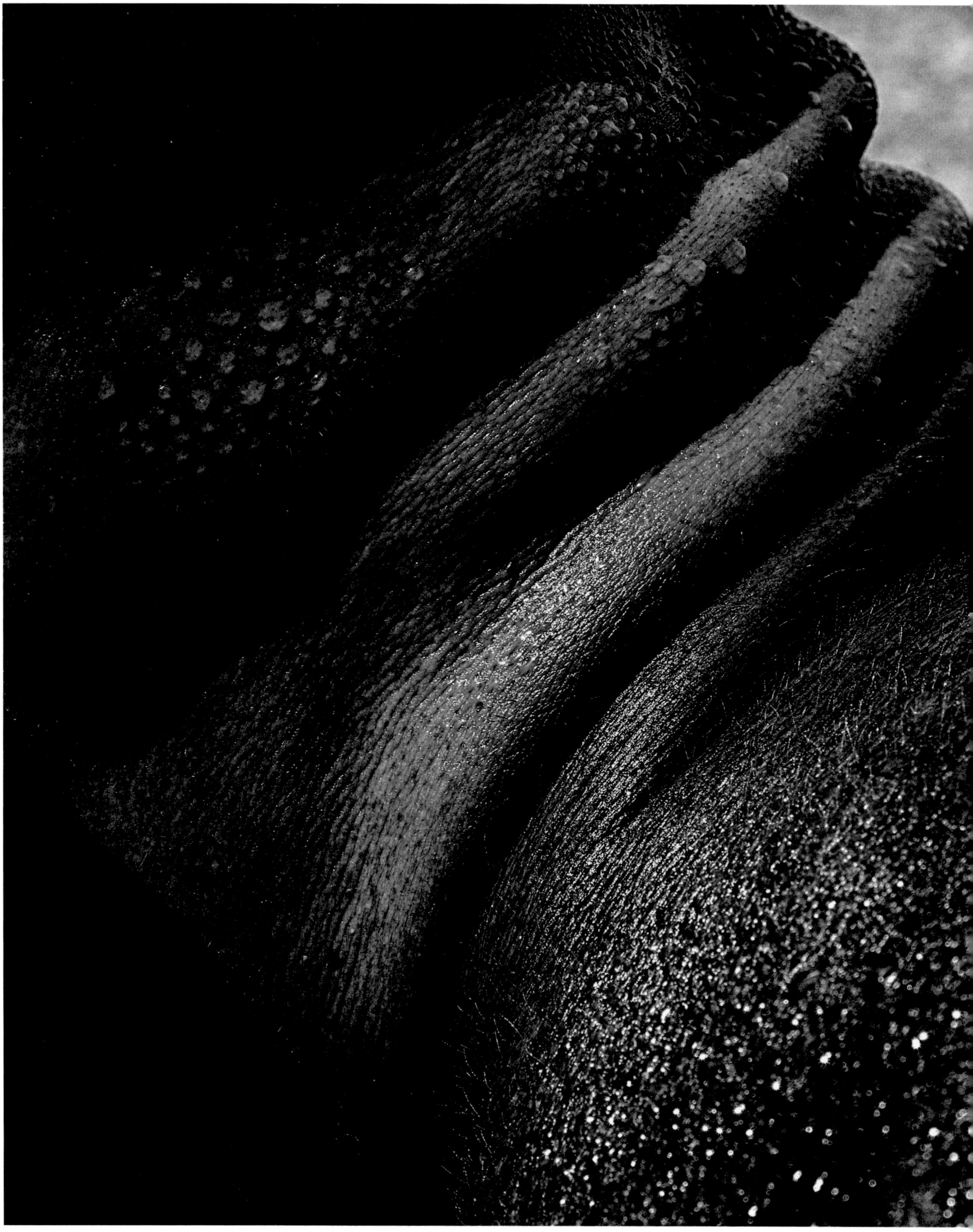

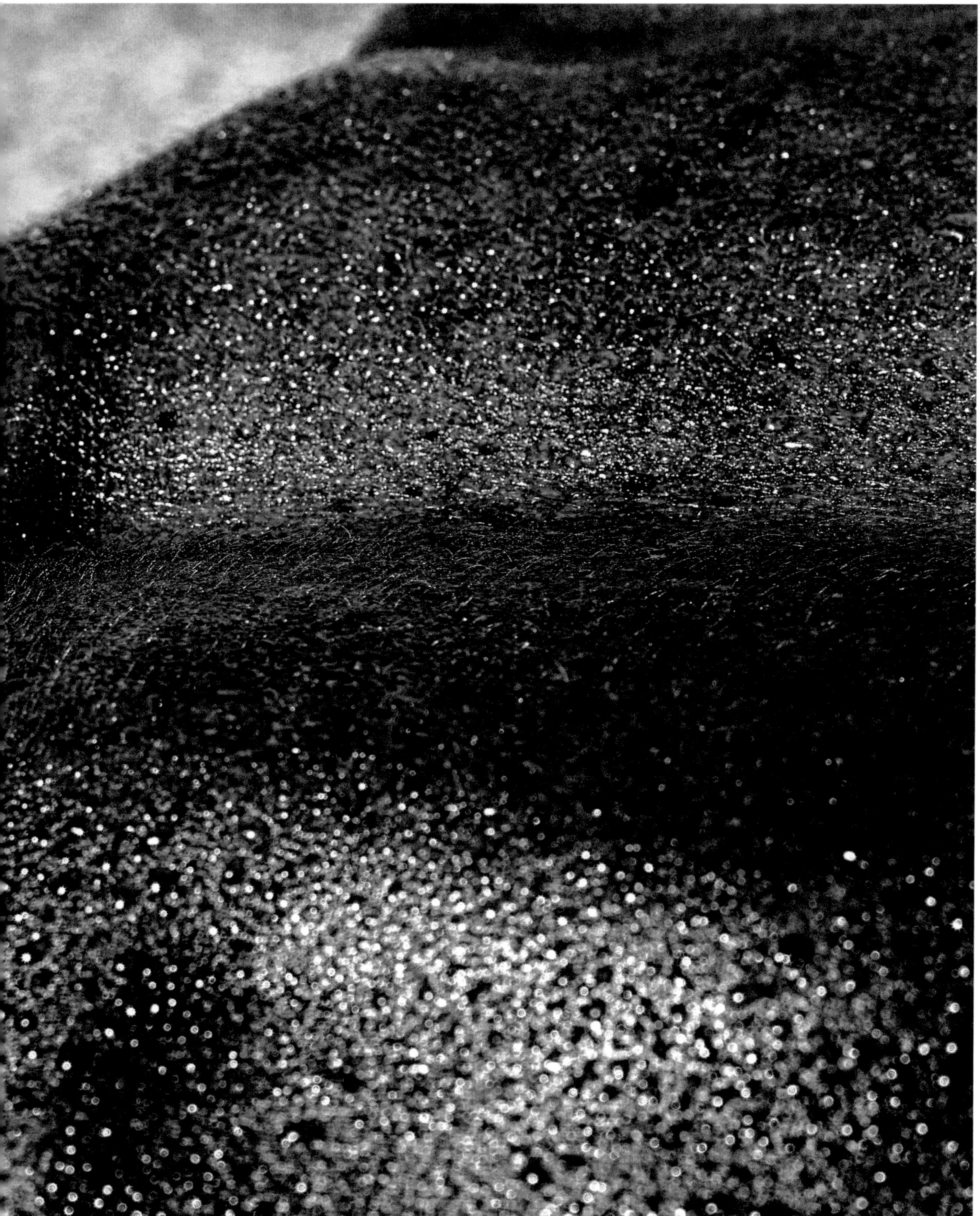

II

STS Kruzenshtern

The STS Kruzenshtern (formerly Padua) was originally a German ship but was surrendered to the USSR in 1946 as a war reparation. She was renamed after the early 19th century Baltic German explorer in Russian service, Adam Johann von Krusenstern.

The Kruzenshtern makes three training voyages annually, each lasting no less than two and no more than four months.

The uniforms of the 120 cadets on board never leave the ship and are handed from one cadet to the next over the years.

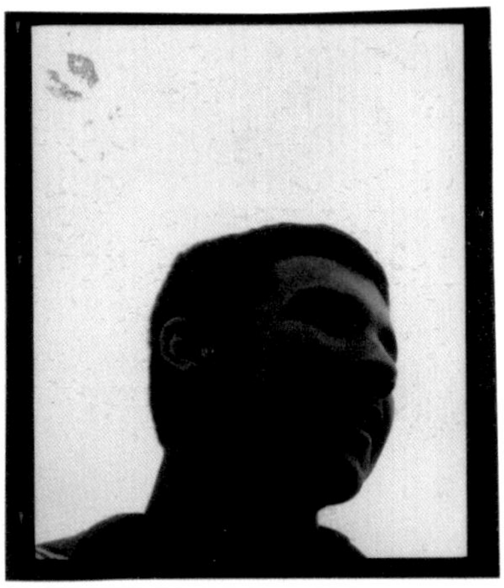
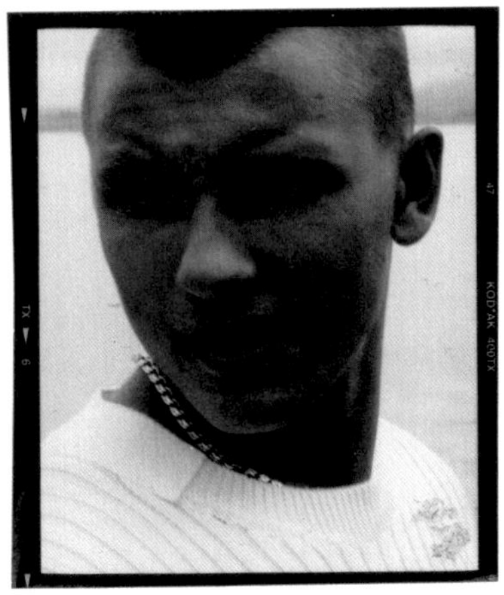
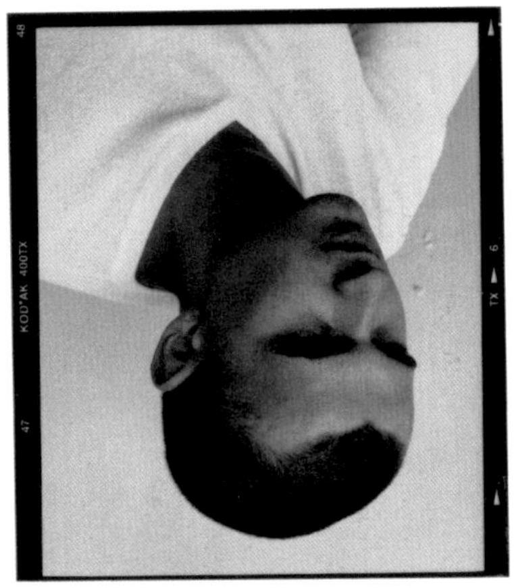
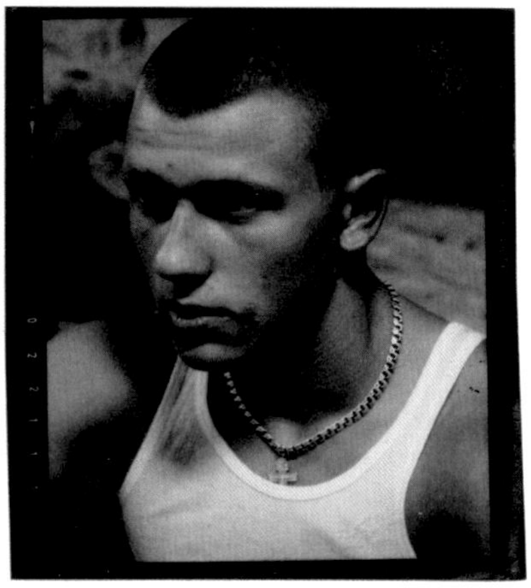
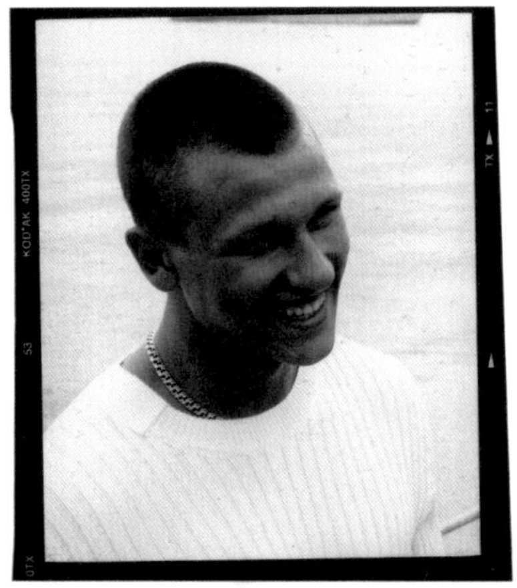
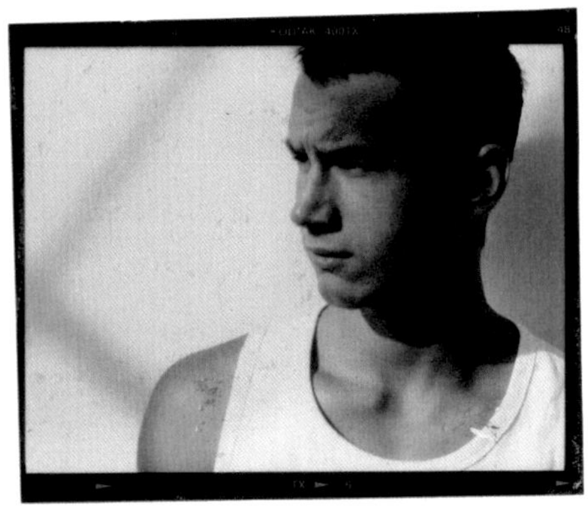
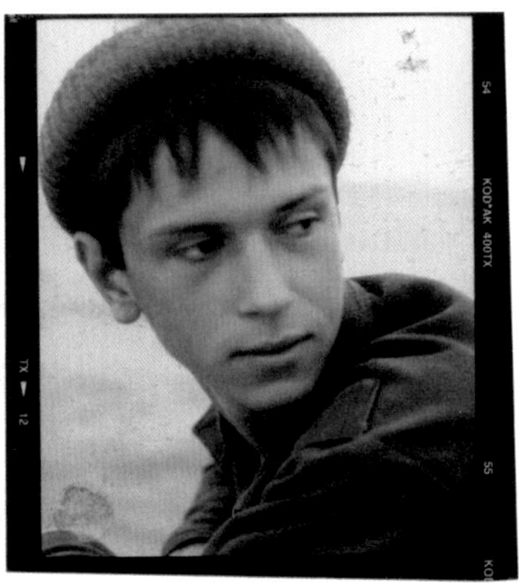
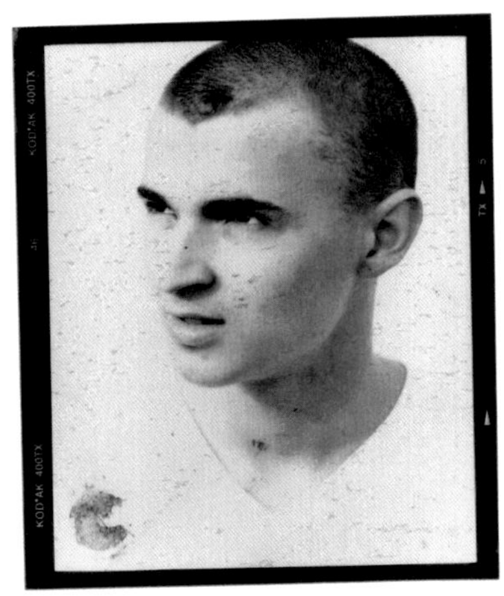

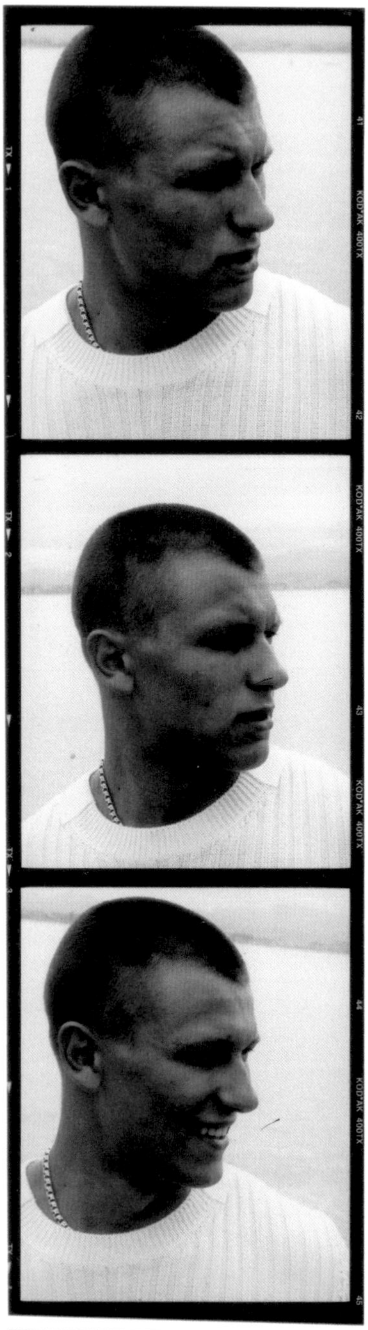

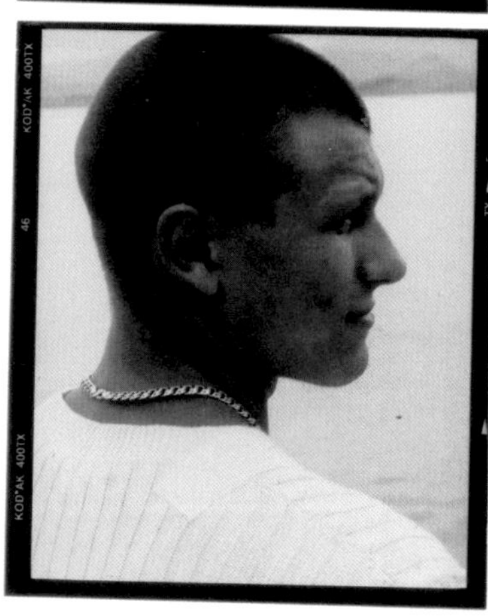

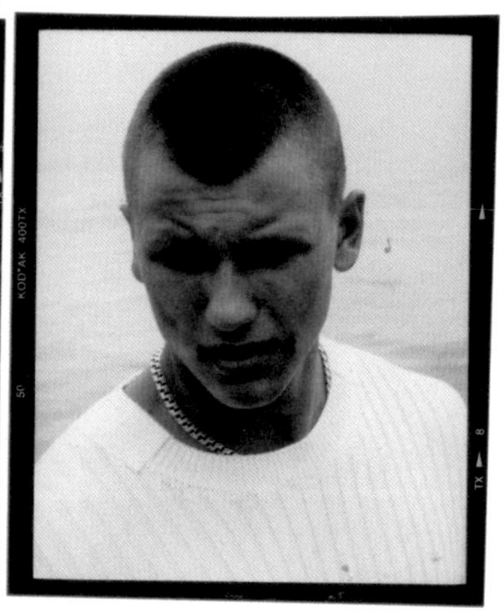

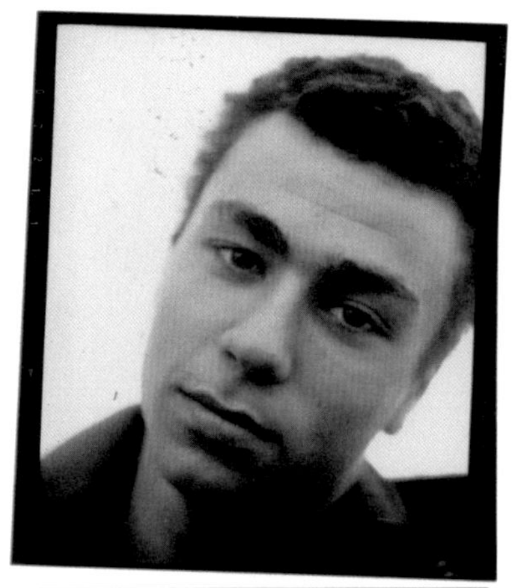

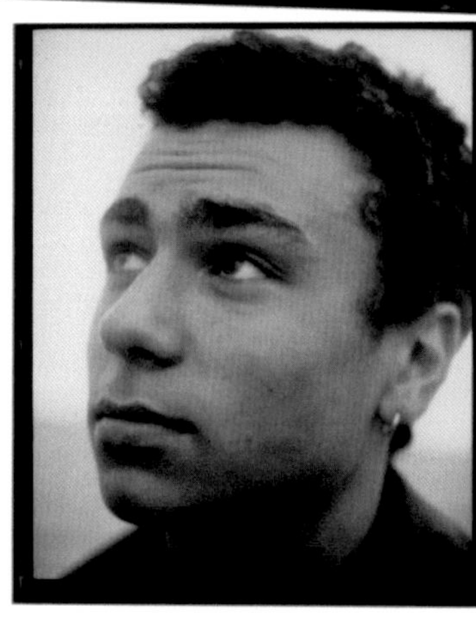

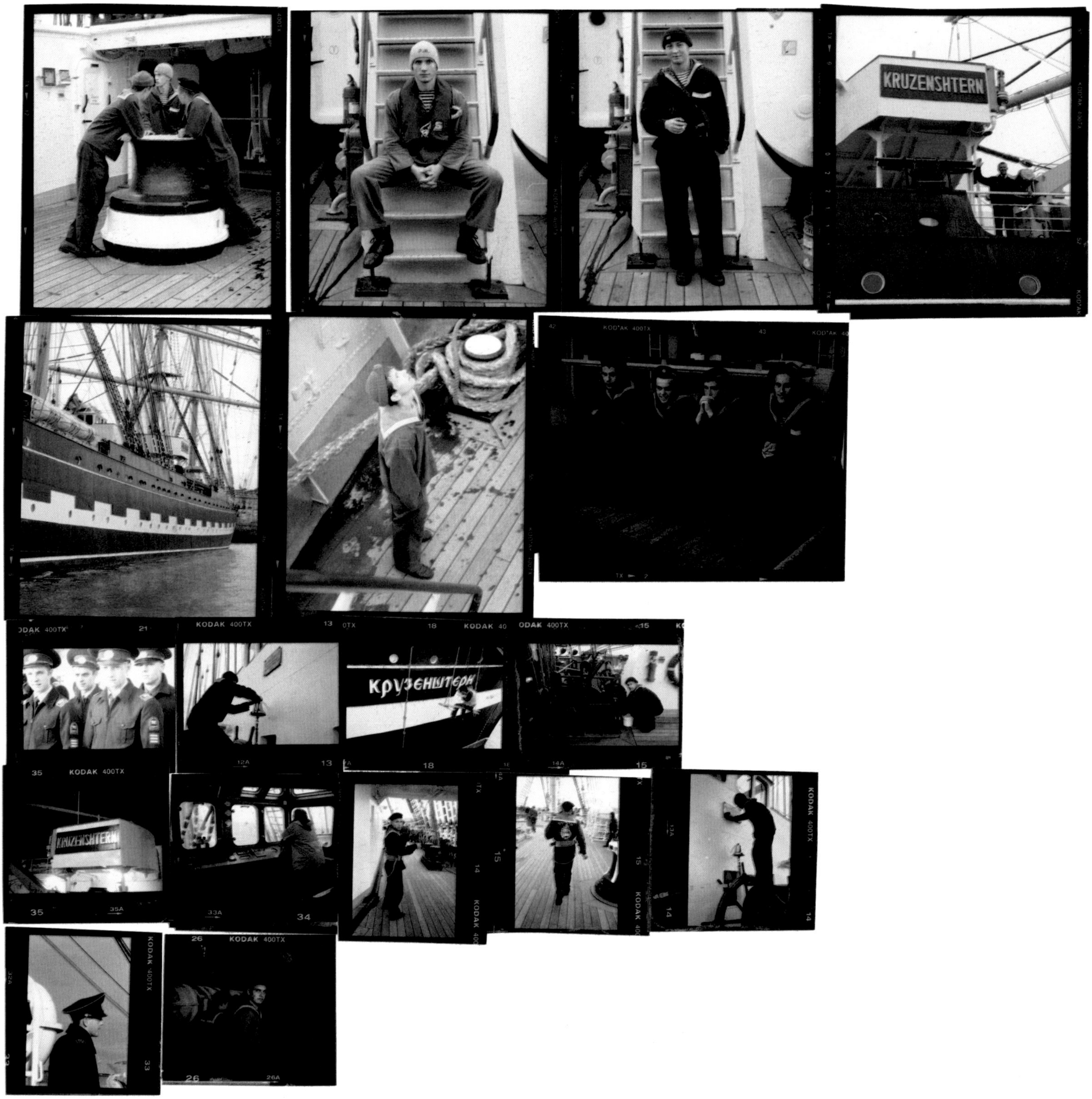
KRUZENSHTERN
Крузенштерн

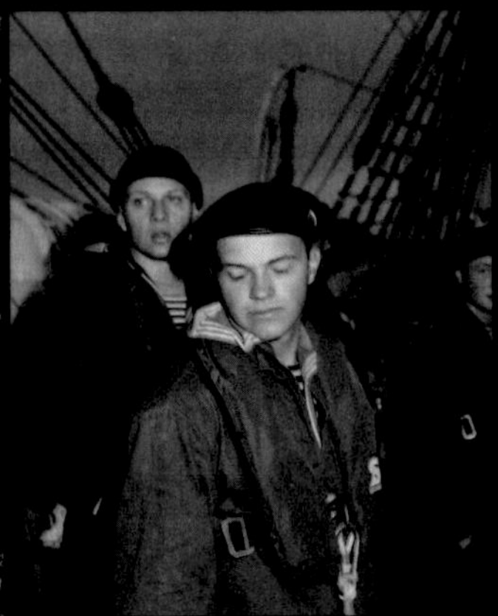
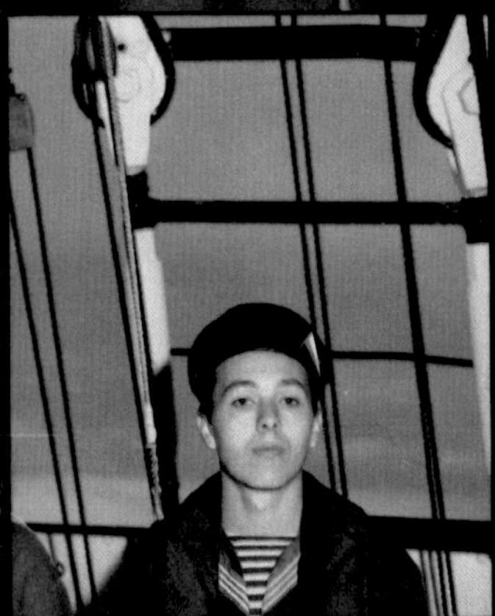
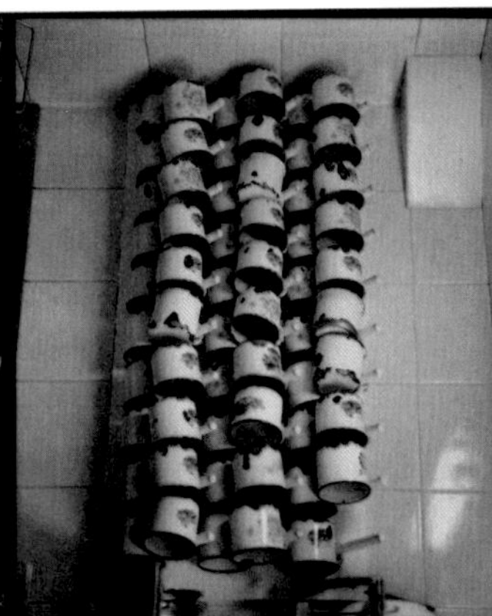
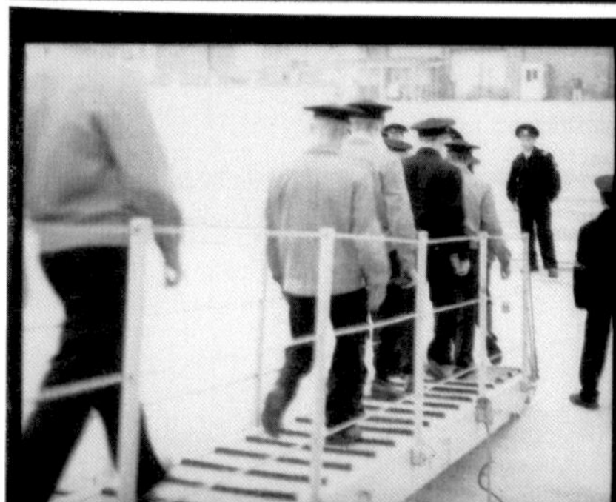
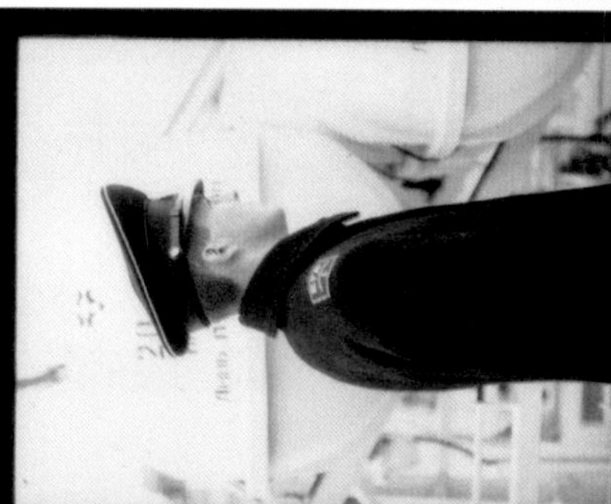
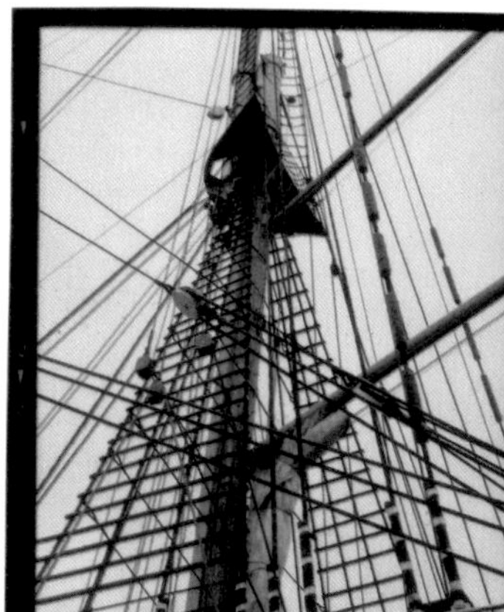
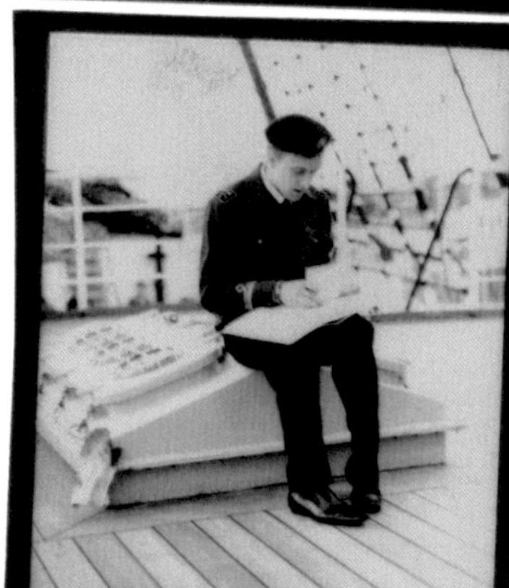

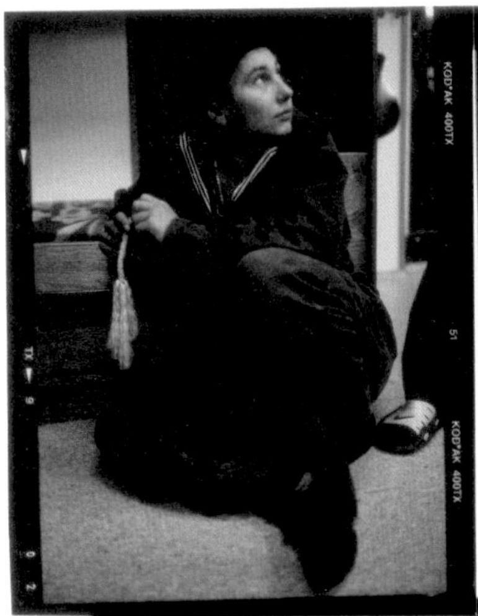

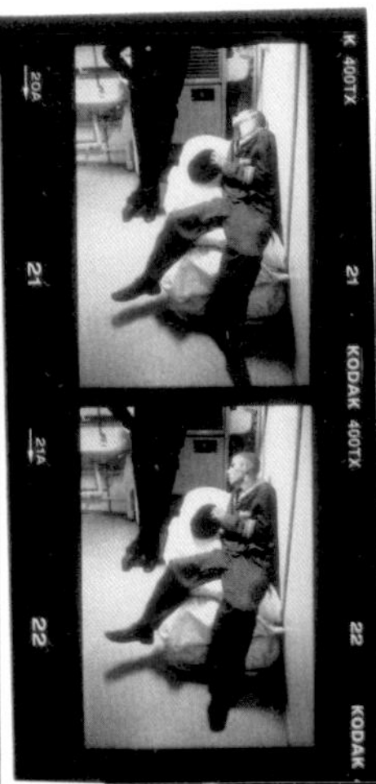

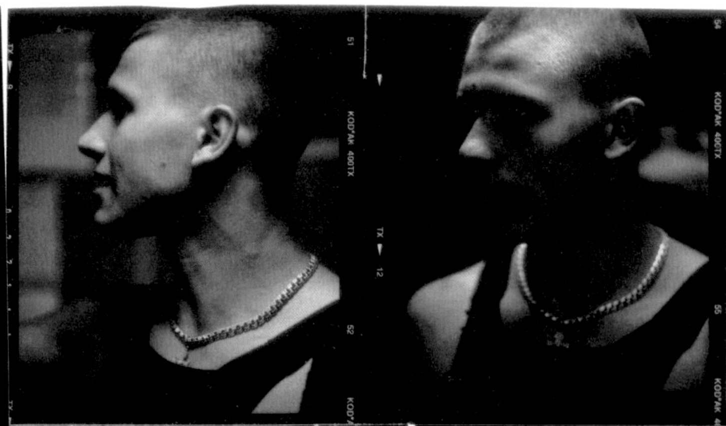

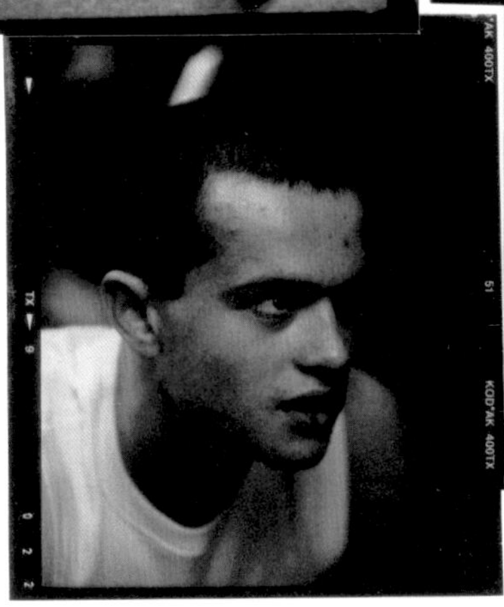

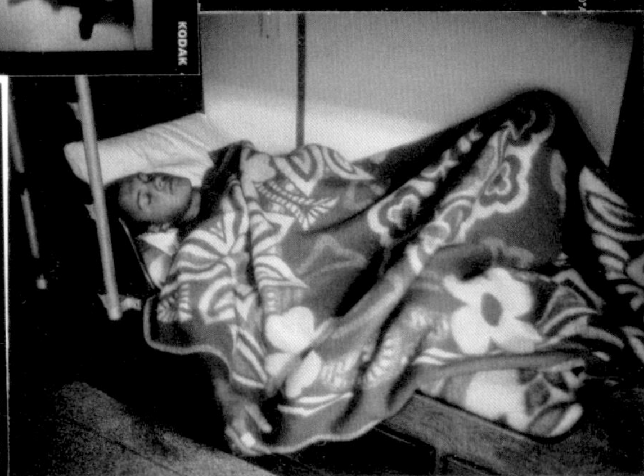

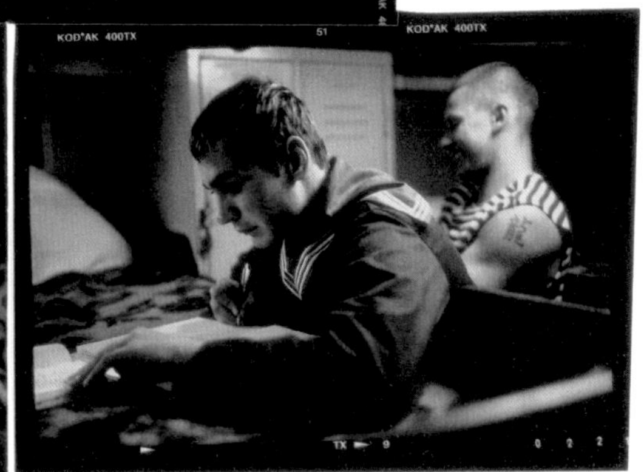

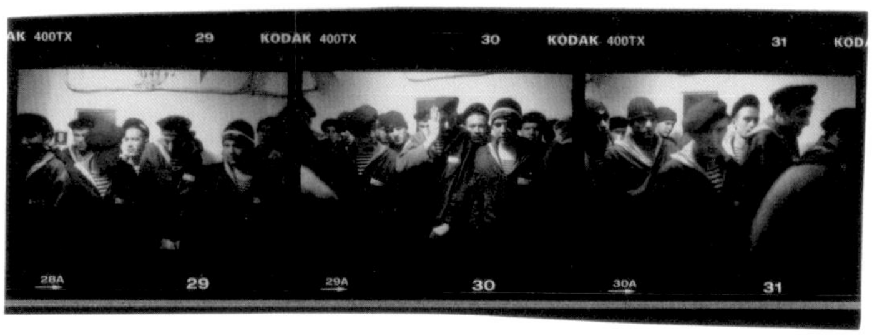
AK 400TX
29
KODAK 400TX
30
KODAK 400TX
31
28A
29
29A
30
30A
31

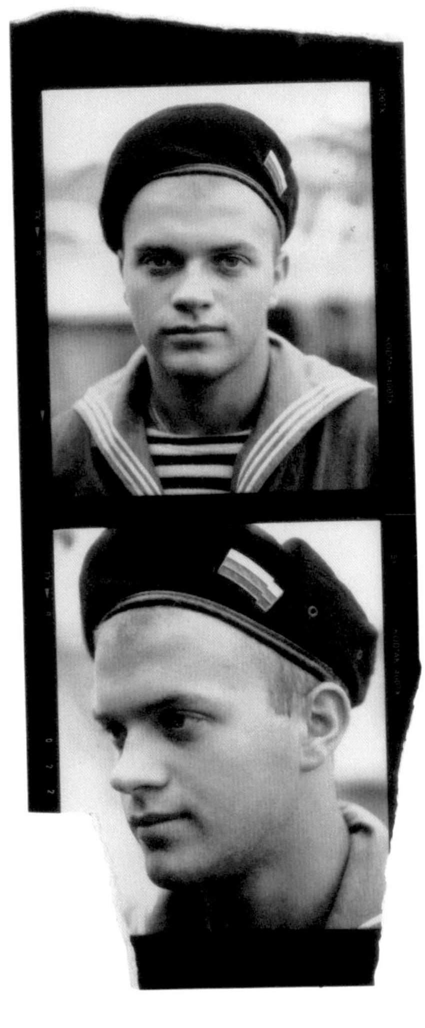

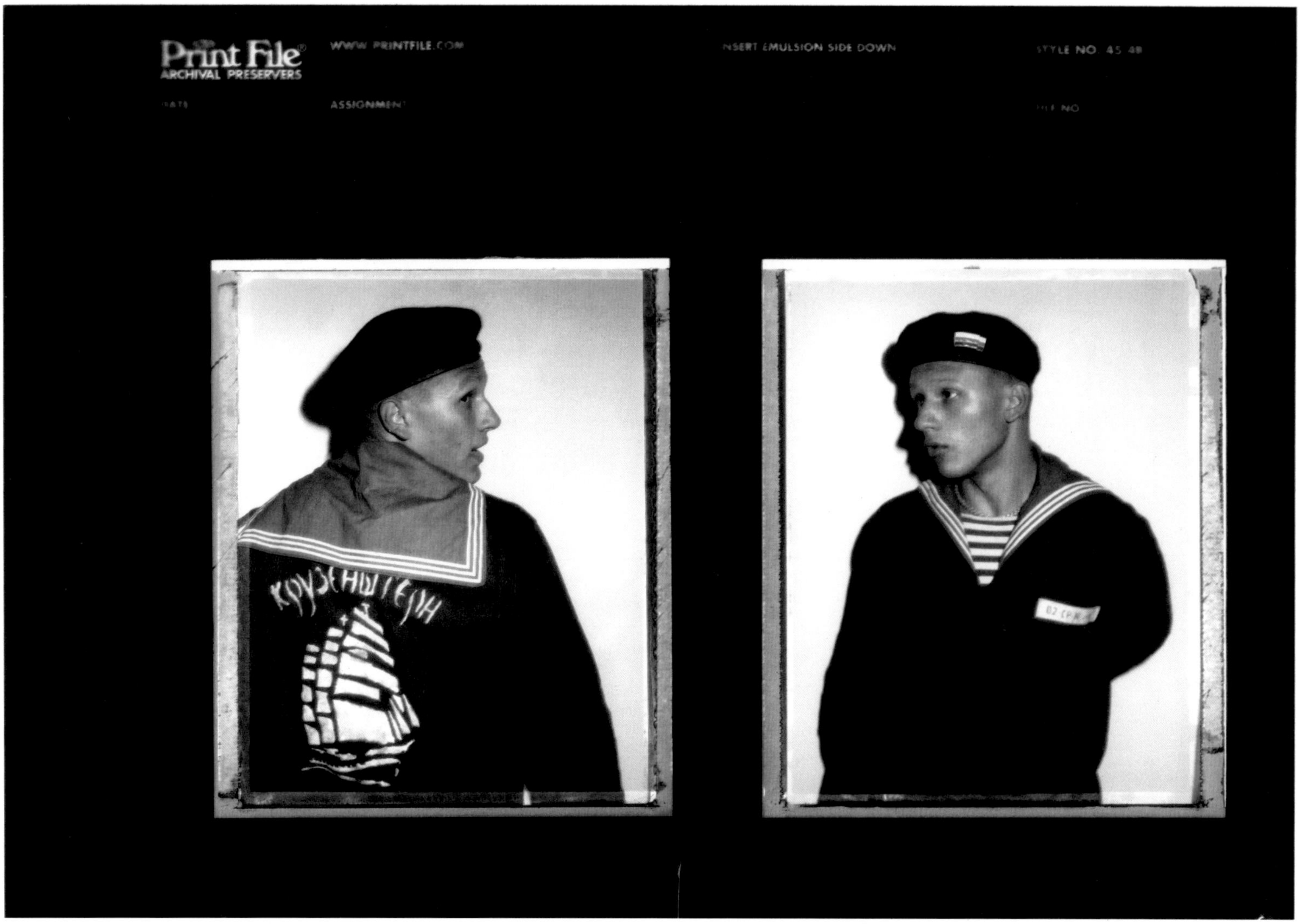
Print File
ARCHIVAL PRESERVERS
WWW.PRINTFILE.COM
NSERT EMULSION SIDE DOWN
STYLE NO. 45 4B
ASSIGNMENT
КРУЗЕНШТЕРН

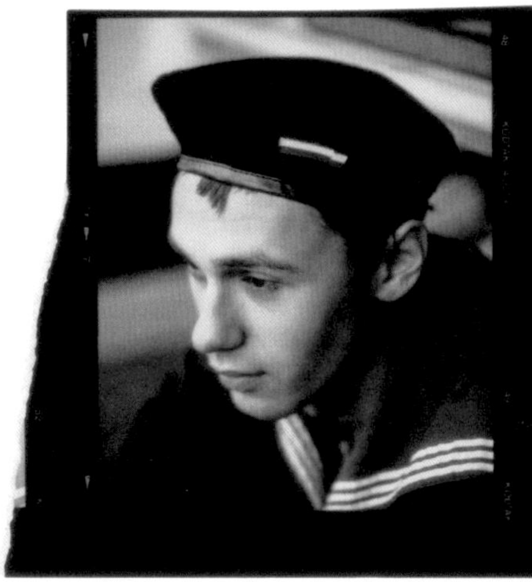
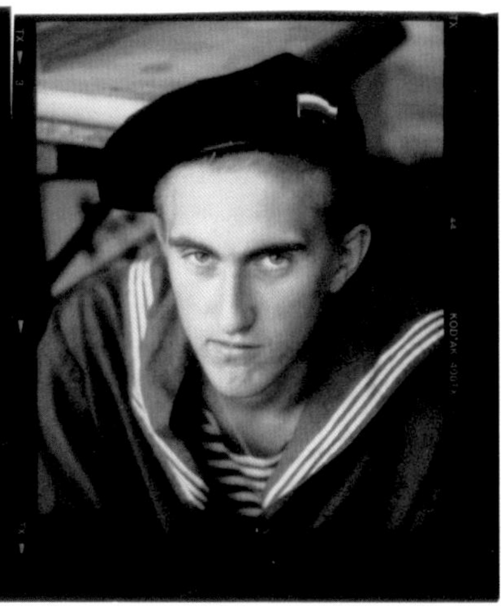
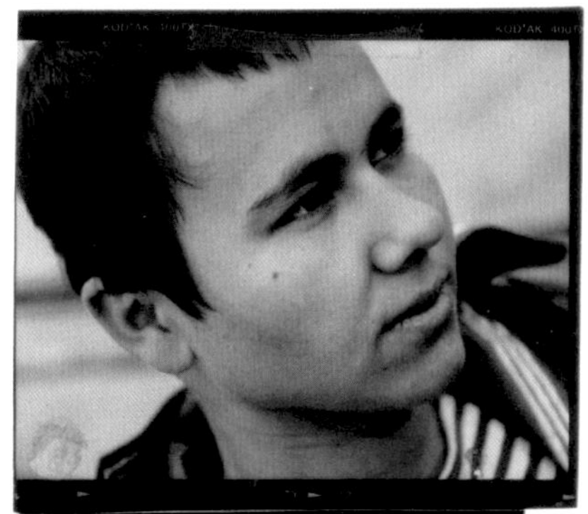
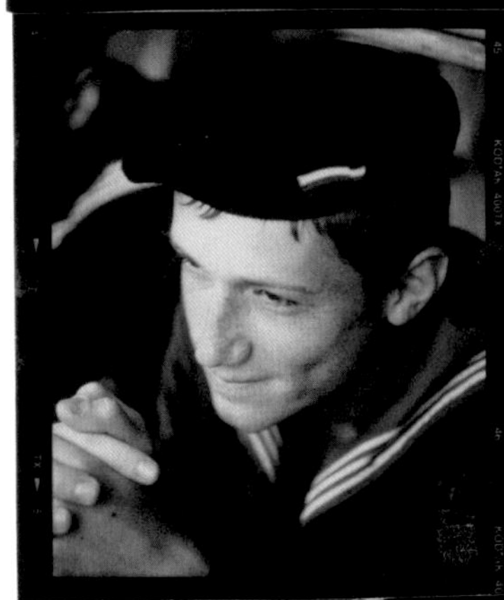
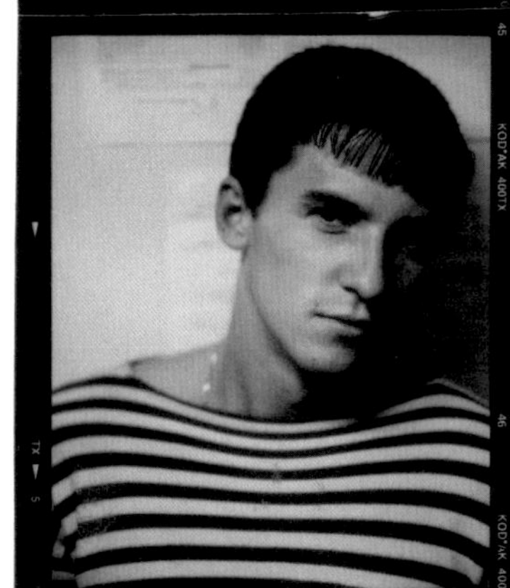
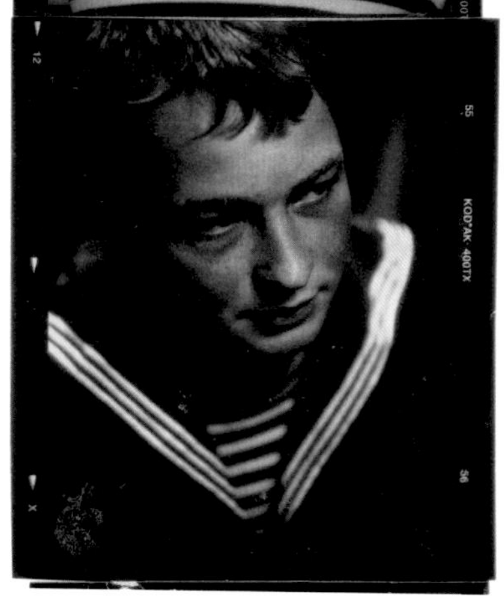
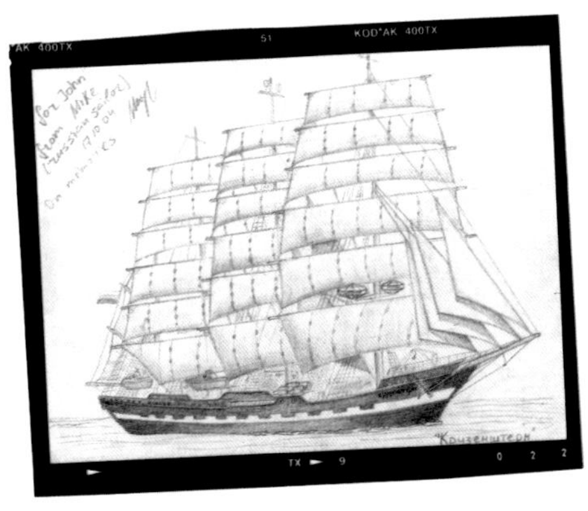

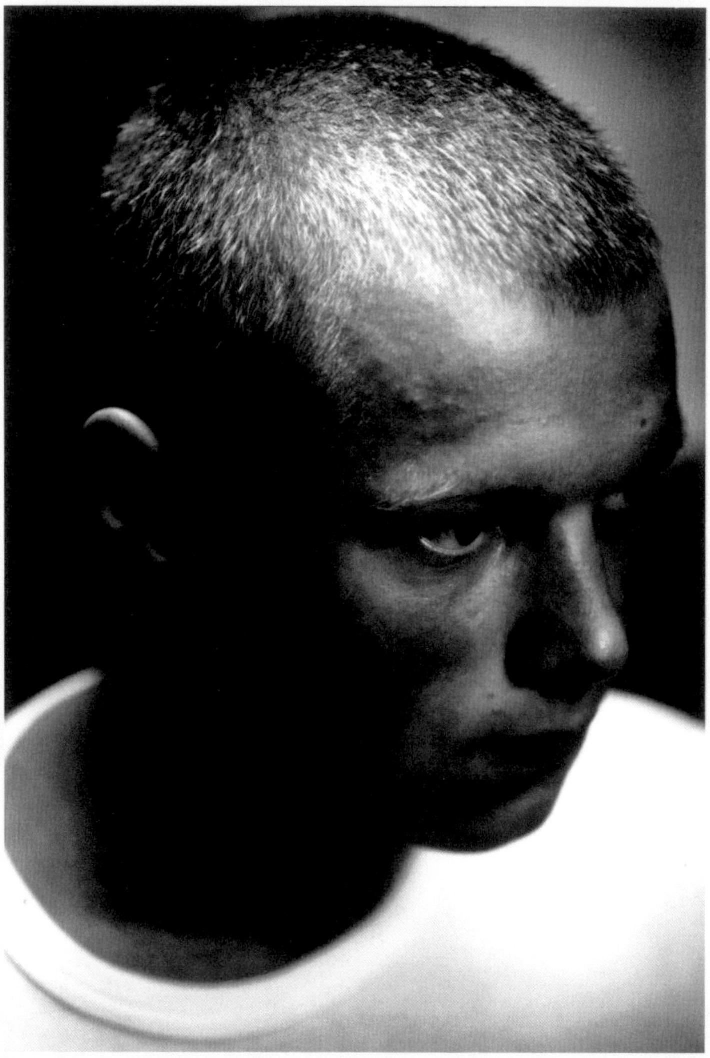

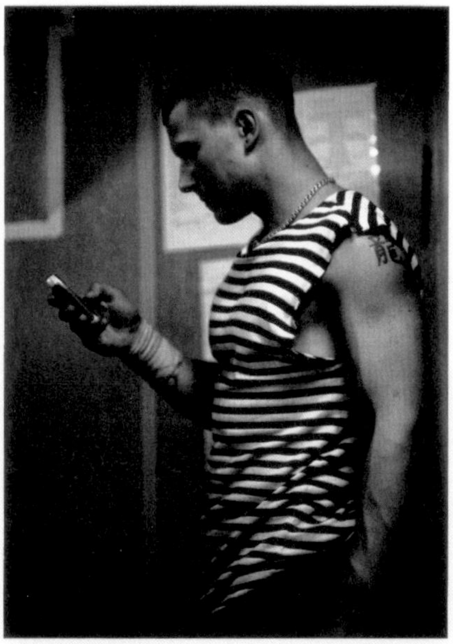

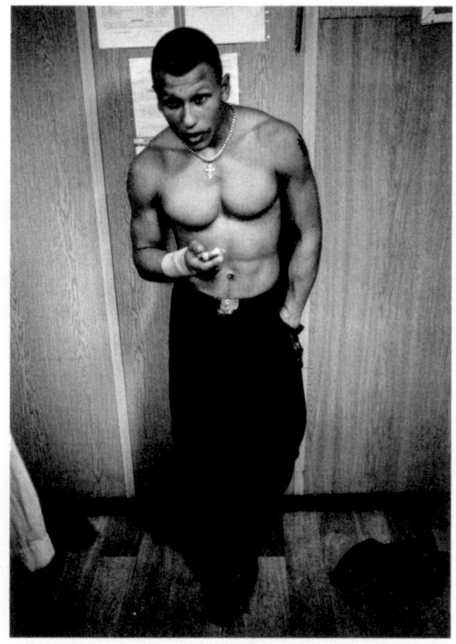

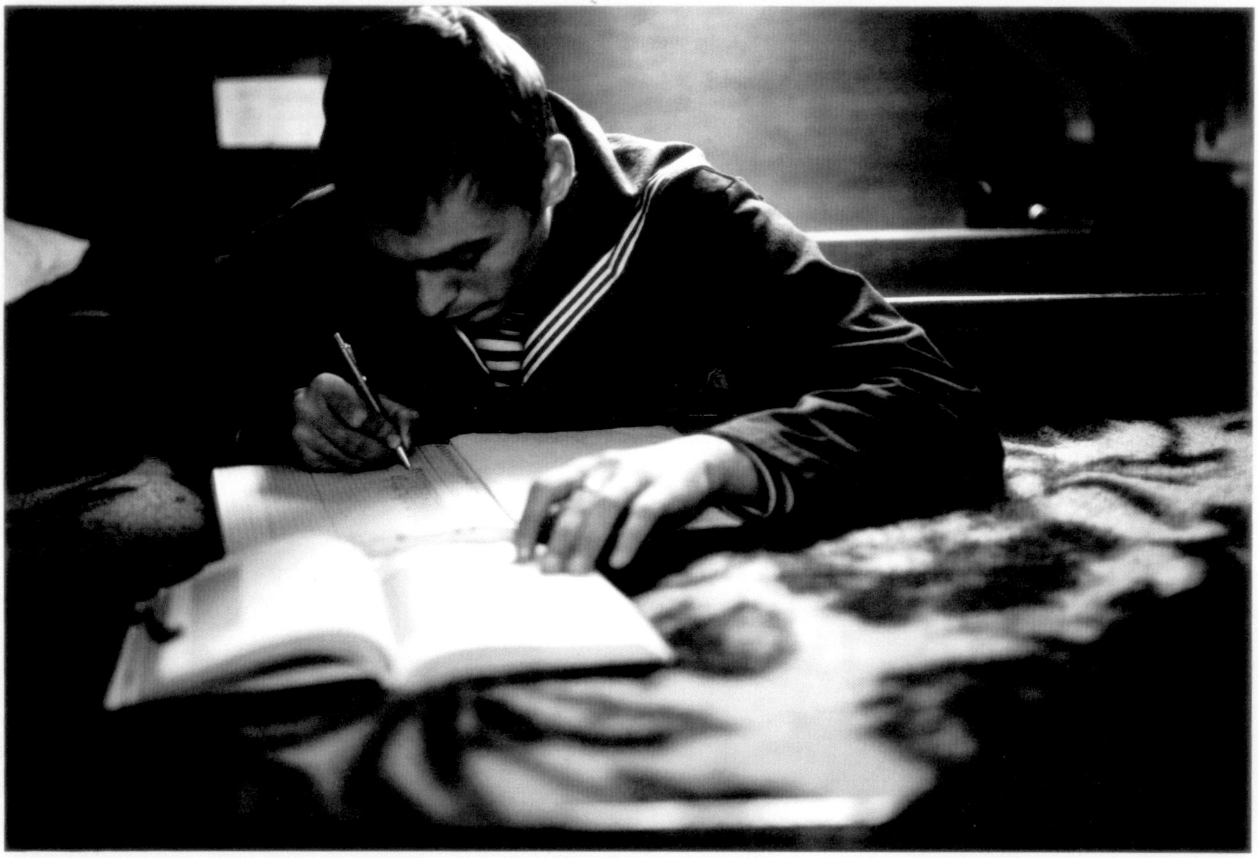

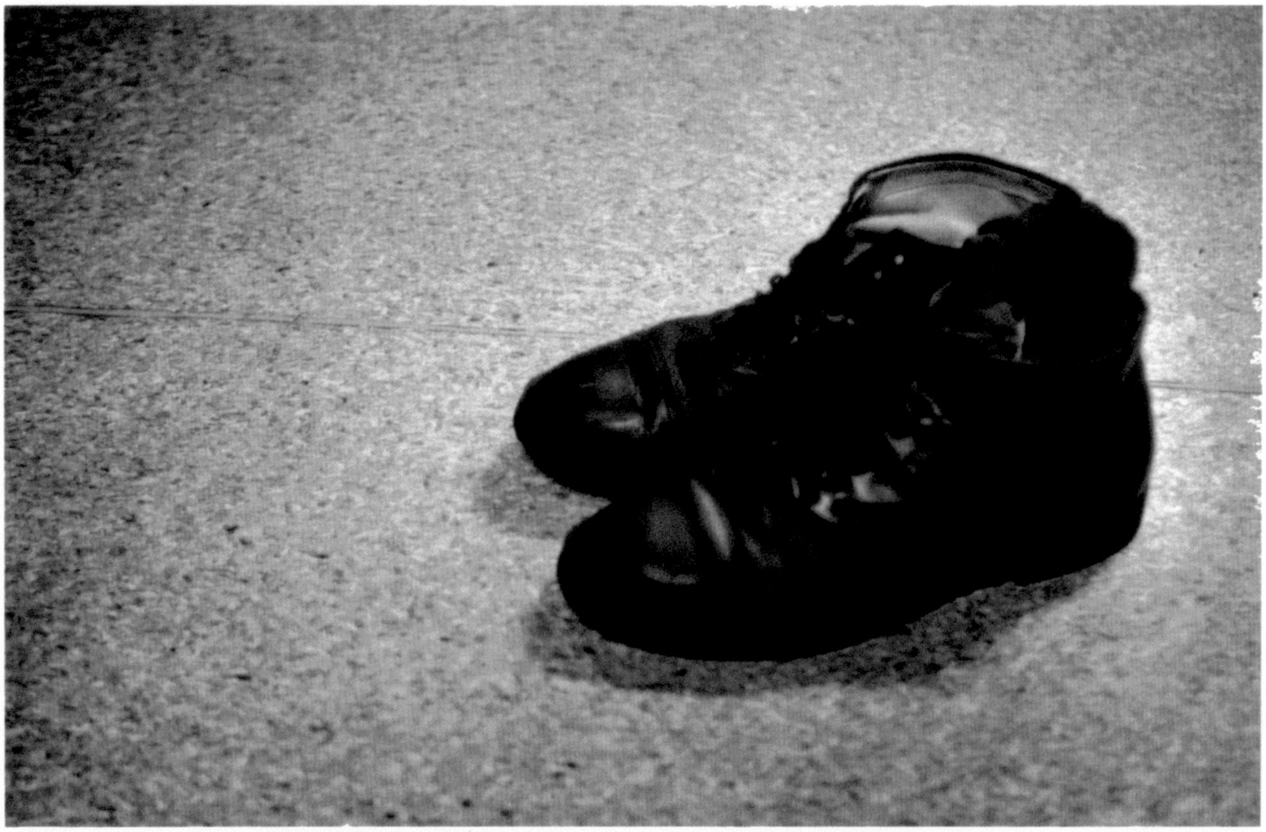

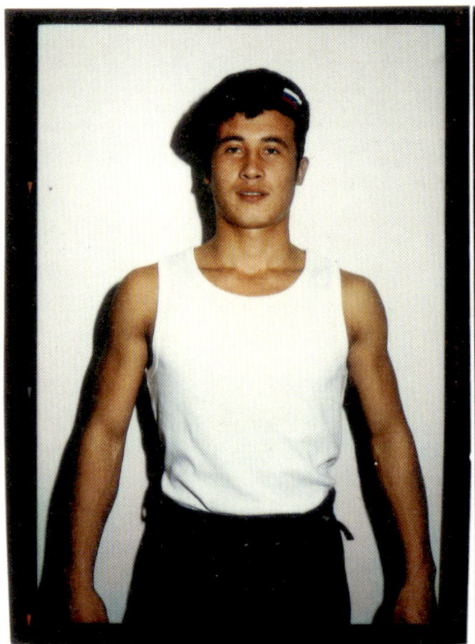

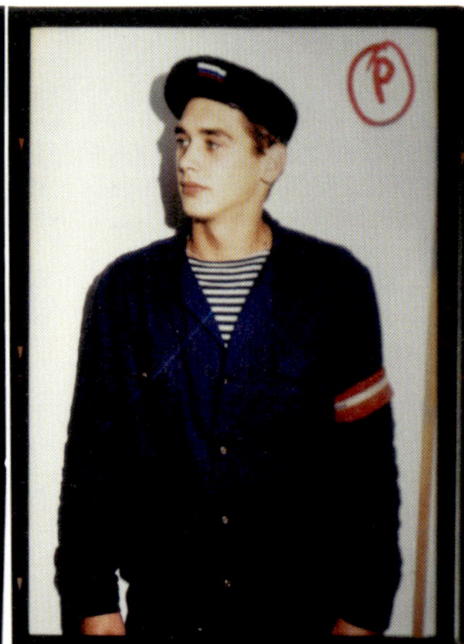

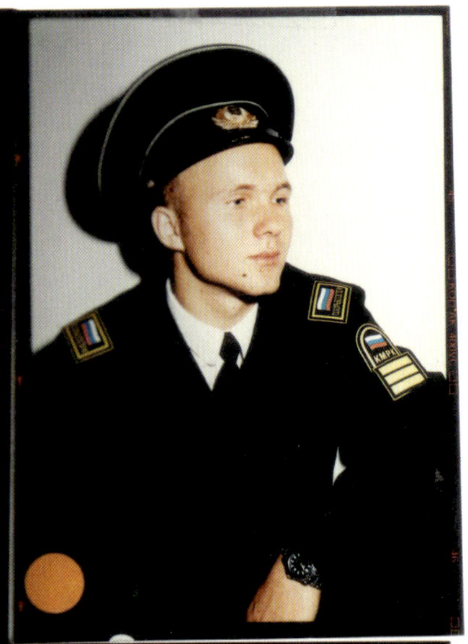

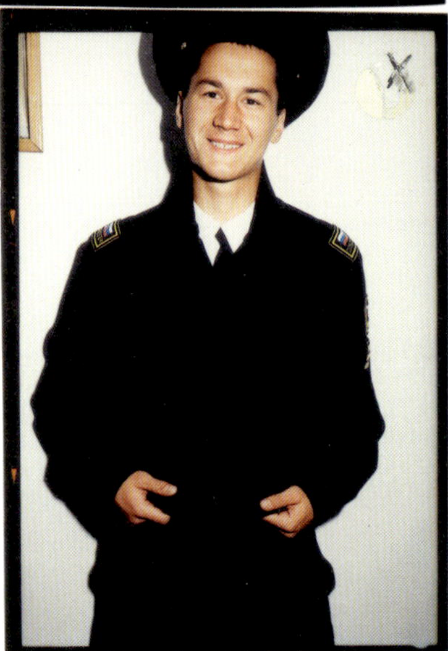

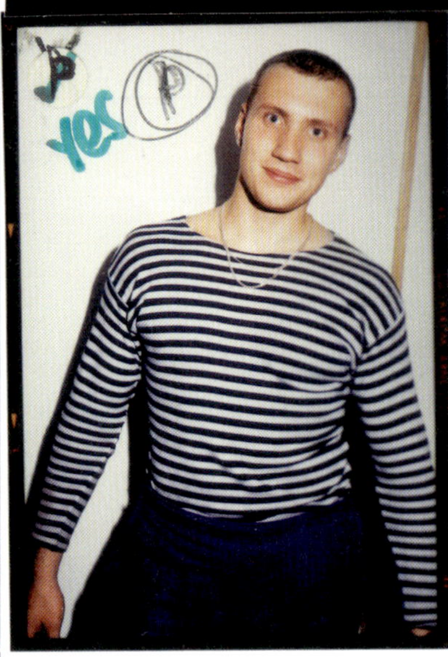
yes

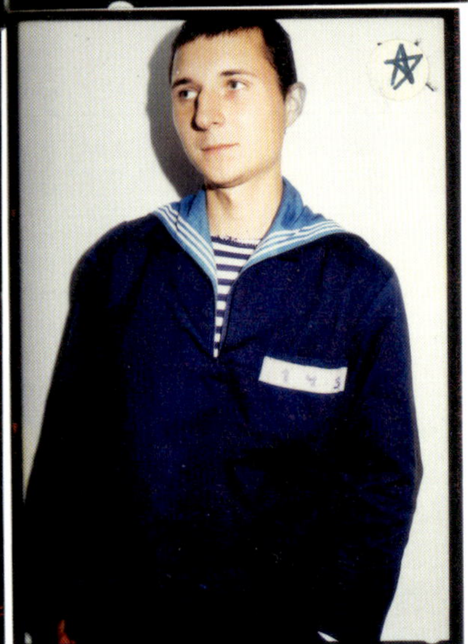

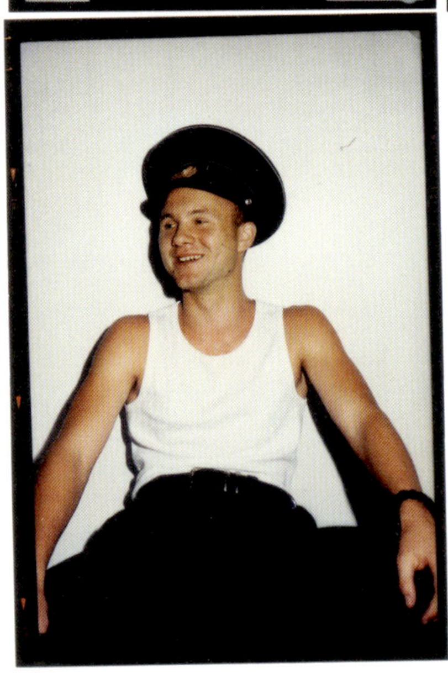

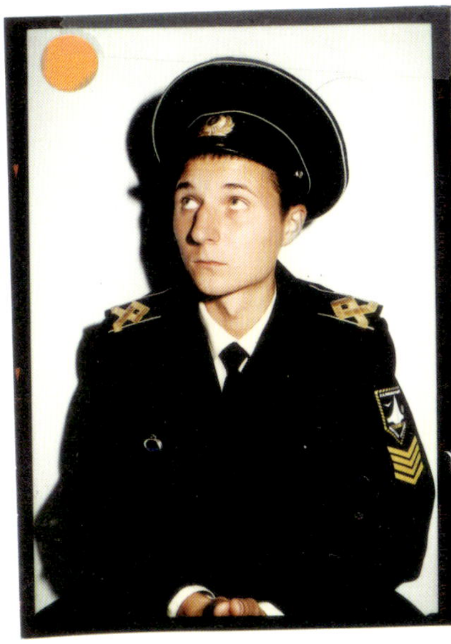
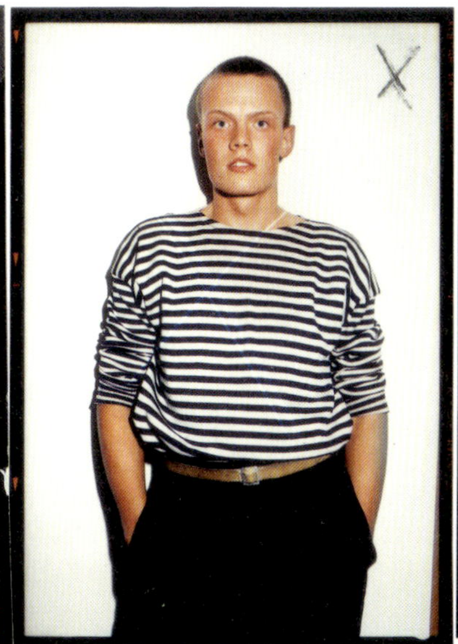
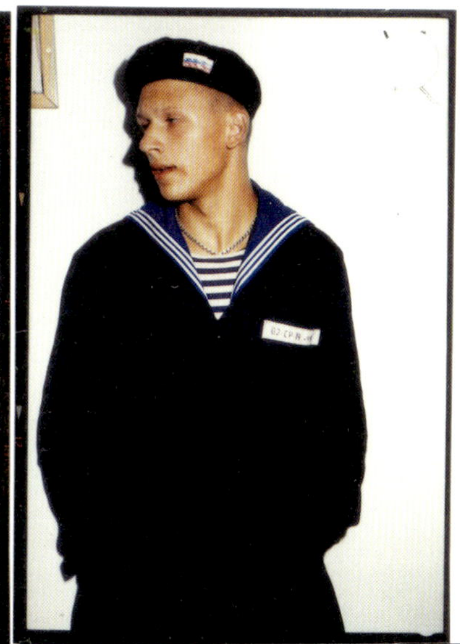
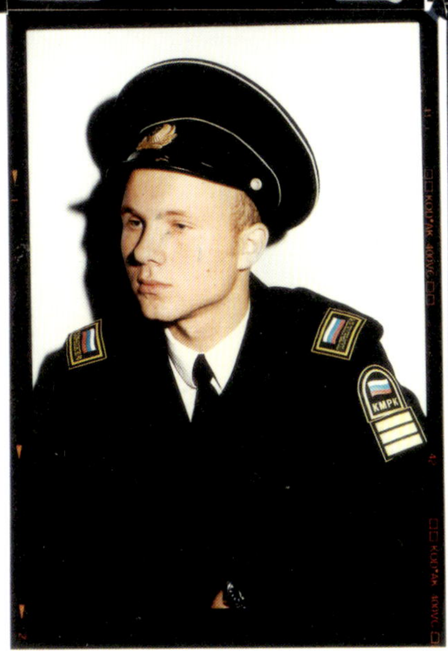
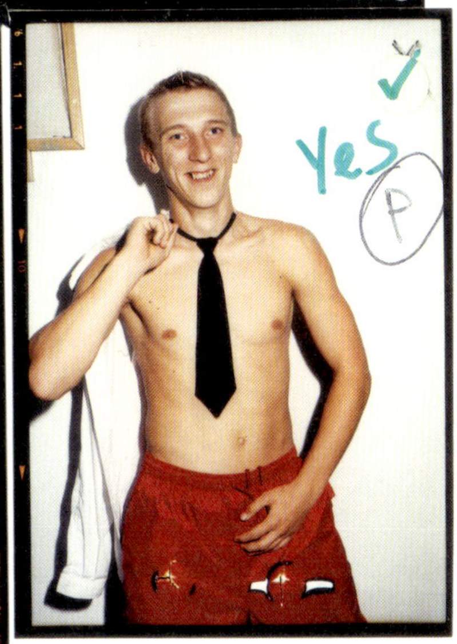
Yes
P

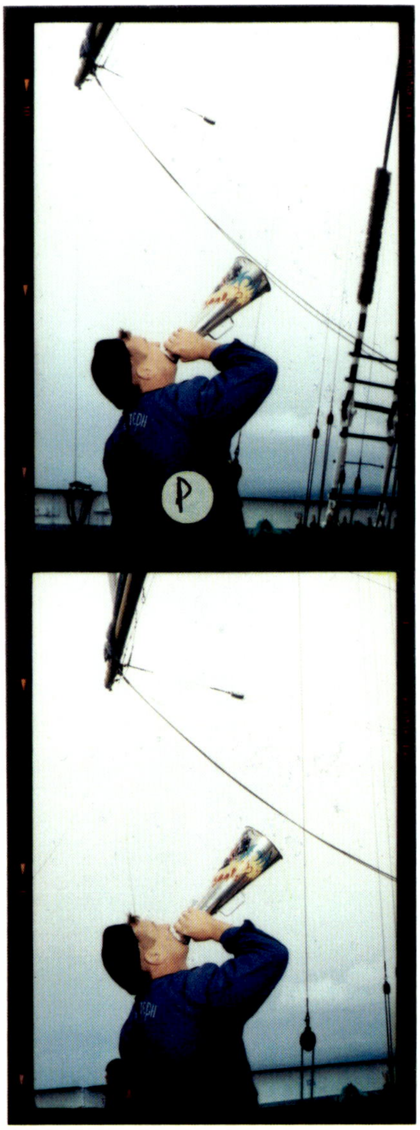

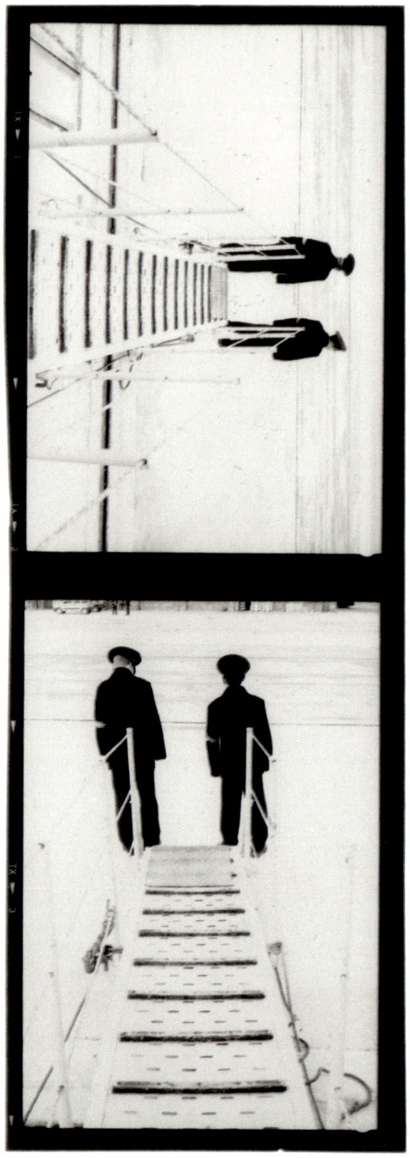

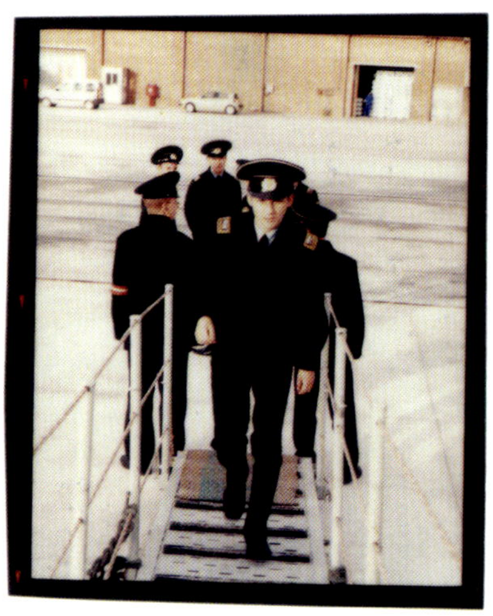

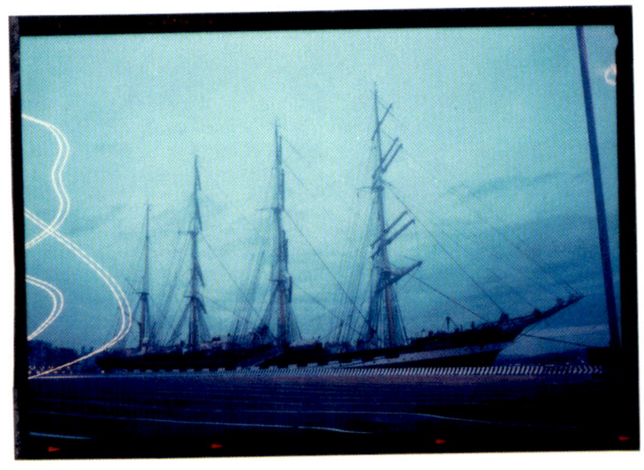

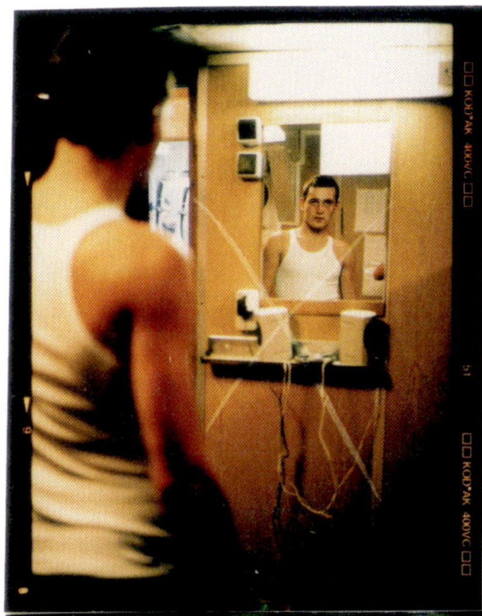
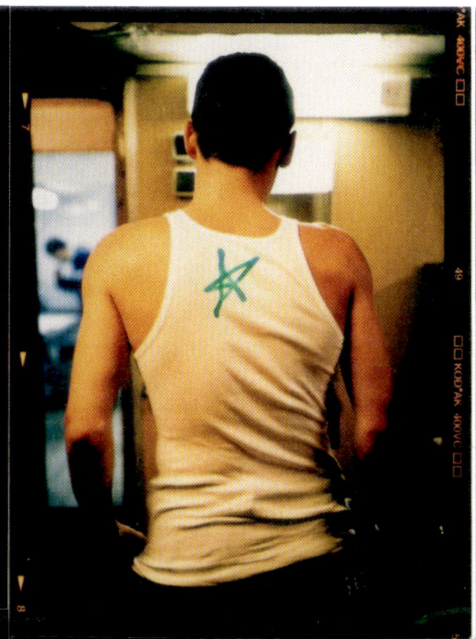
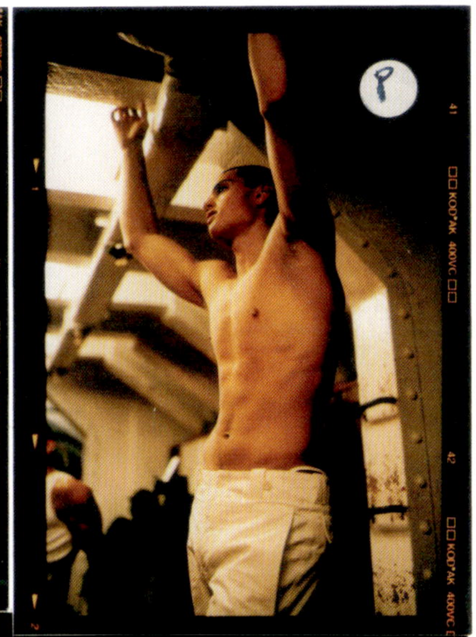
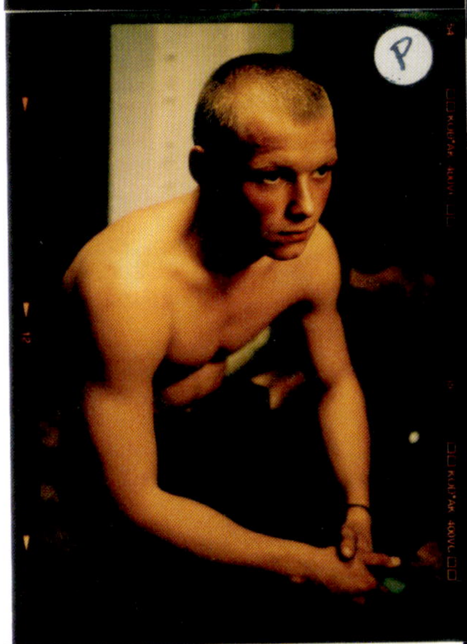
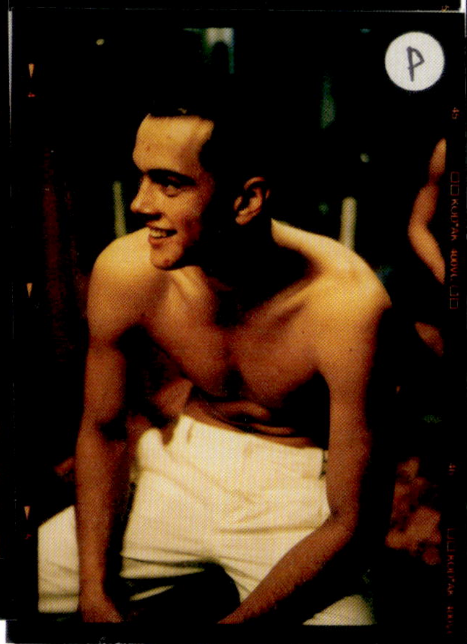
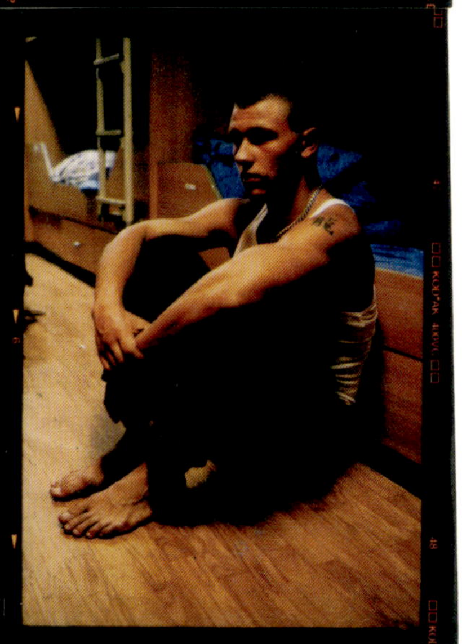
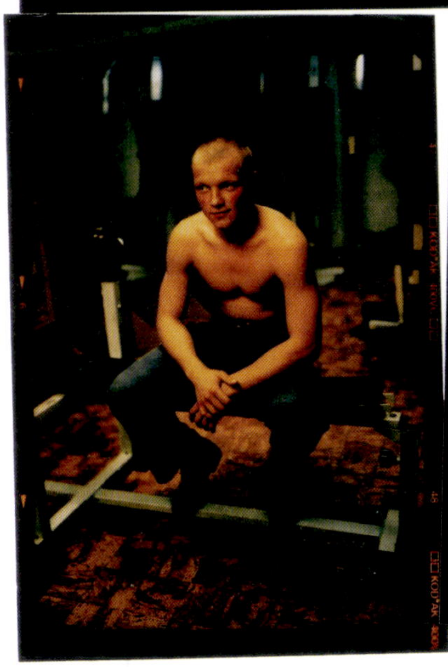
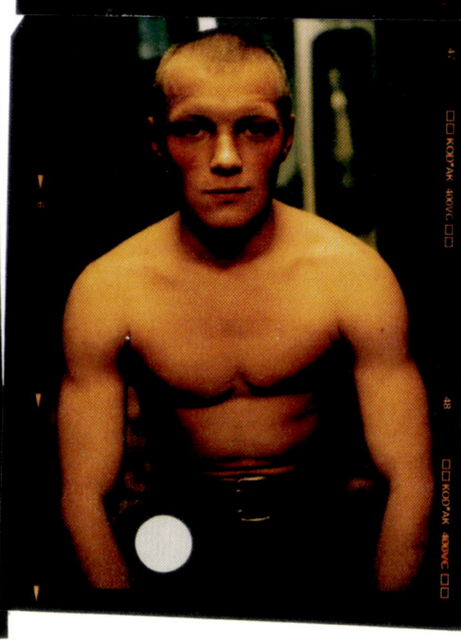
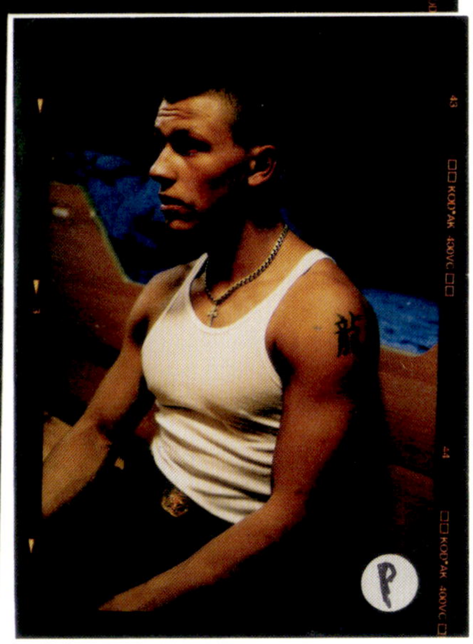

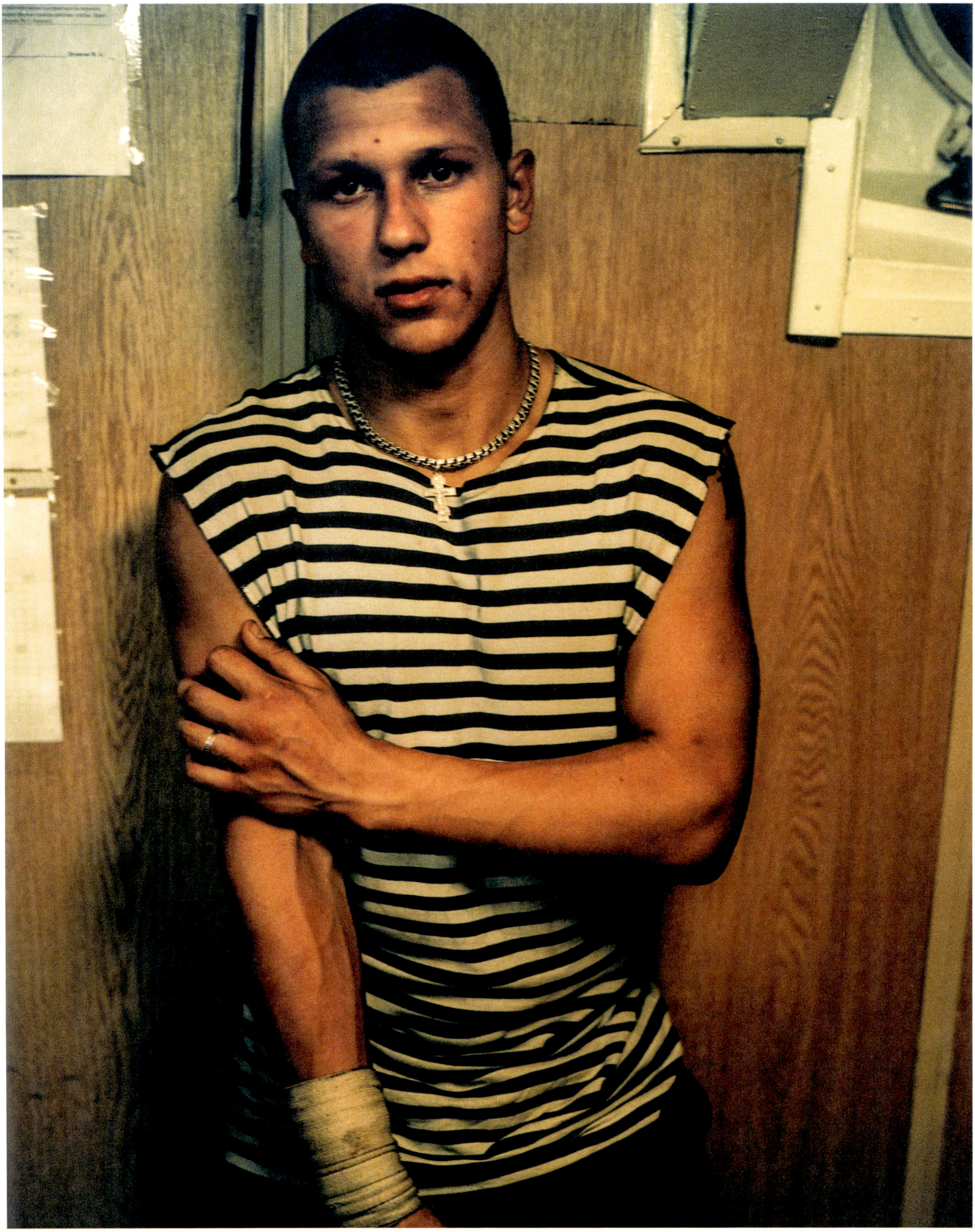

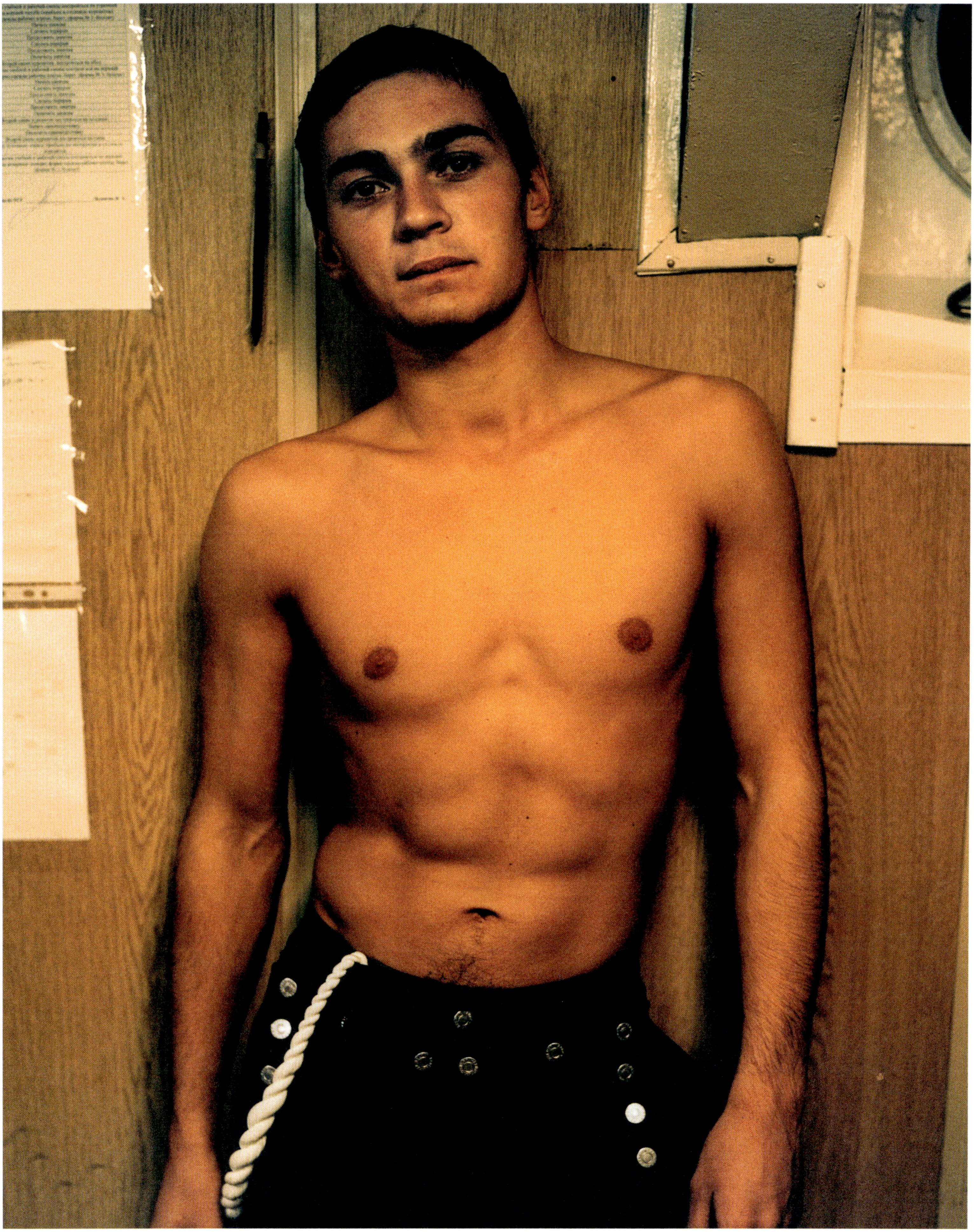

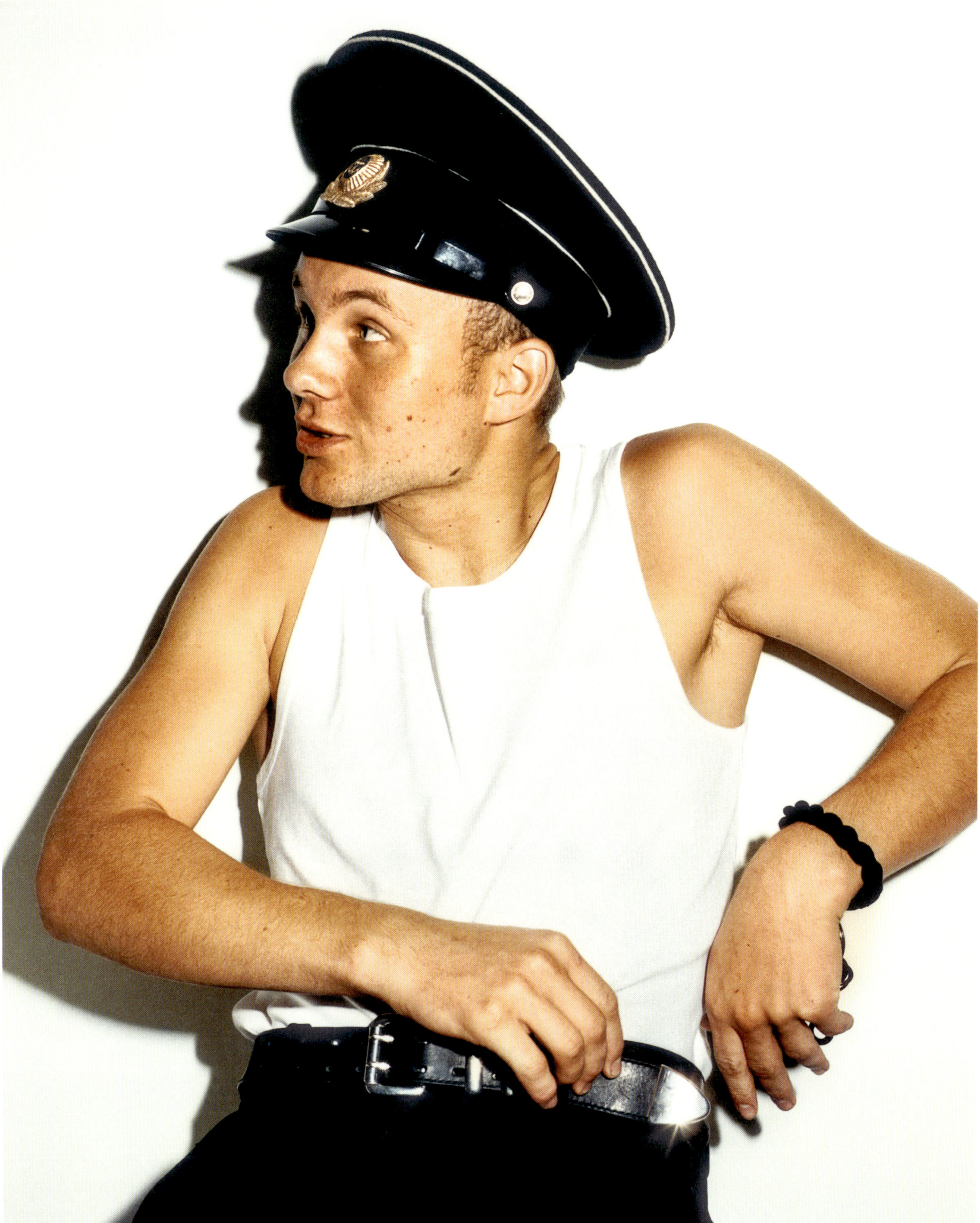

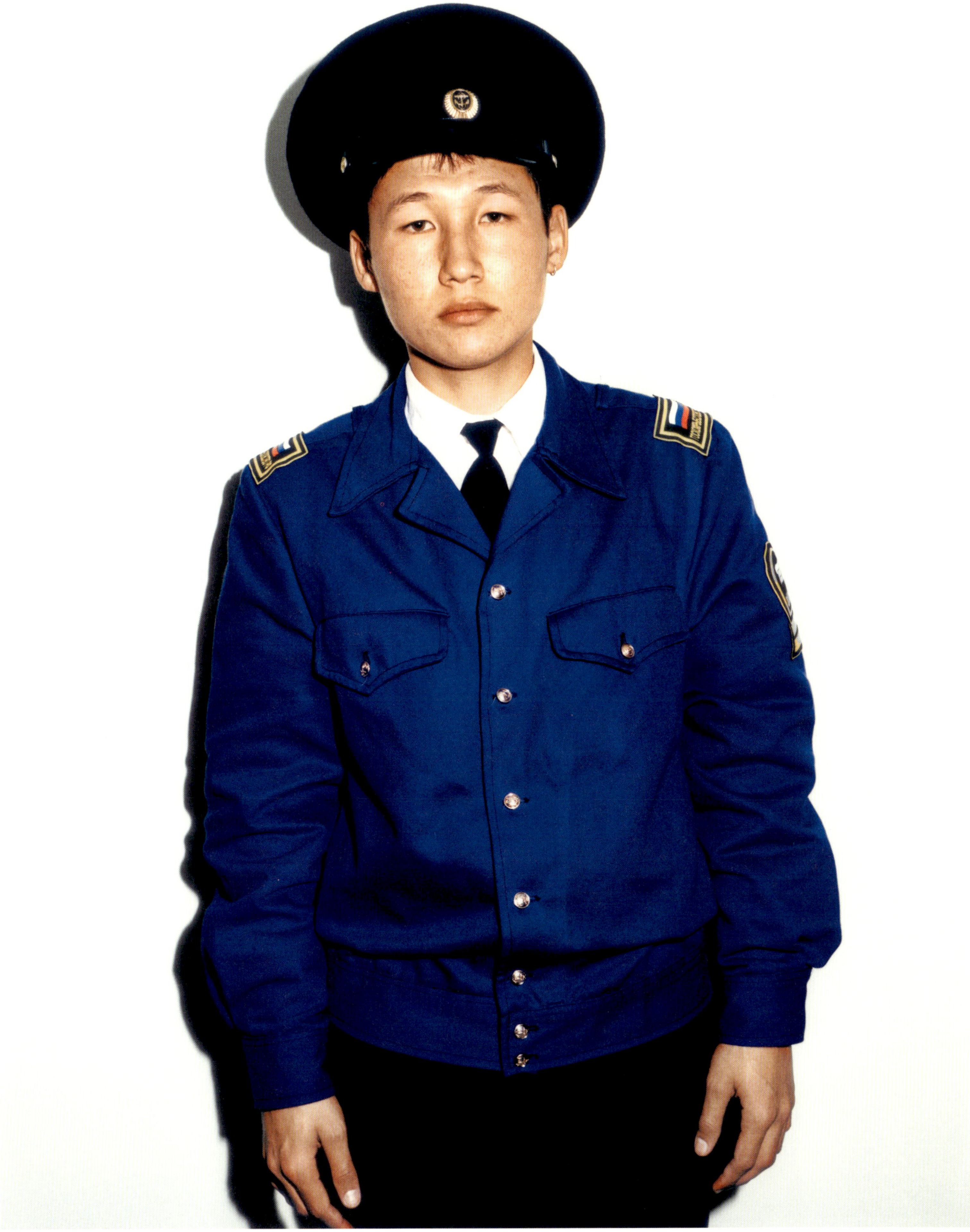

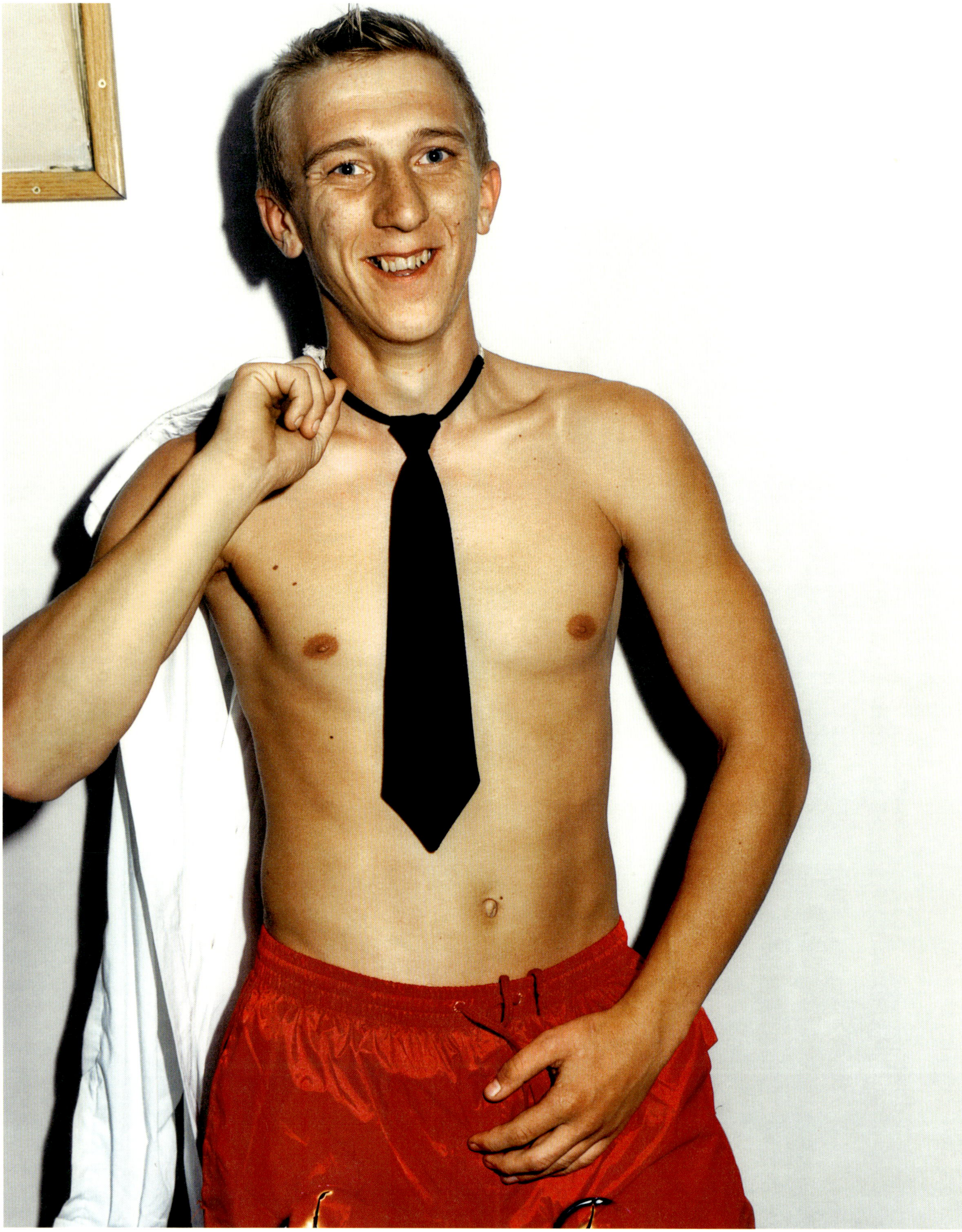

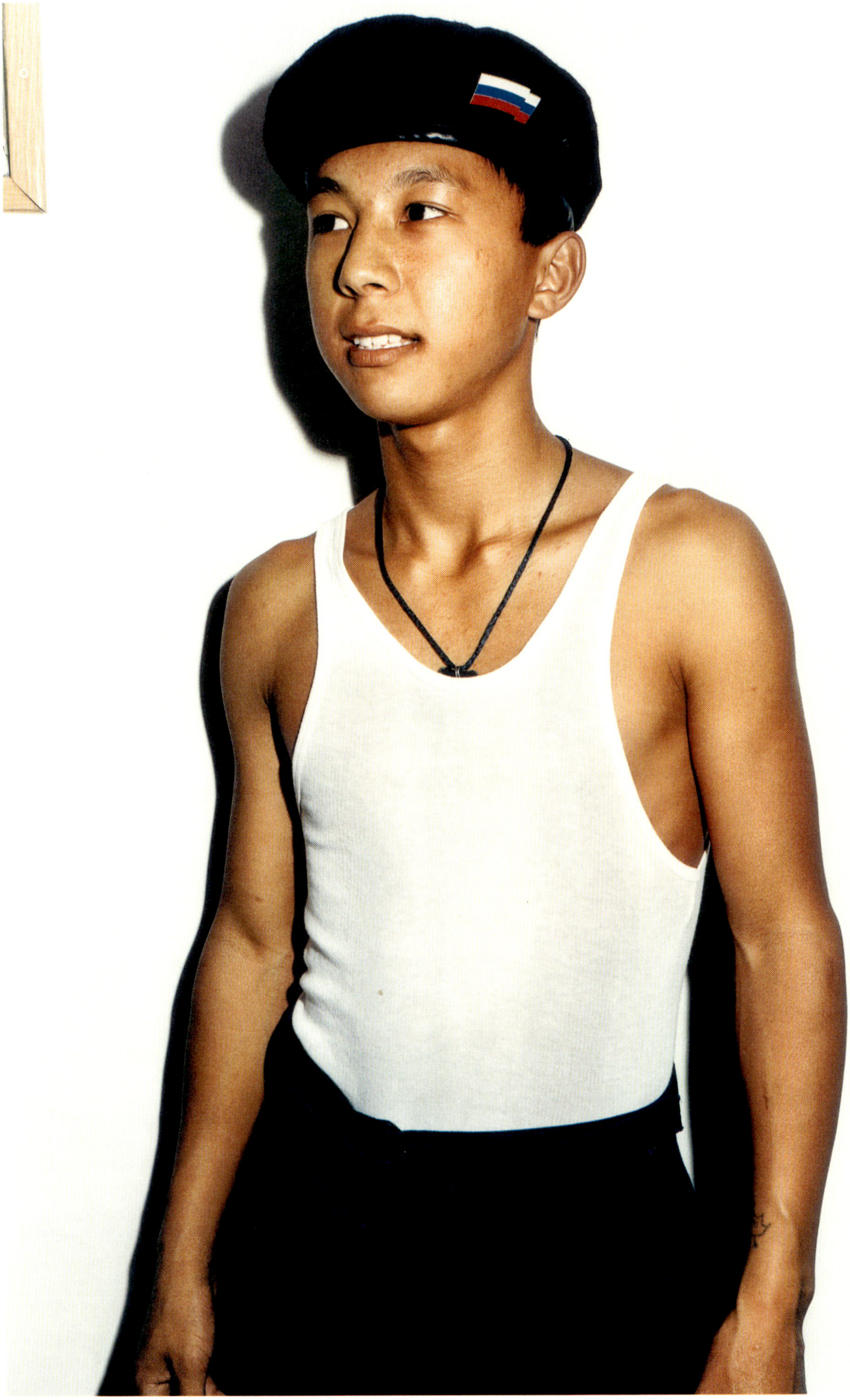

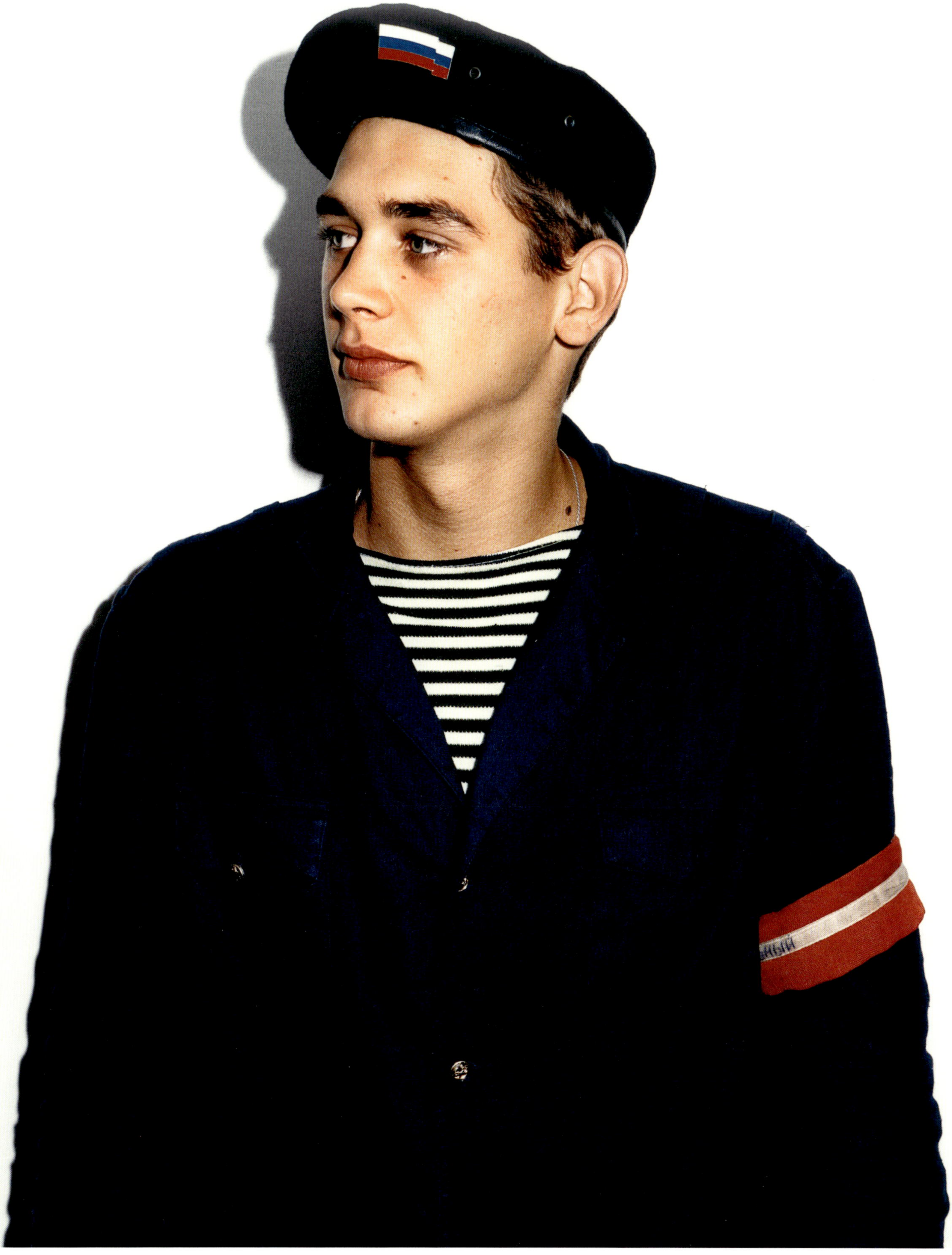

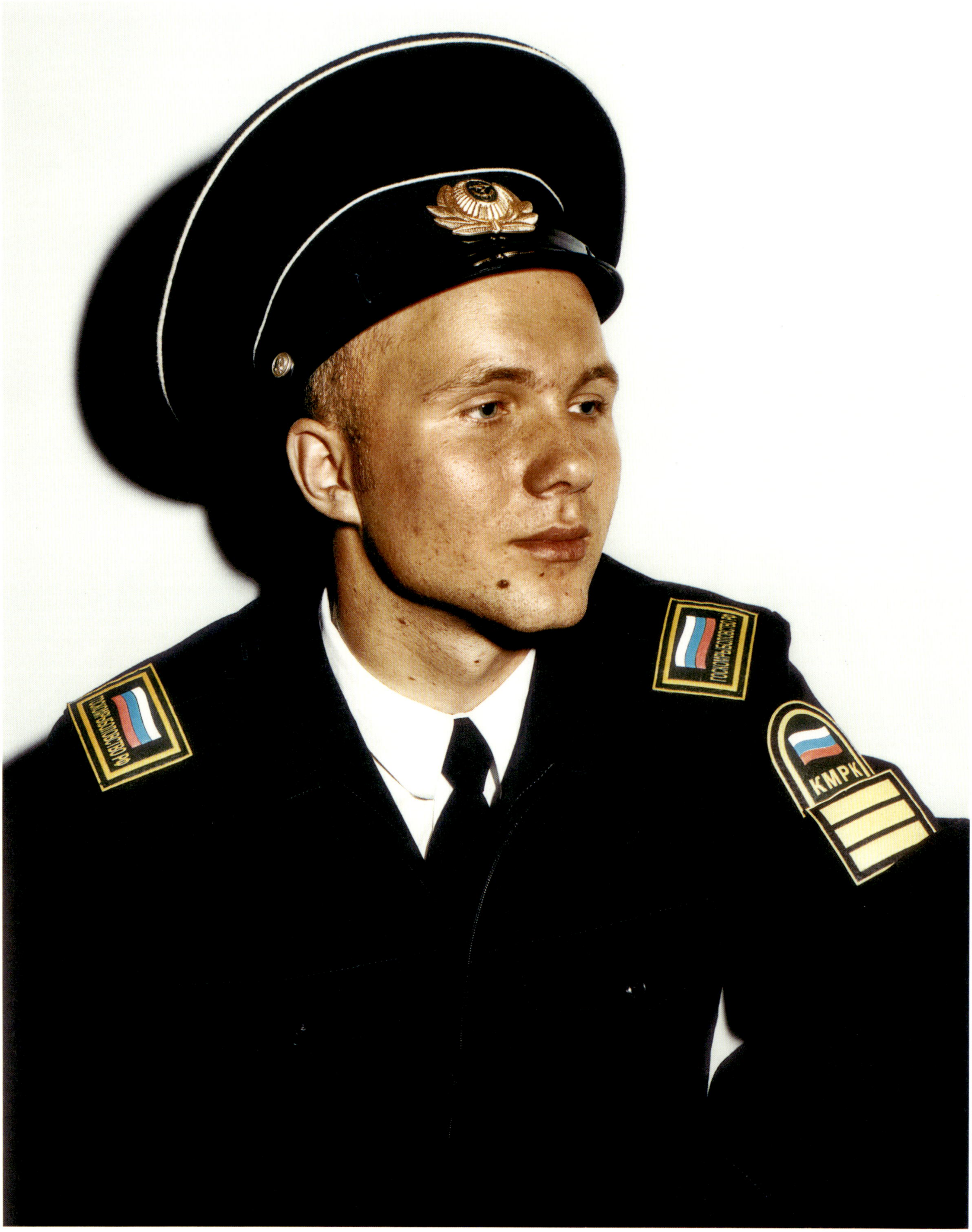
КМРК

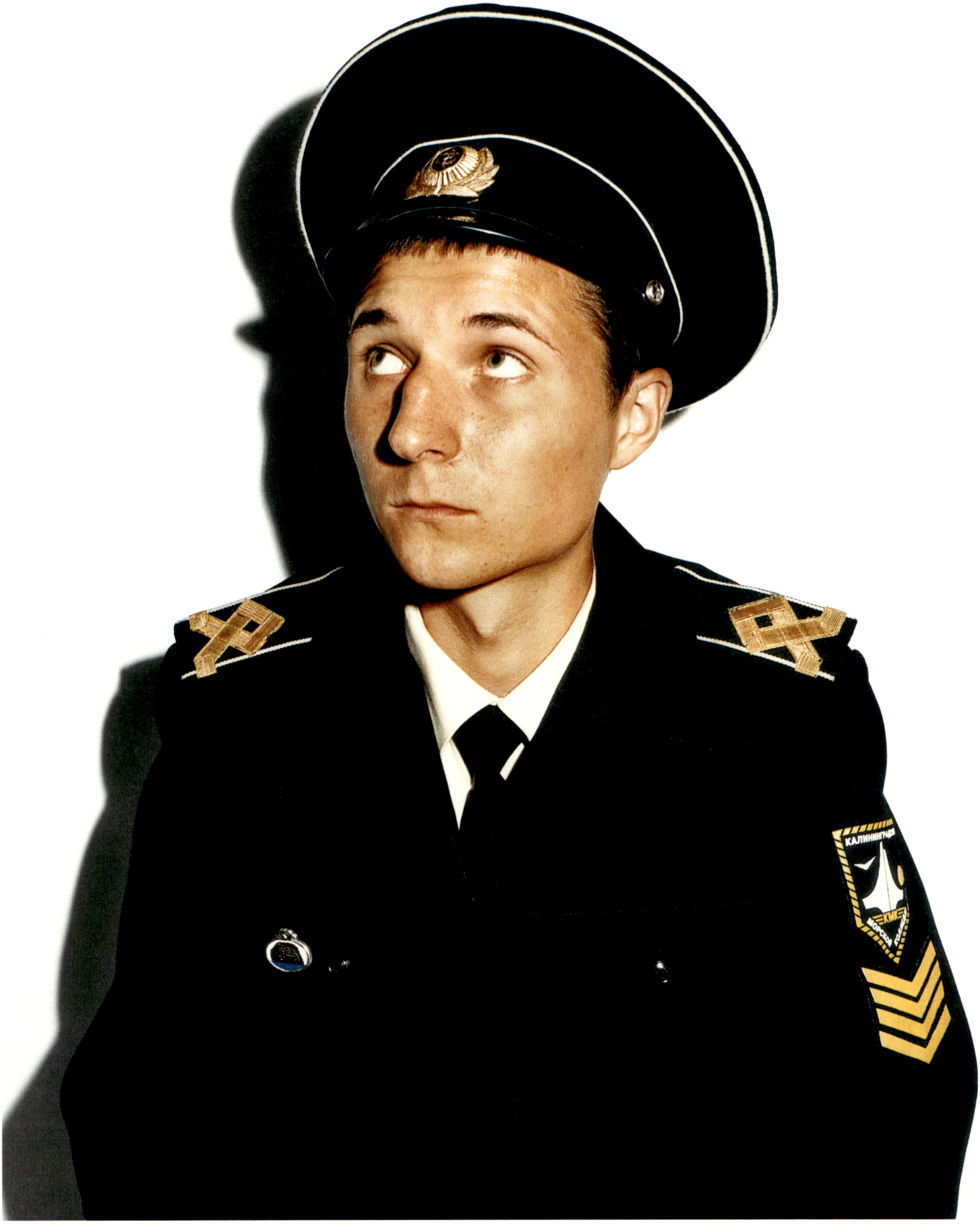

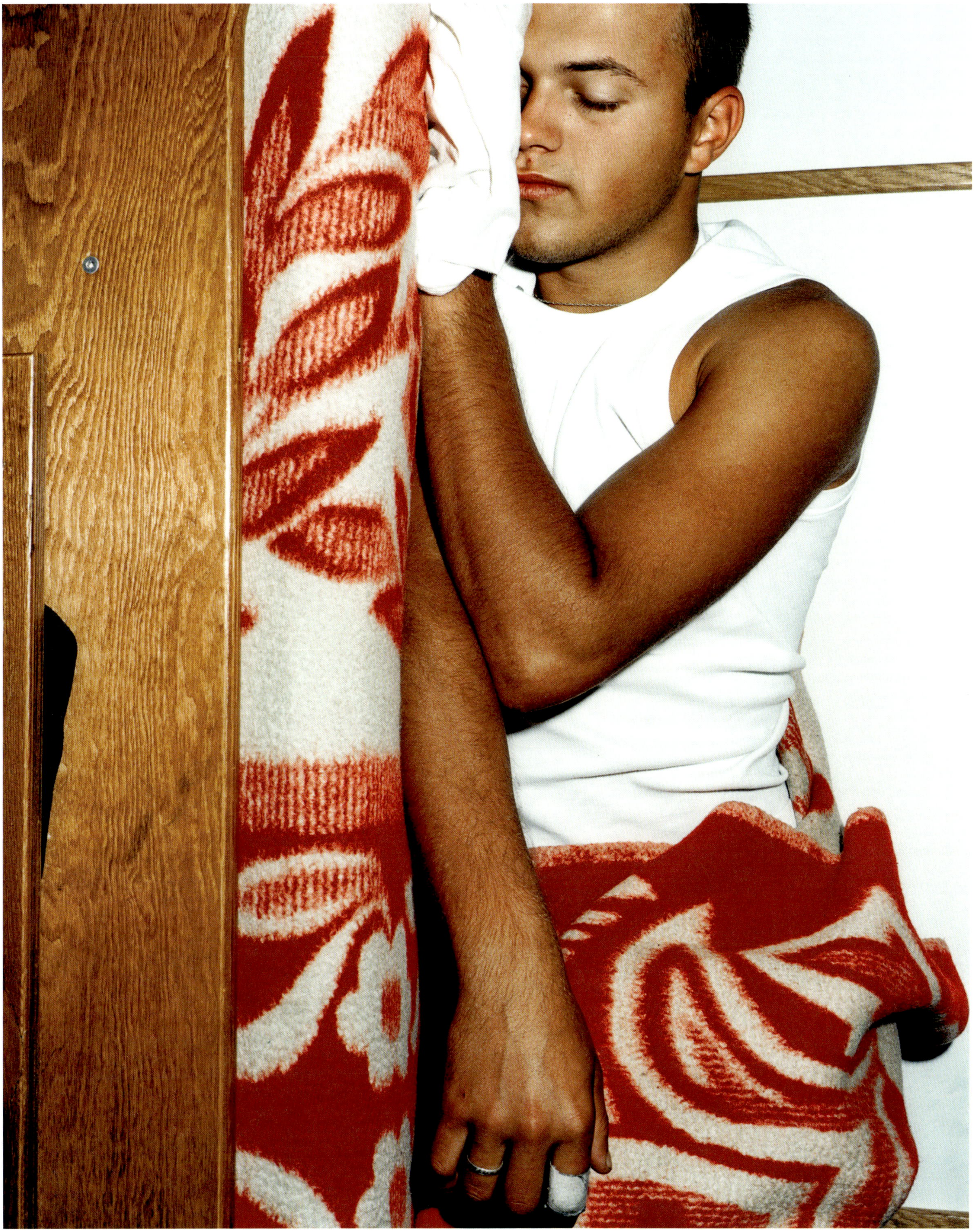

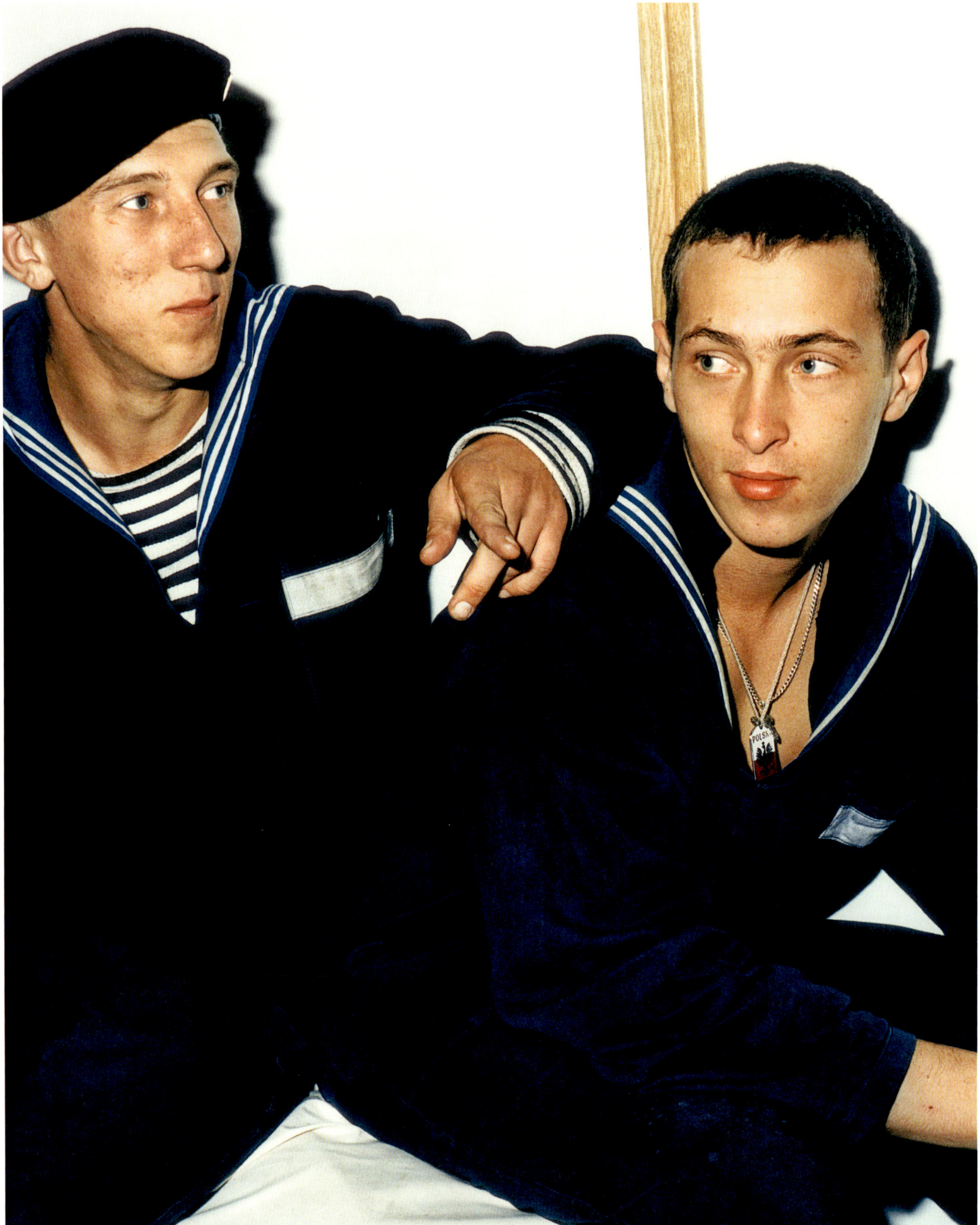
POLSKA

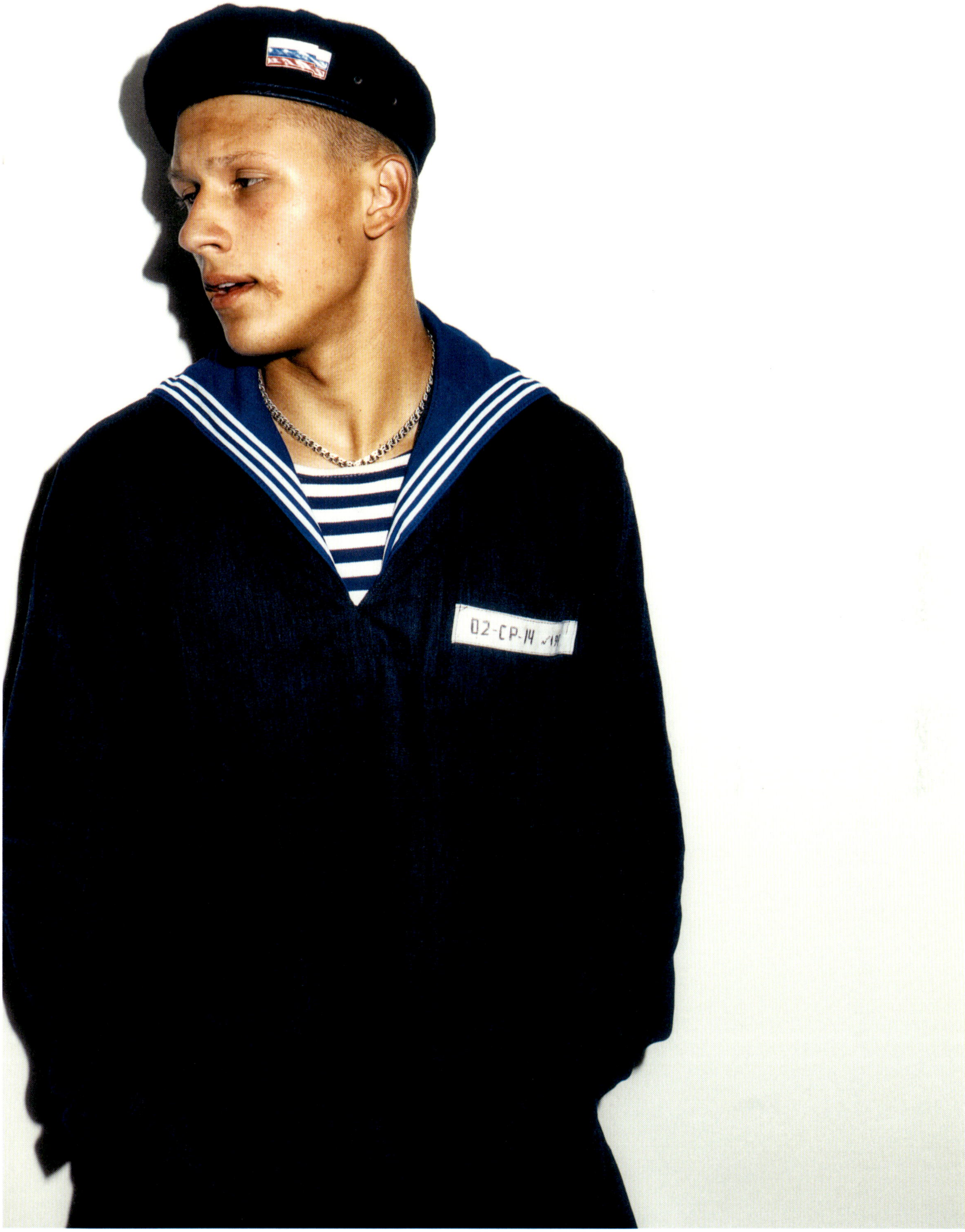
02-CP-14

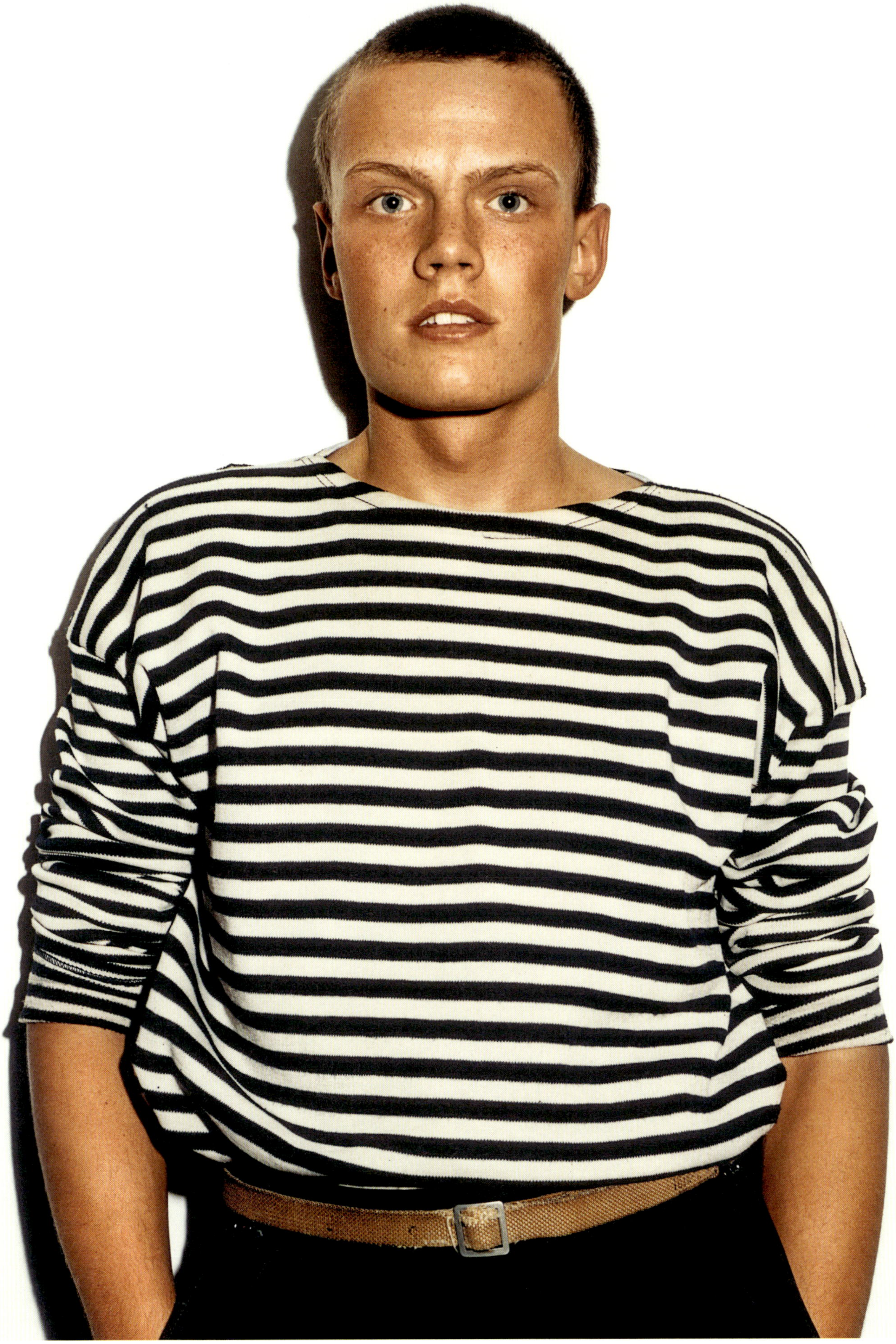

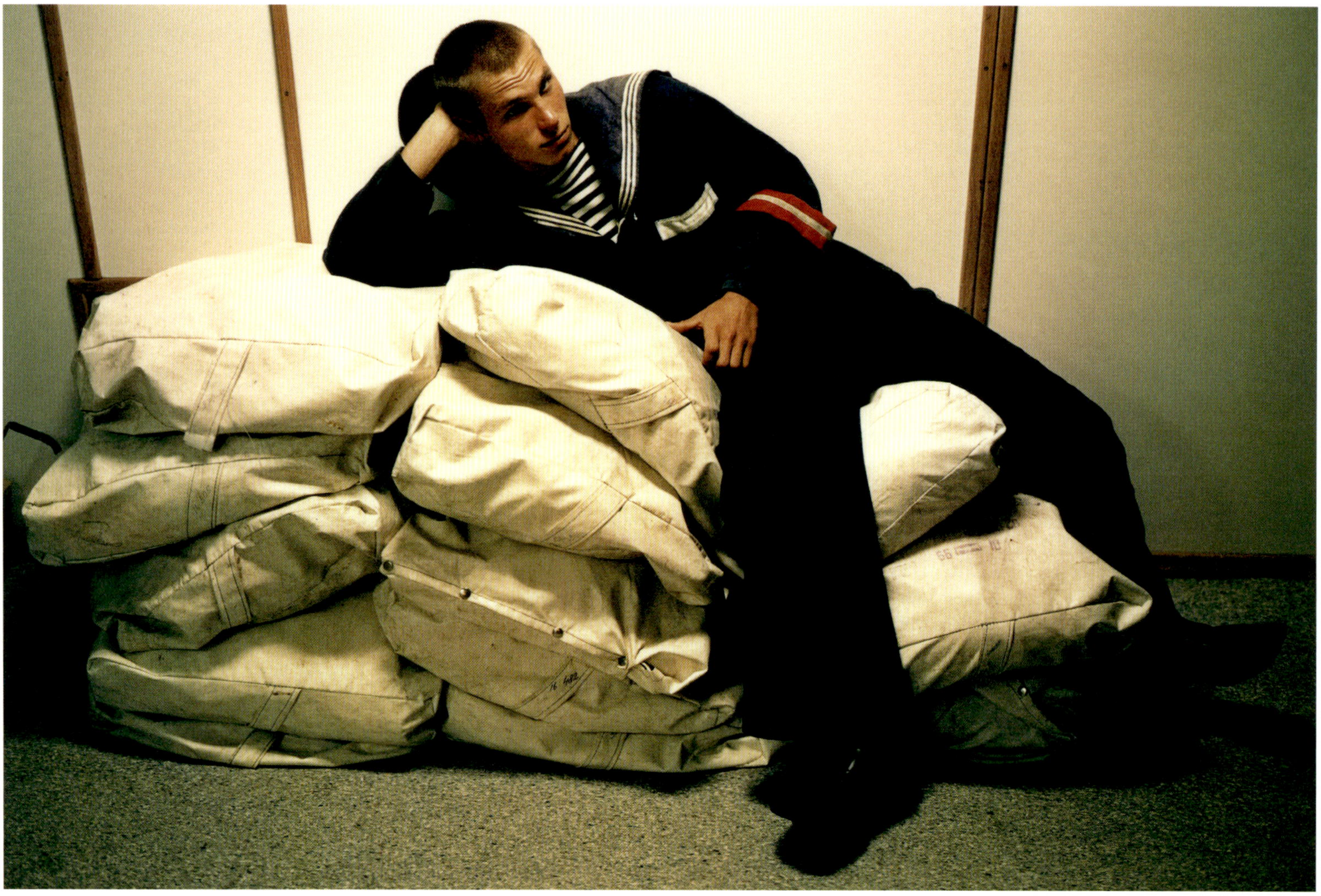

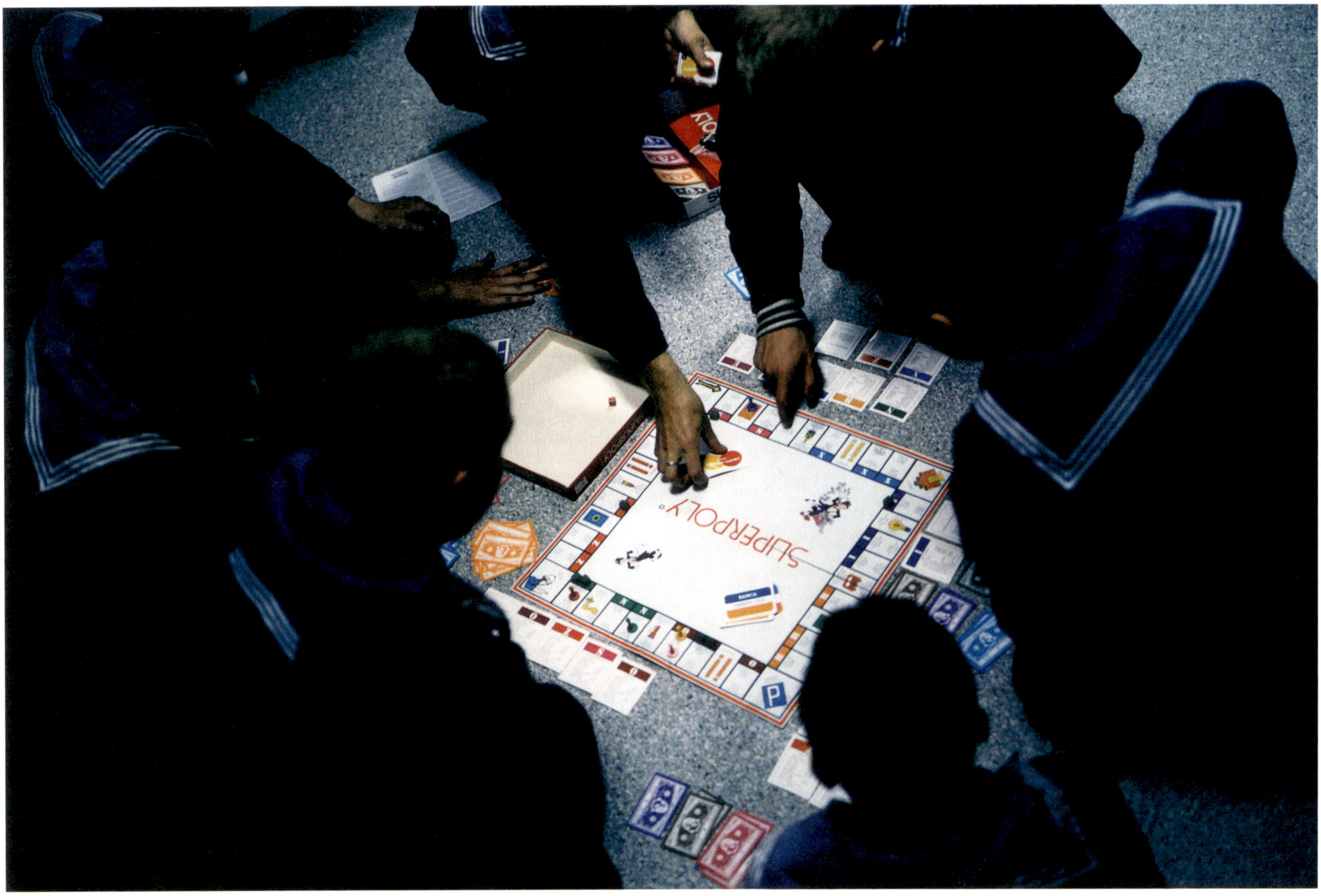
SUPERPOLY

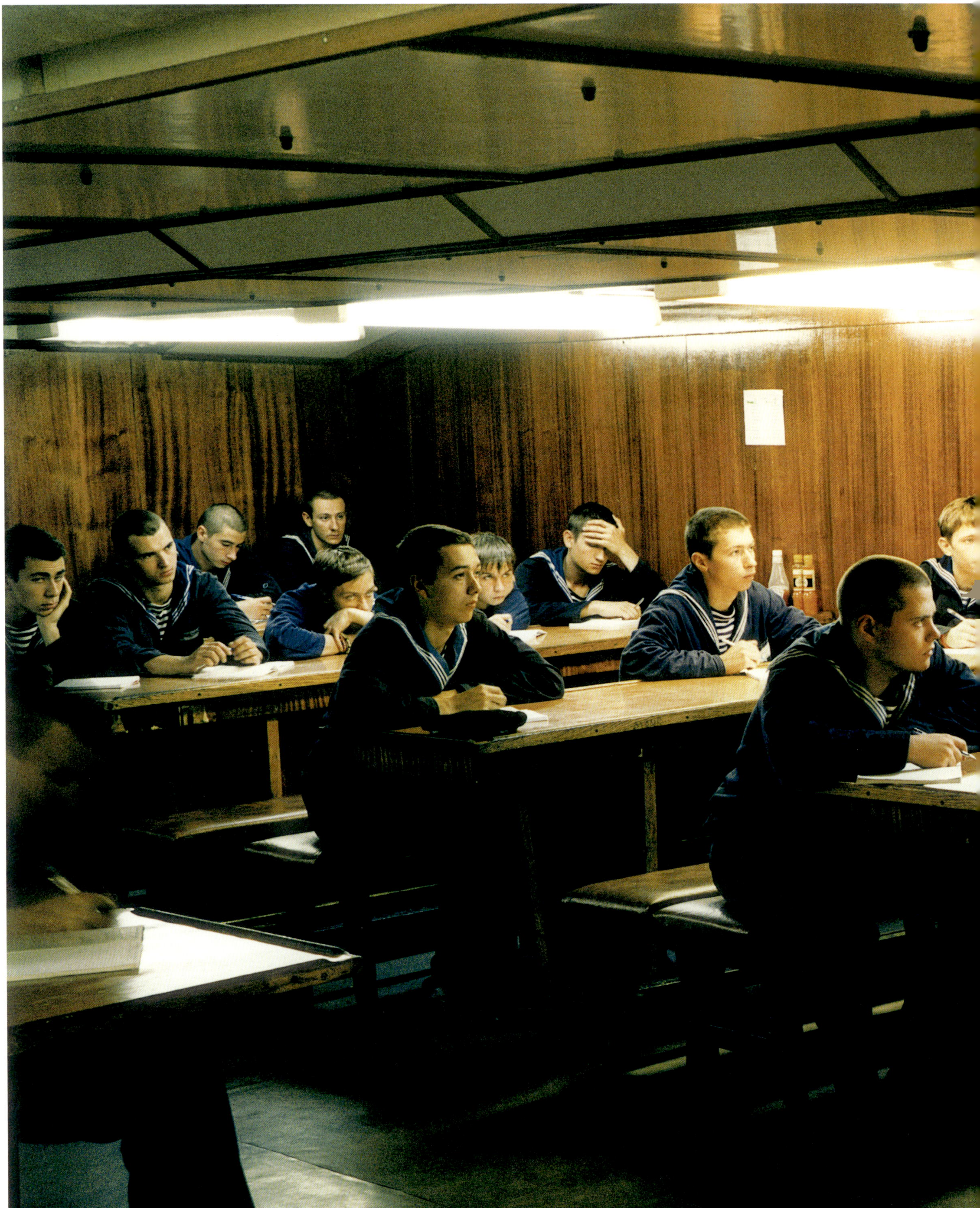

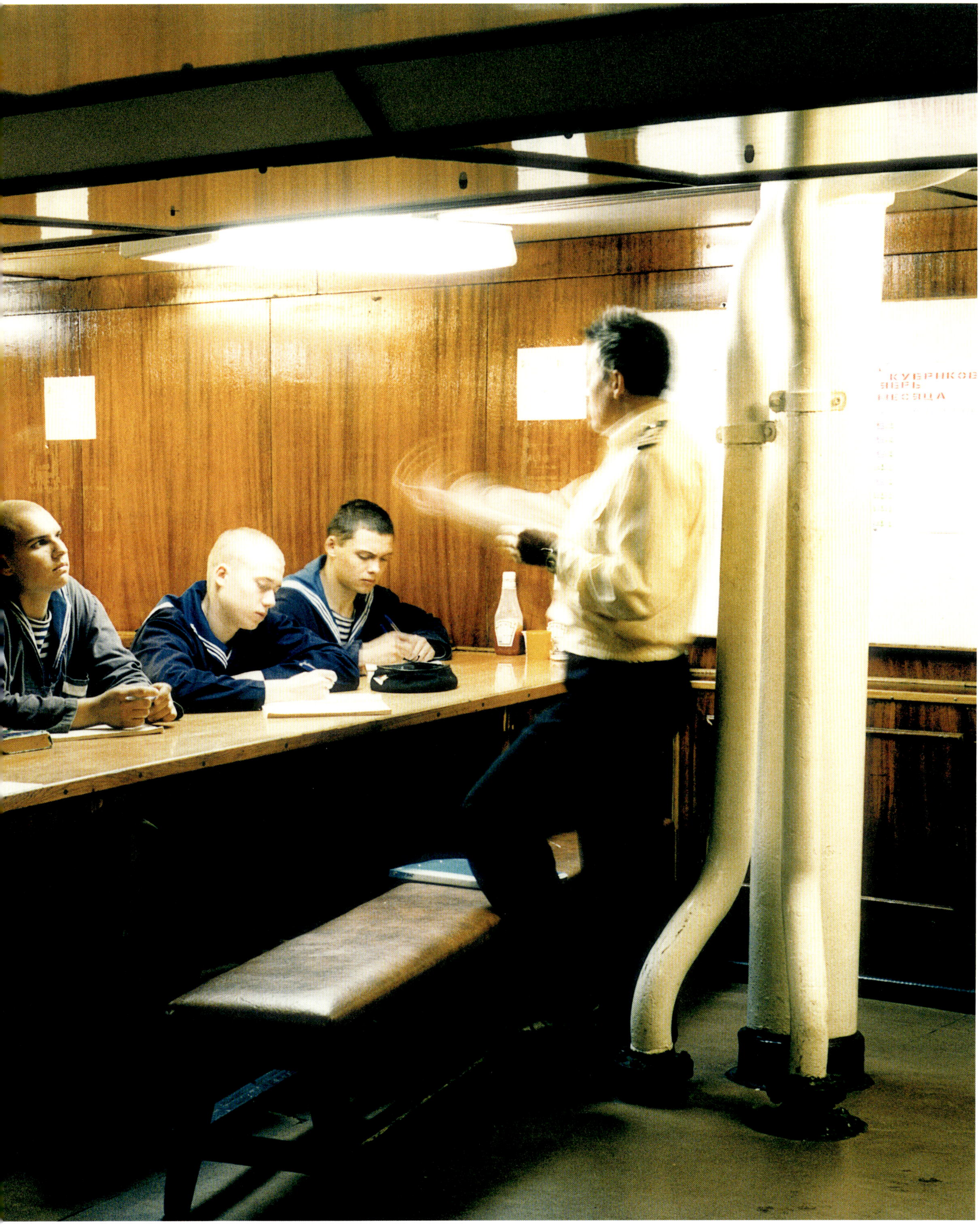

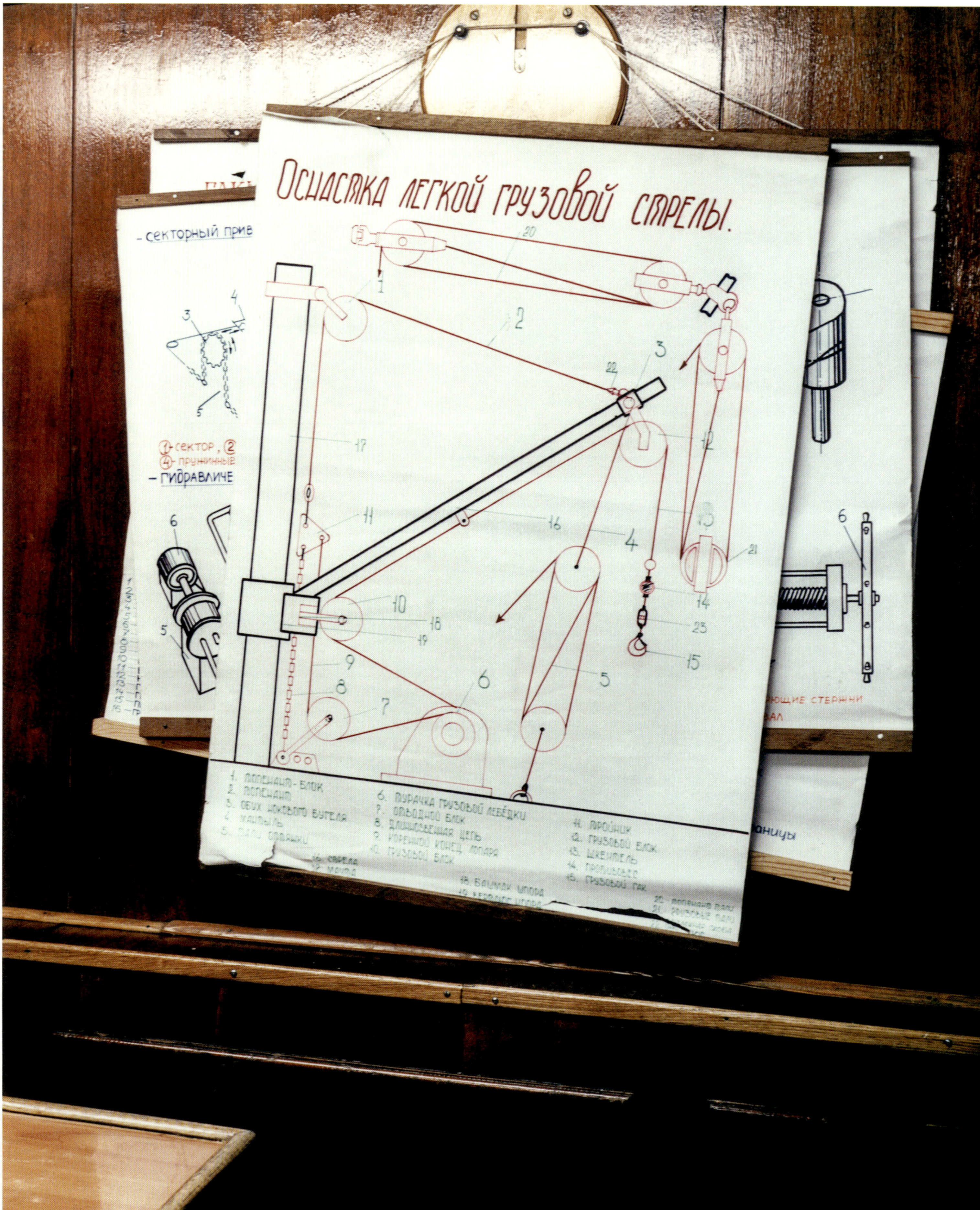
Оснастка легкой грузовой стрелы.
1. Топенант-блок
2. Топенант
6. Турачка грузовой лебёдки
7. Отводной блок
10. Грузовой блок
11. Тройник
12. Грузовой блок
13. Шкентель
14. Противовес
15. Грузовой гак

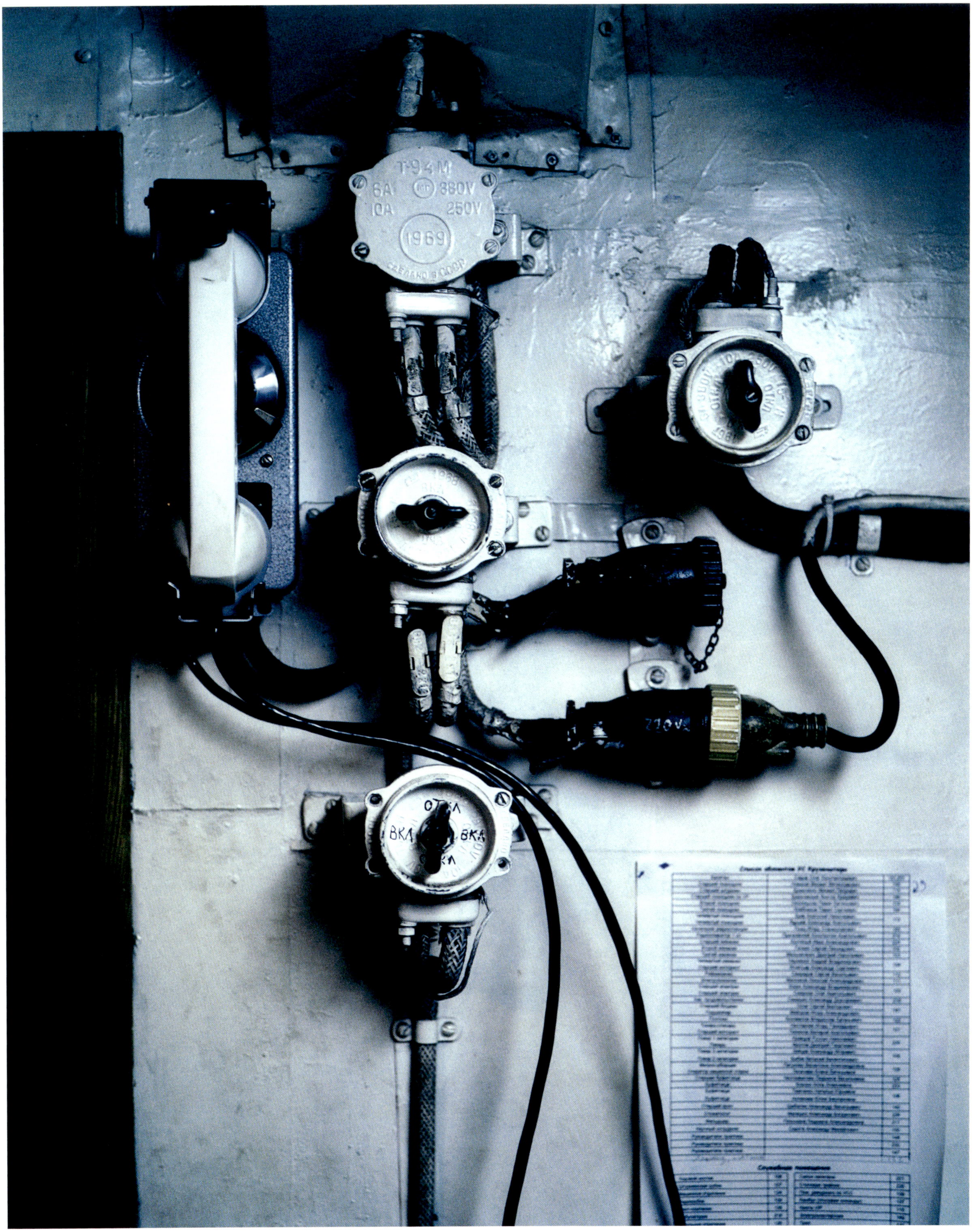
T-94M
6A 380V
10A 250V
1969
ОТКЛ
ВКЛ
ВКЛ

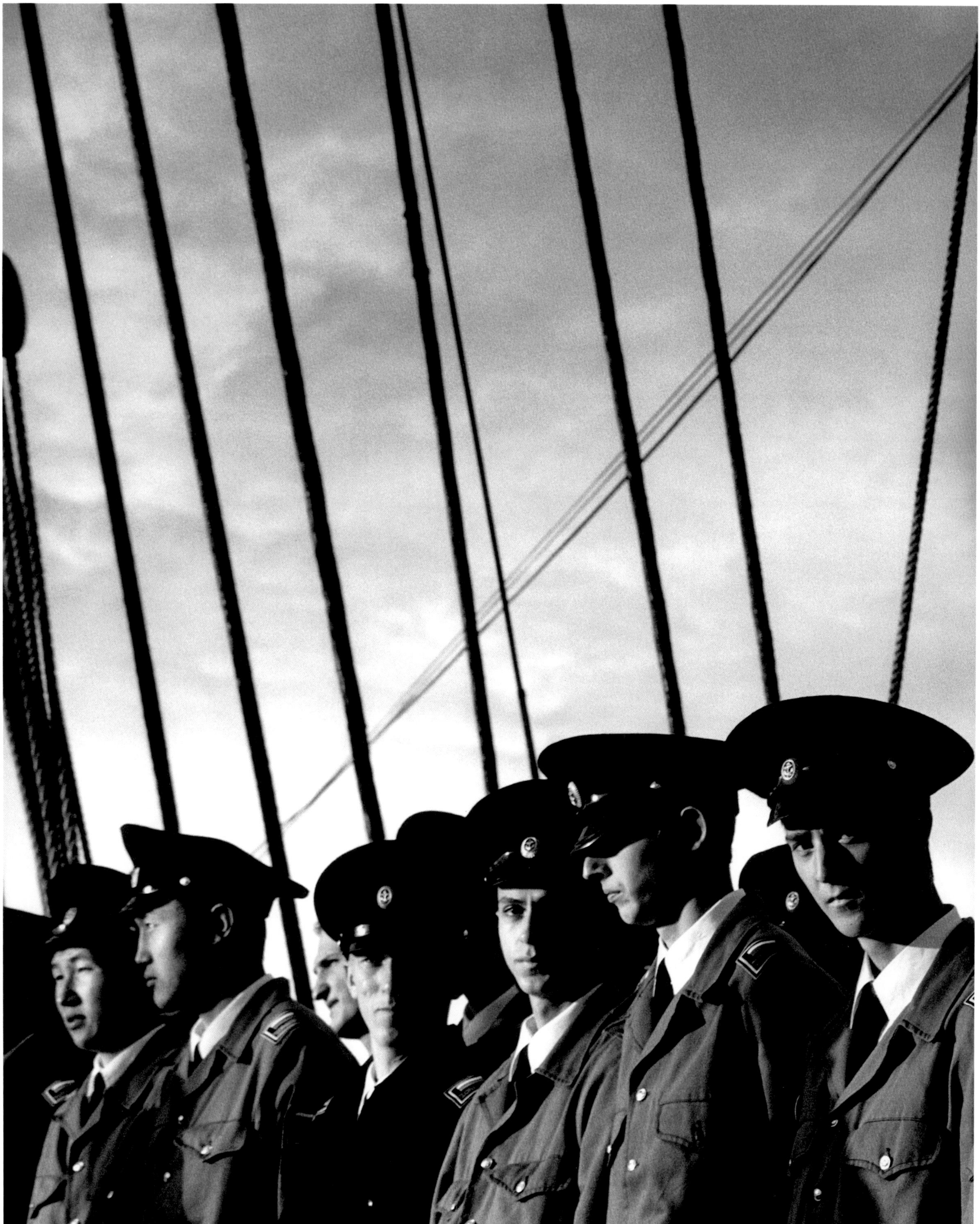

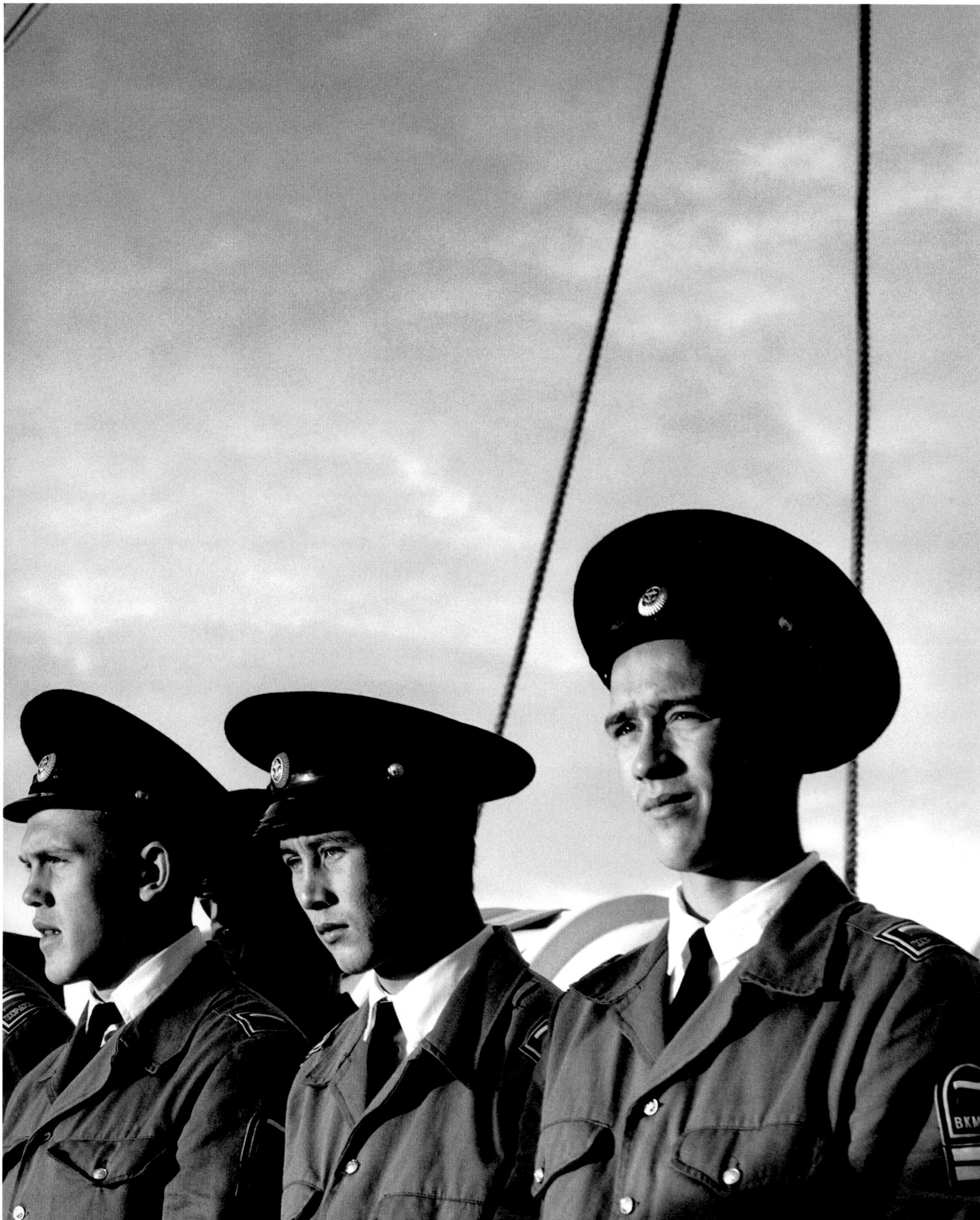
BKM

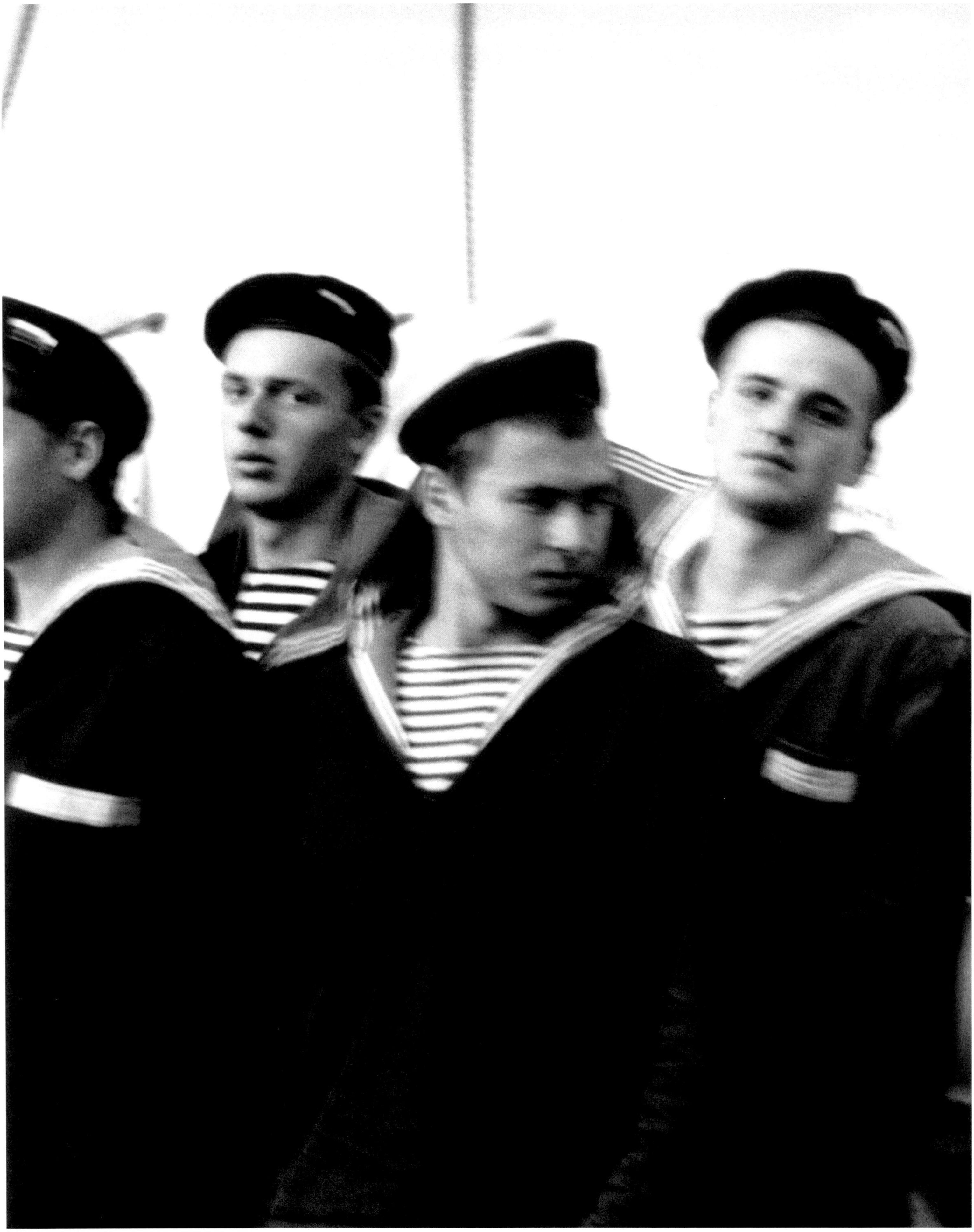

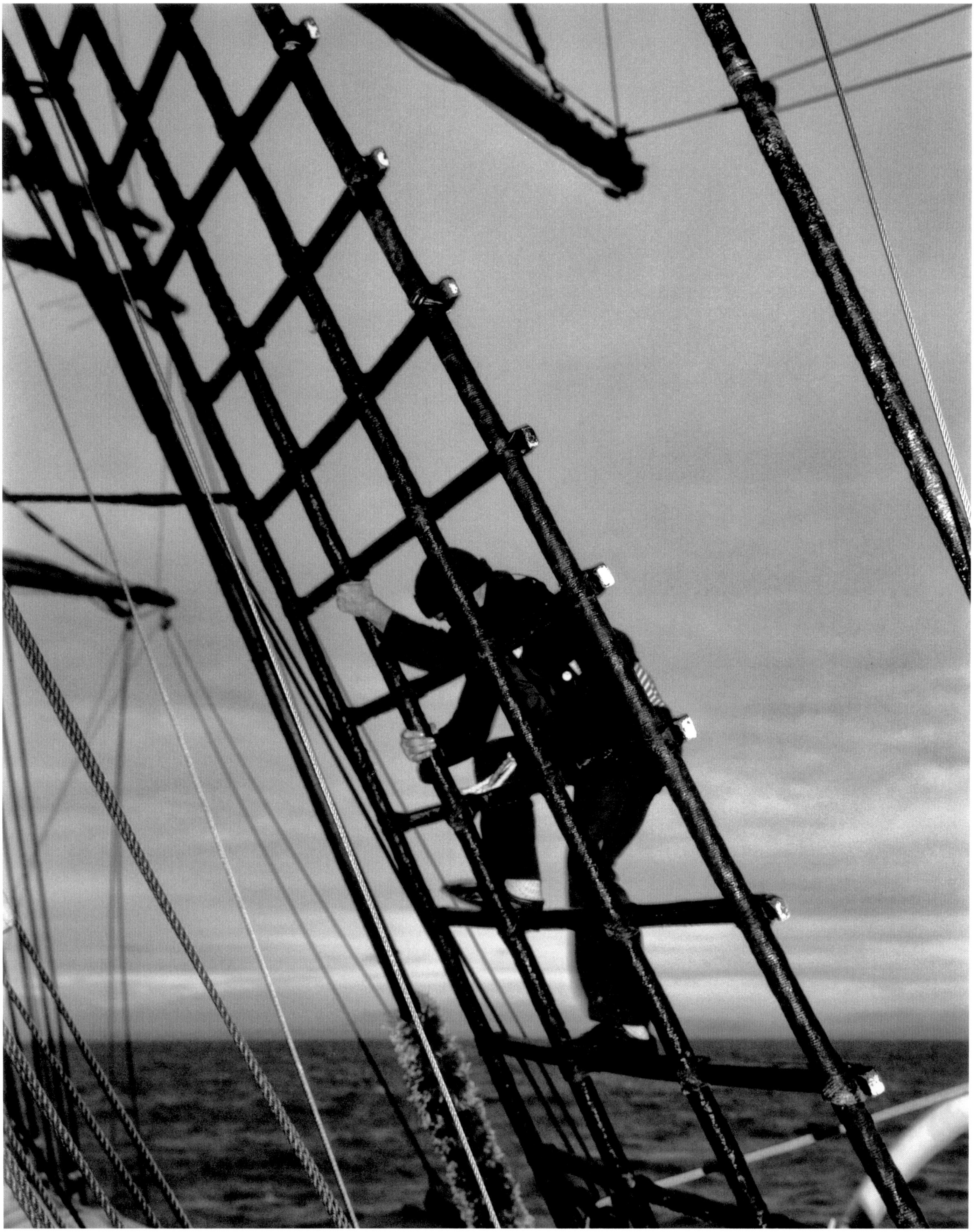

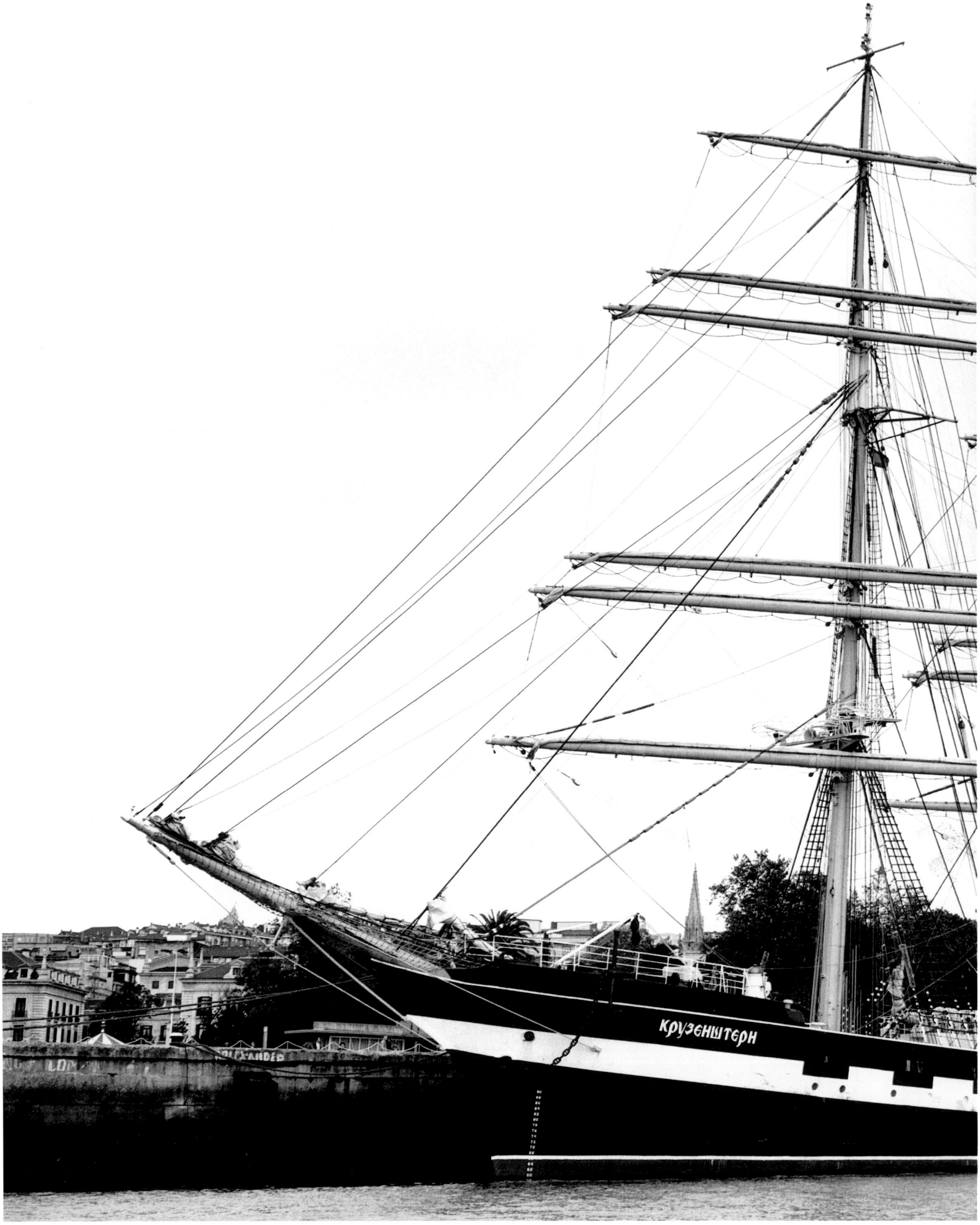
КРУЗЕНШТЕРН

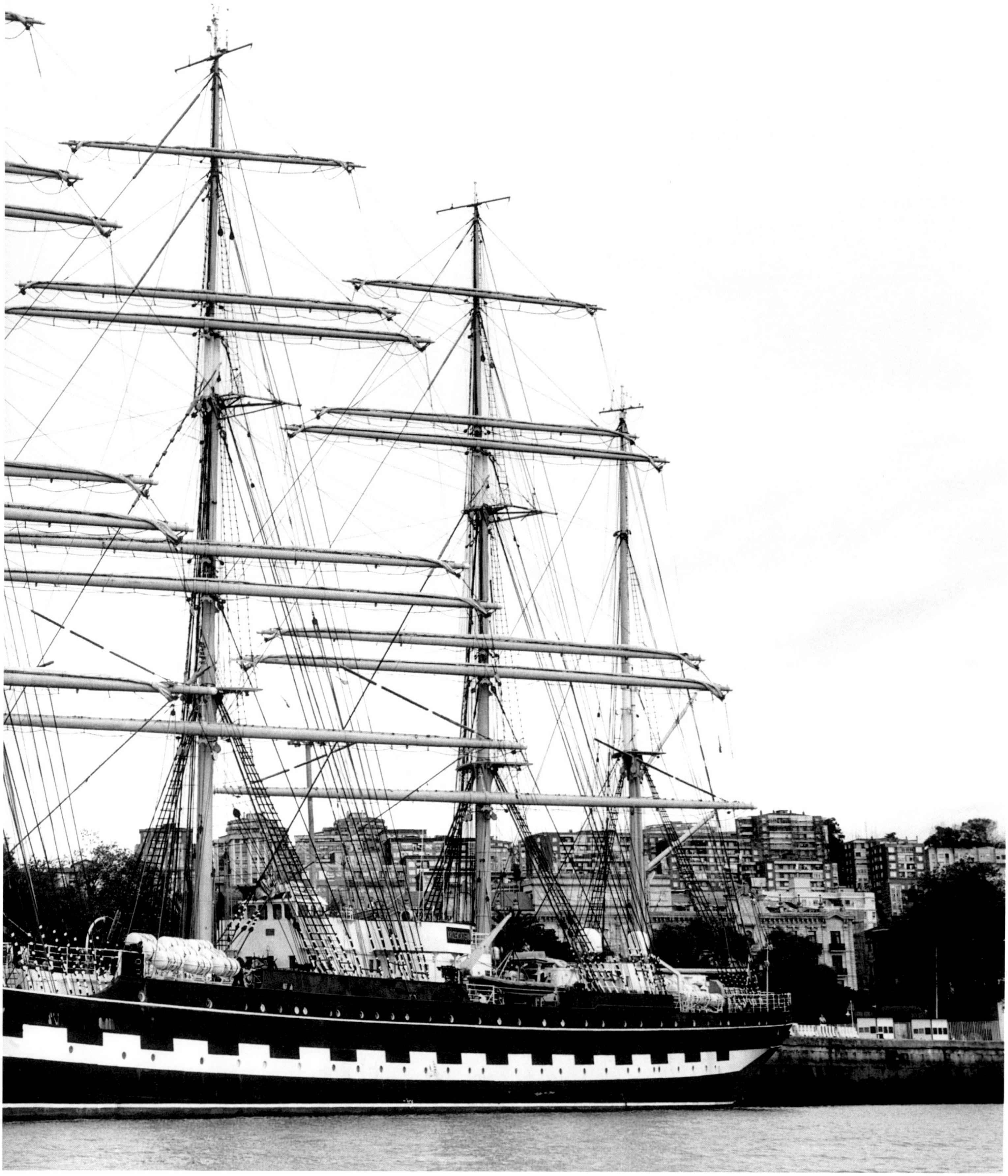

III

Paul R. Tregurtha

The MV Paul R. Tregurtha, the longest ship operating on the Great Lakes complex, is a bulk carrier freighter unofficially known as the 'Queen of the Lakes.' Due to her size, the Tregurtha is restricted to the Great Lakes Waterway, and is unable to navigate the St. Lawrence Seaway which connects to the Atlantic Ocean.

Since the late 19th century, boats (or lakers), like the Tregurtha have carried bulk cargoes of materials such as limestone, iron ore, grain, coal, or salt back and forth from the mines and fields of the upper Great Lakes to the populated industrial areas and steel-making towns farther east.

Because the waves on the Great Lakes do not reach the size of ocean waves, particularly the waves' height, lakers are in less danger of being suspended between two waves and breaking, so the ratio between the ship's length, beam and its depth is often larger than that of seafaring ships.

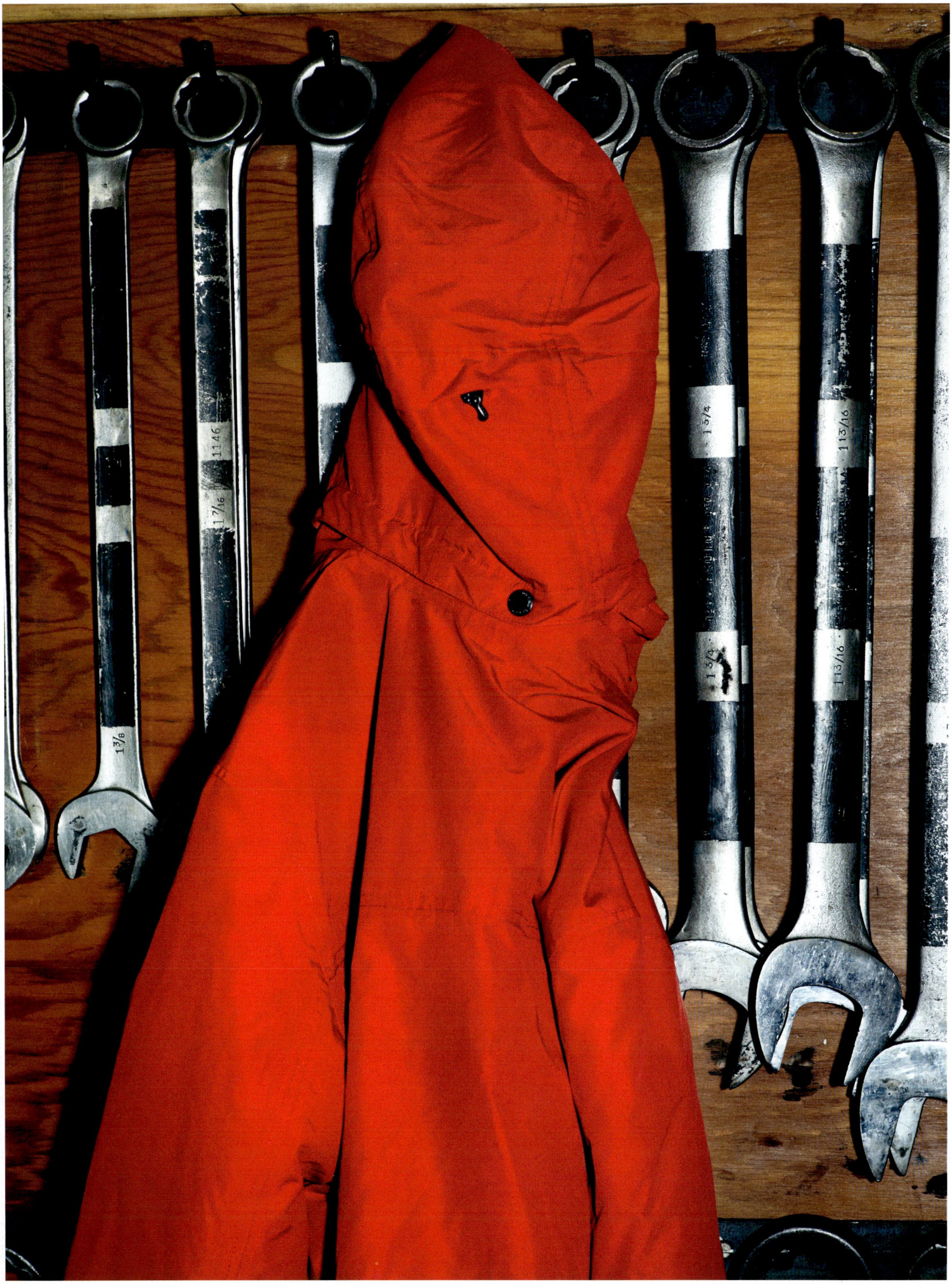

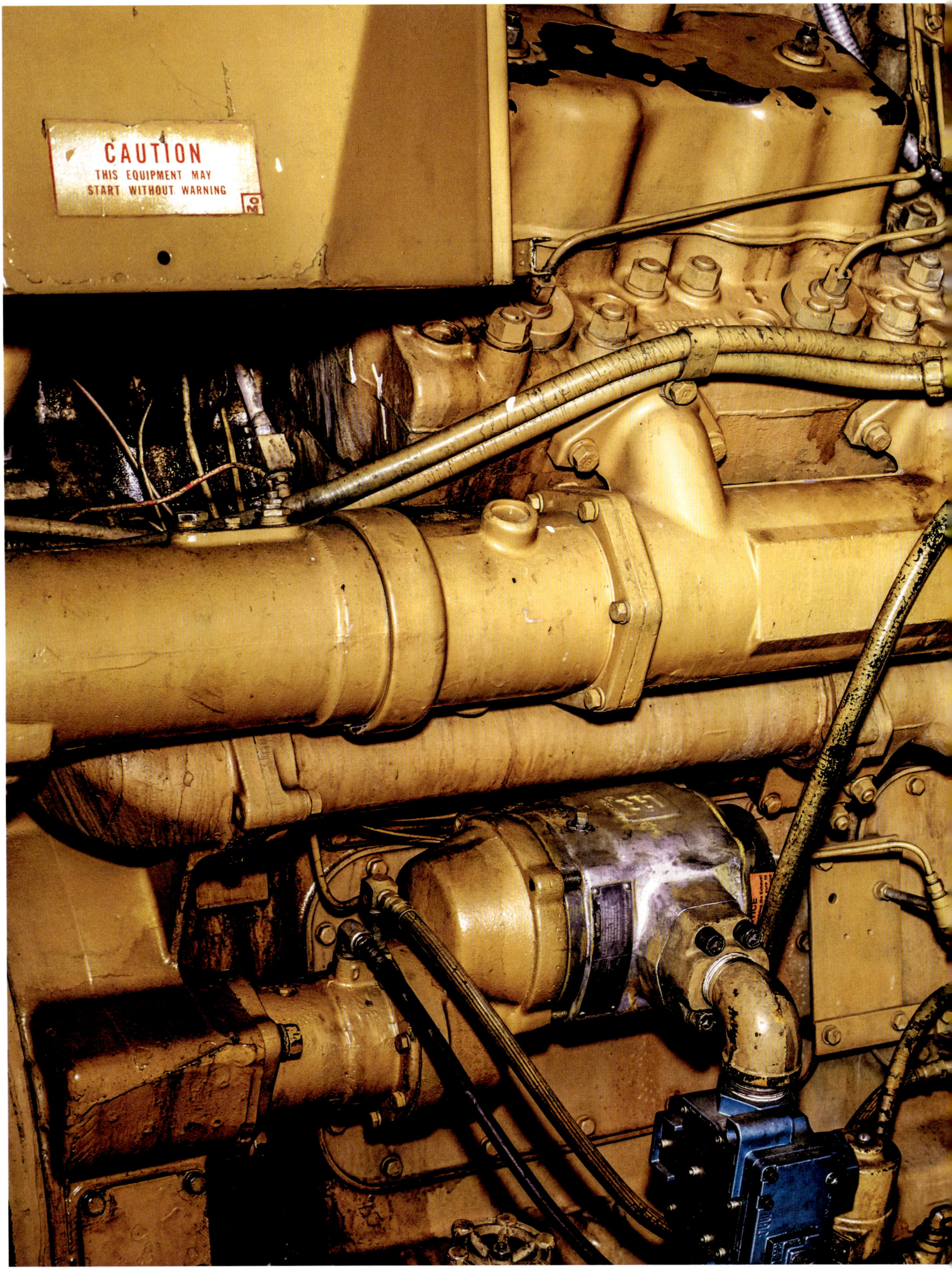
CAUTION
THIS EQUIPMENT MAY
START WITHOUT WARNING

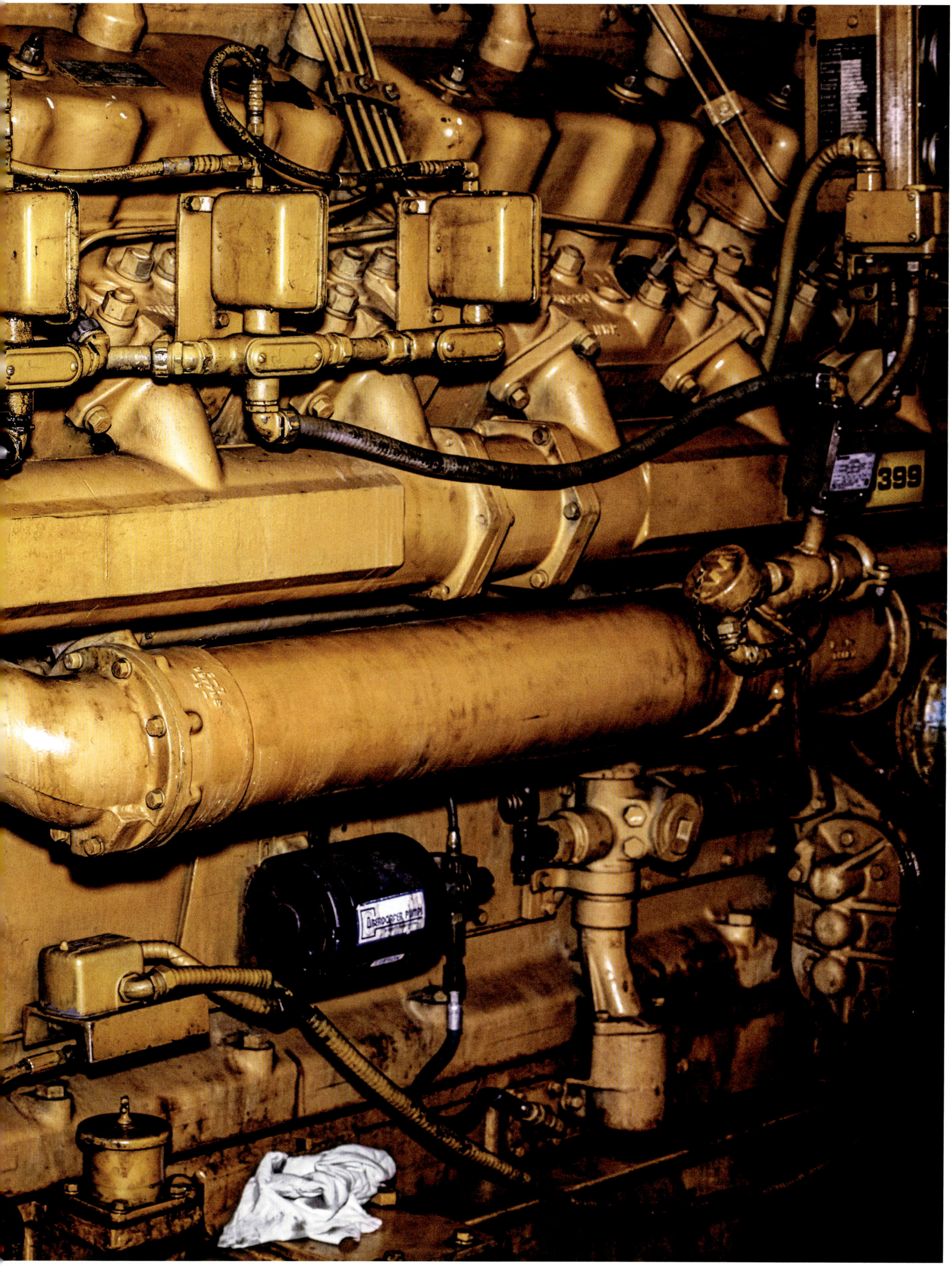
399

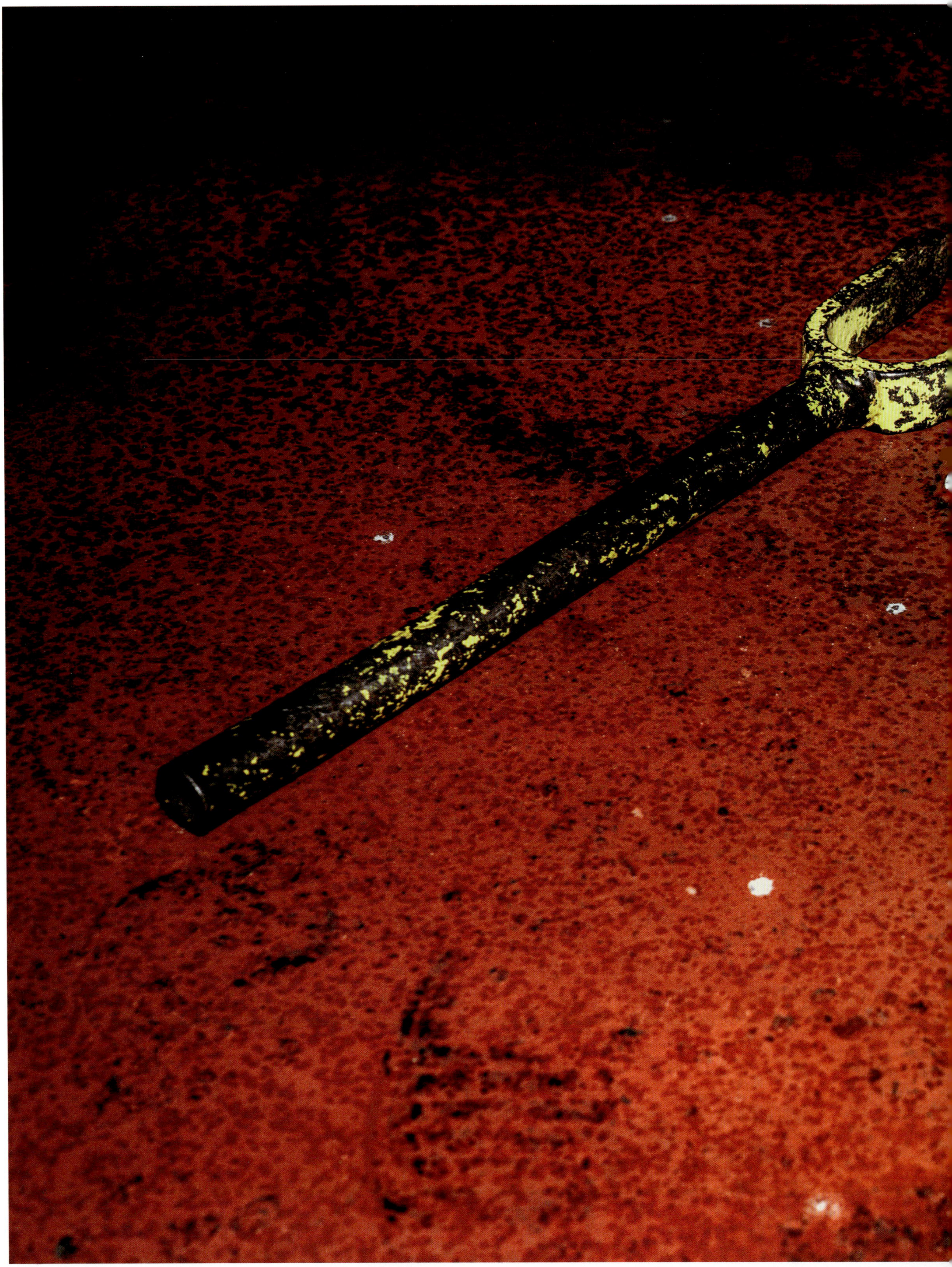

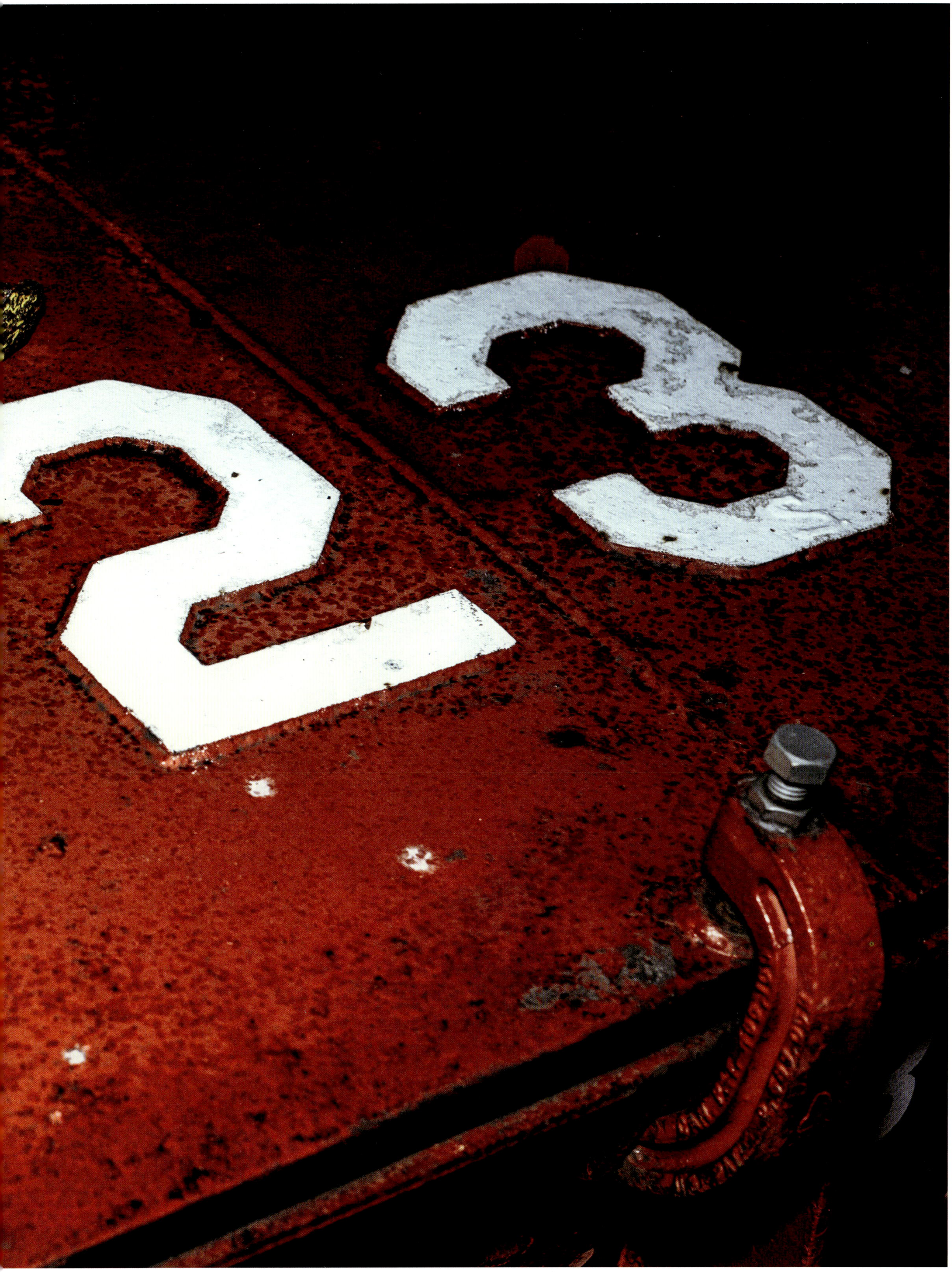
2
3

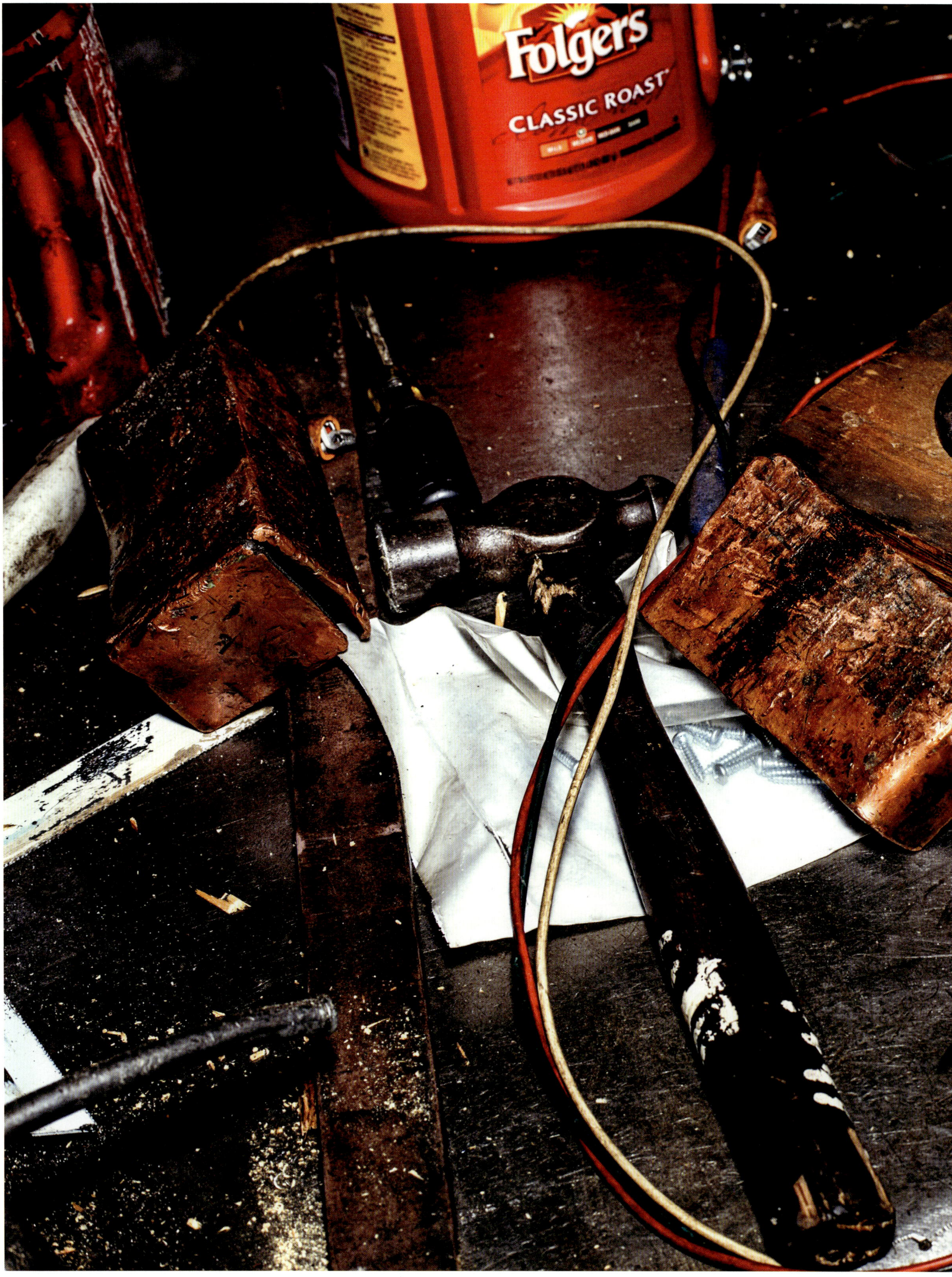
Folgers
CLASSIC ROAST

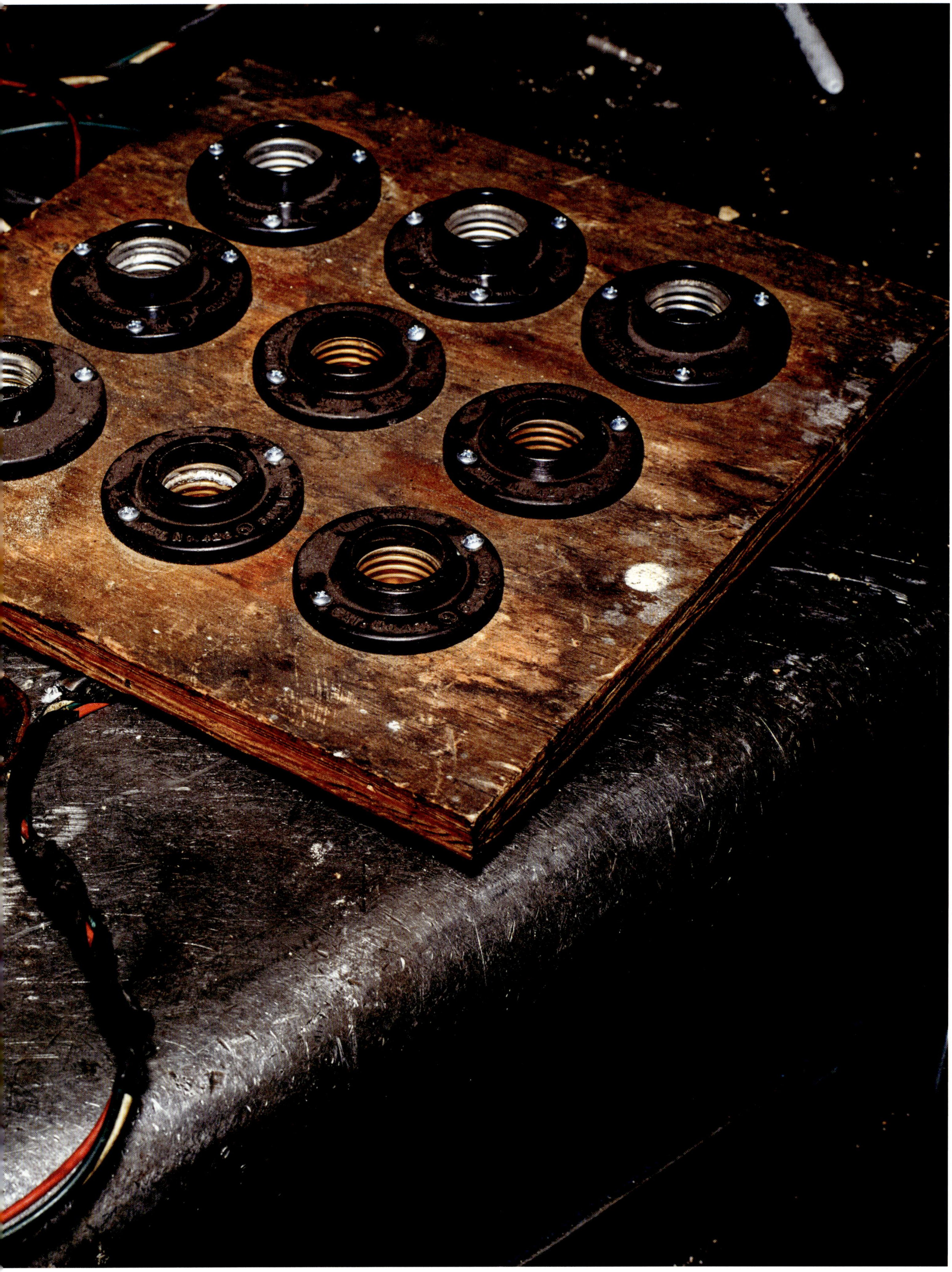

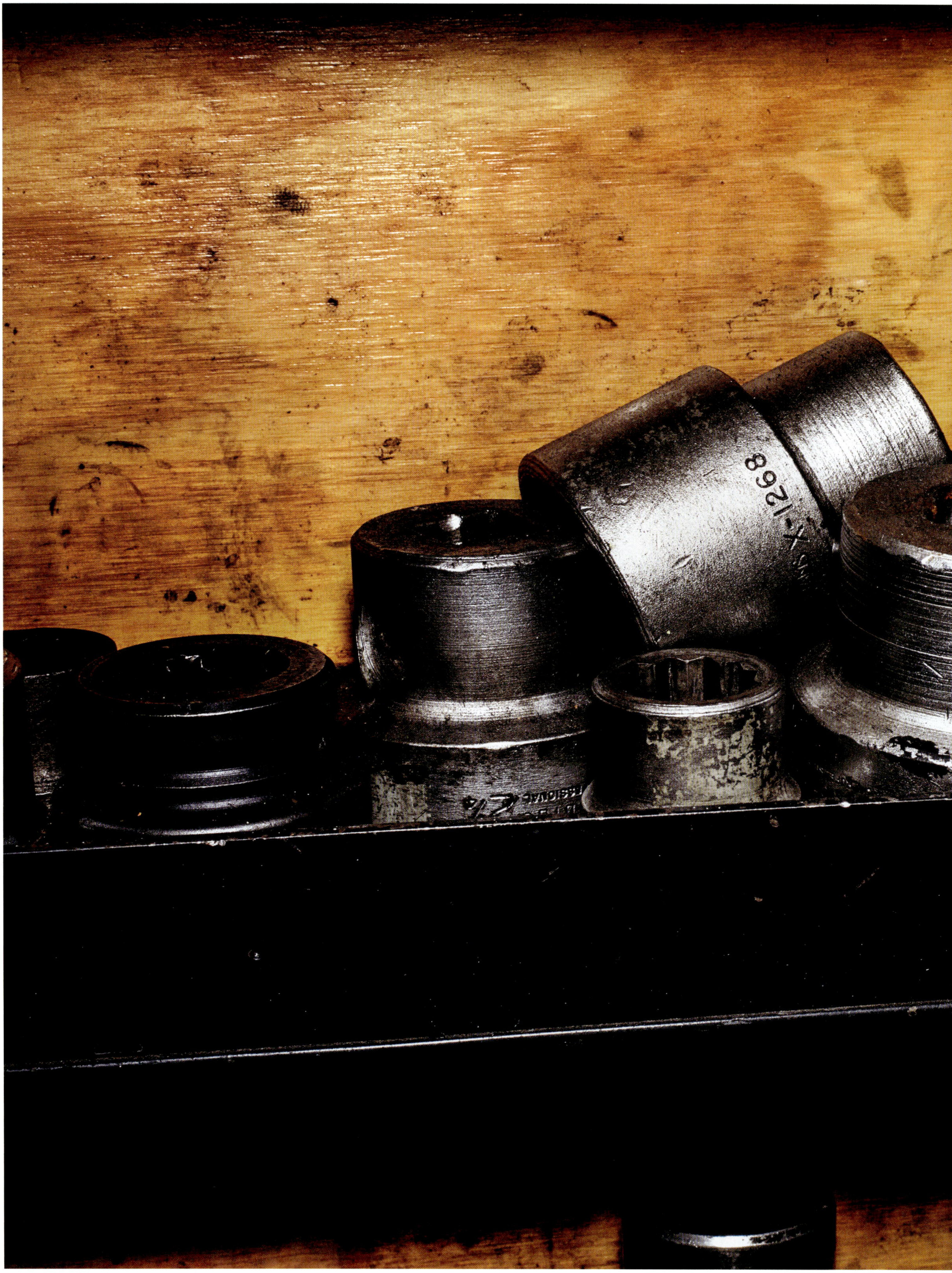
X-1268

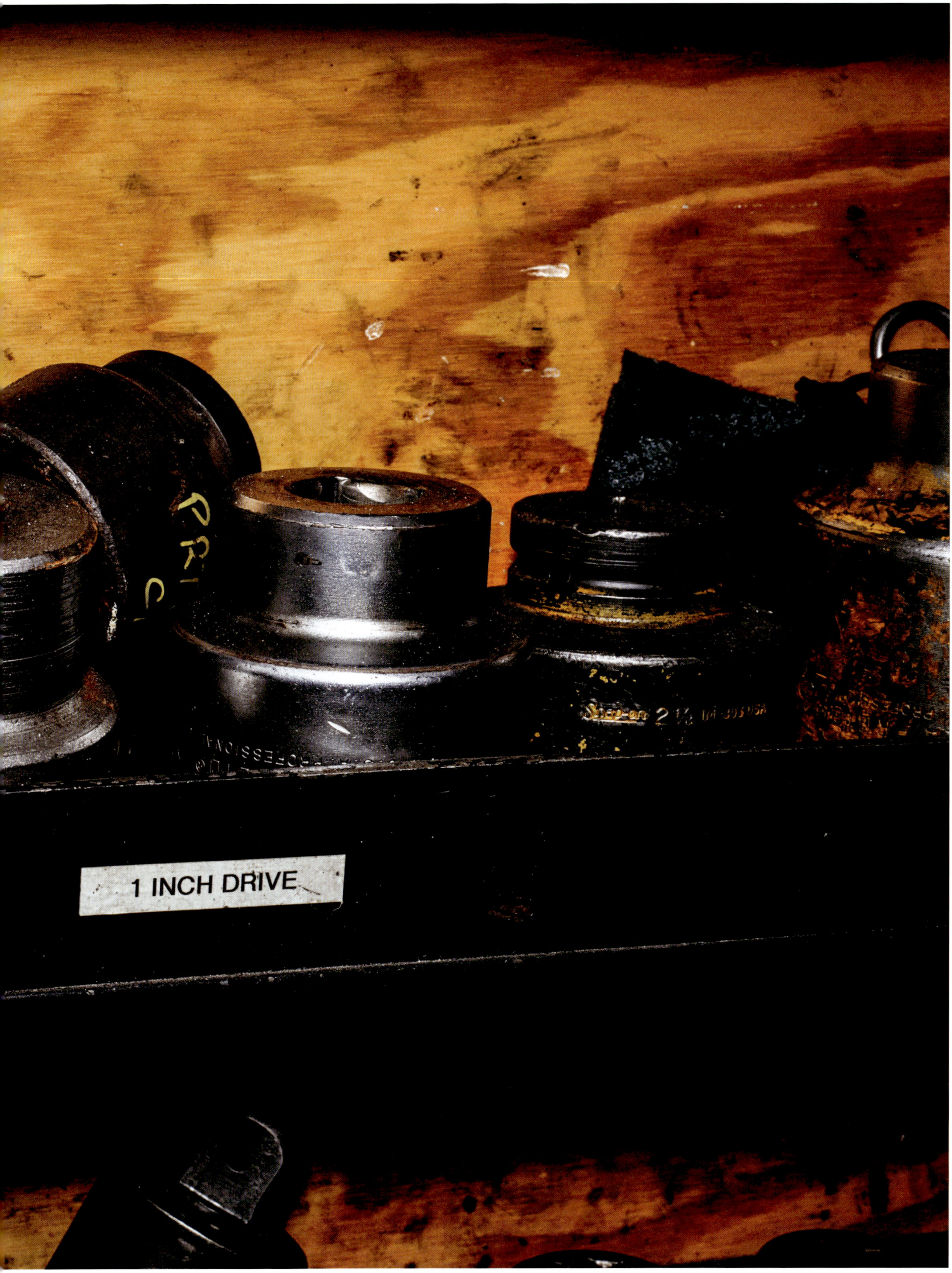
1 INCH DRIVE

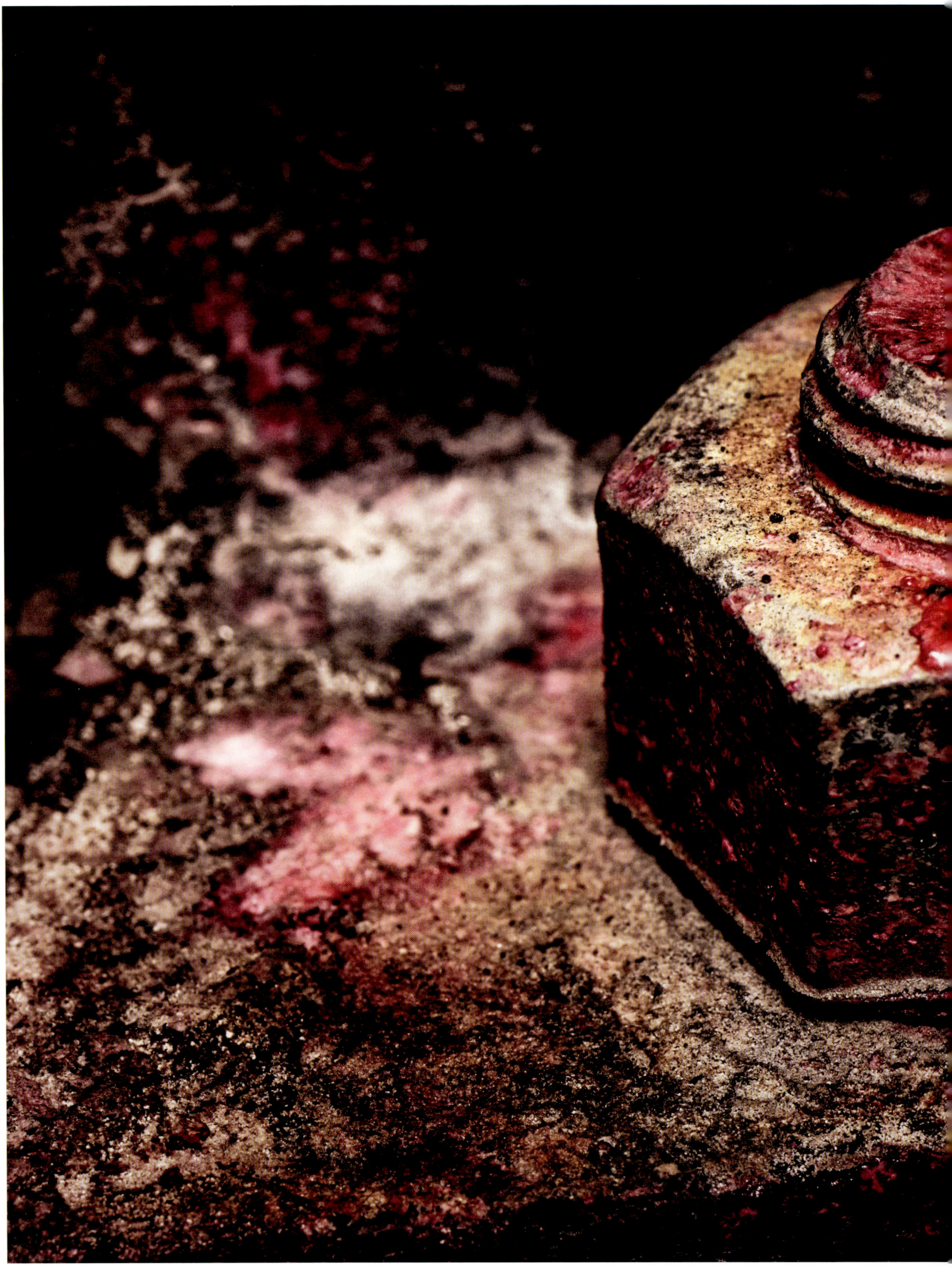

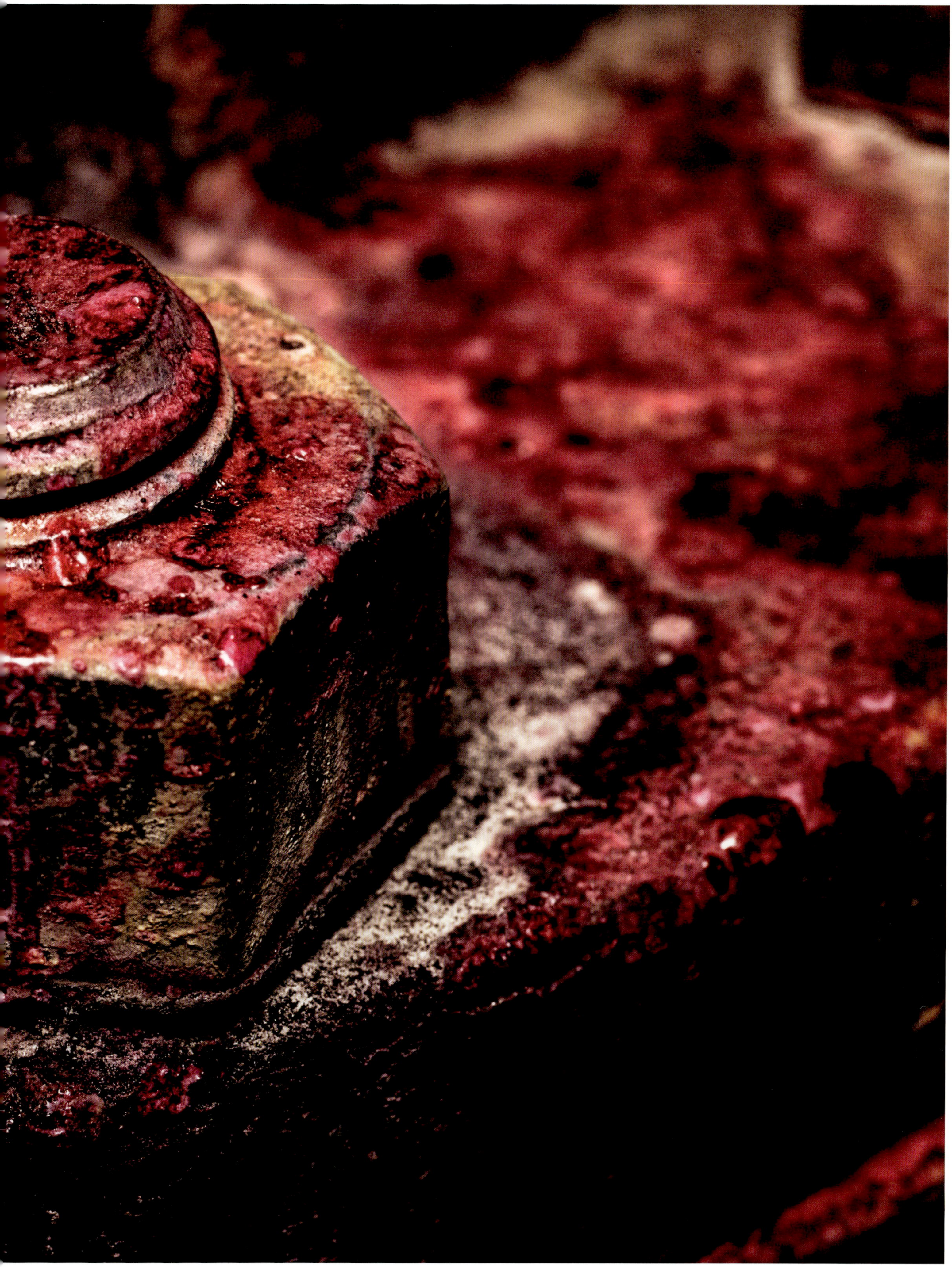

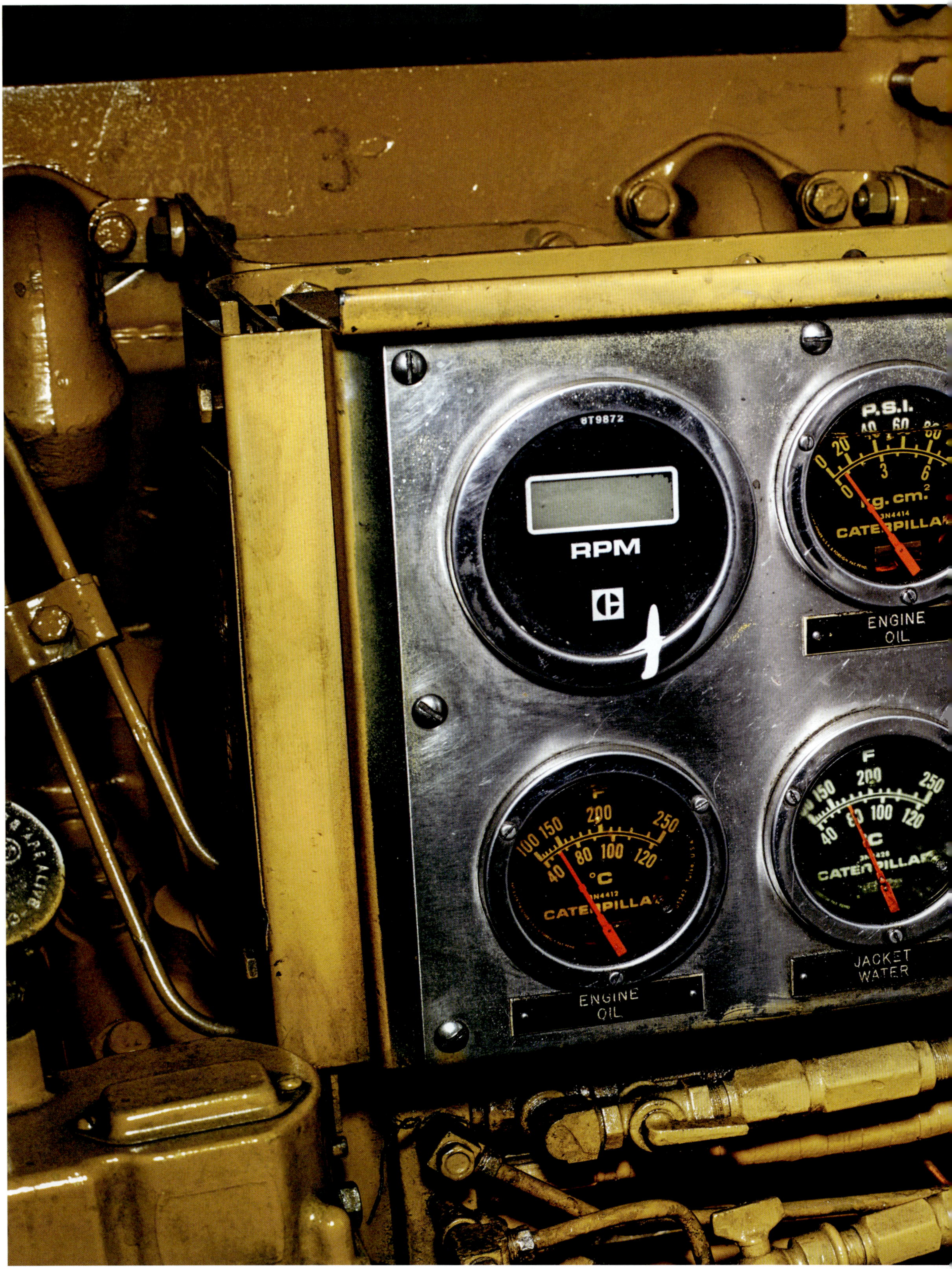
8T9872
RPM
P.S.I.
kg.cm.
ENGINE
OIL
ENGINE
OIL
JACKET
WATER

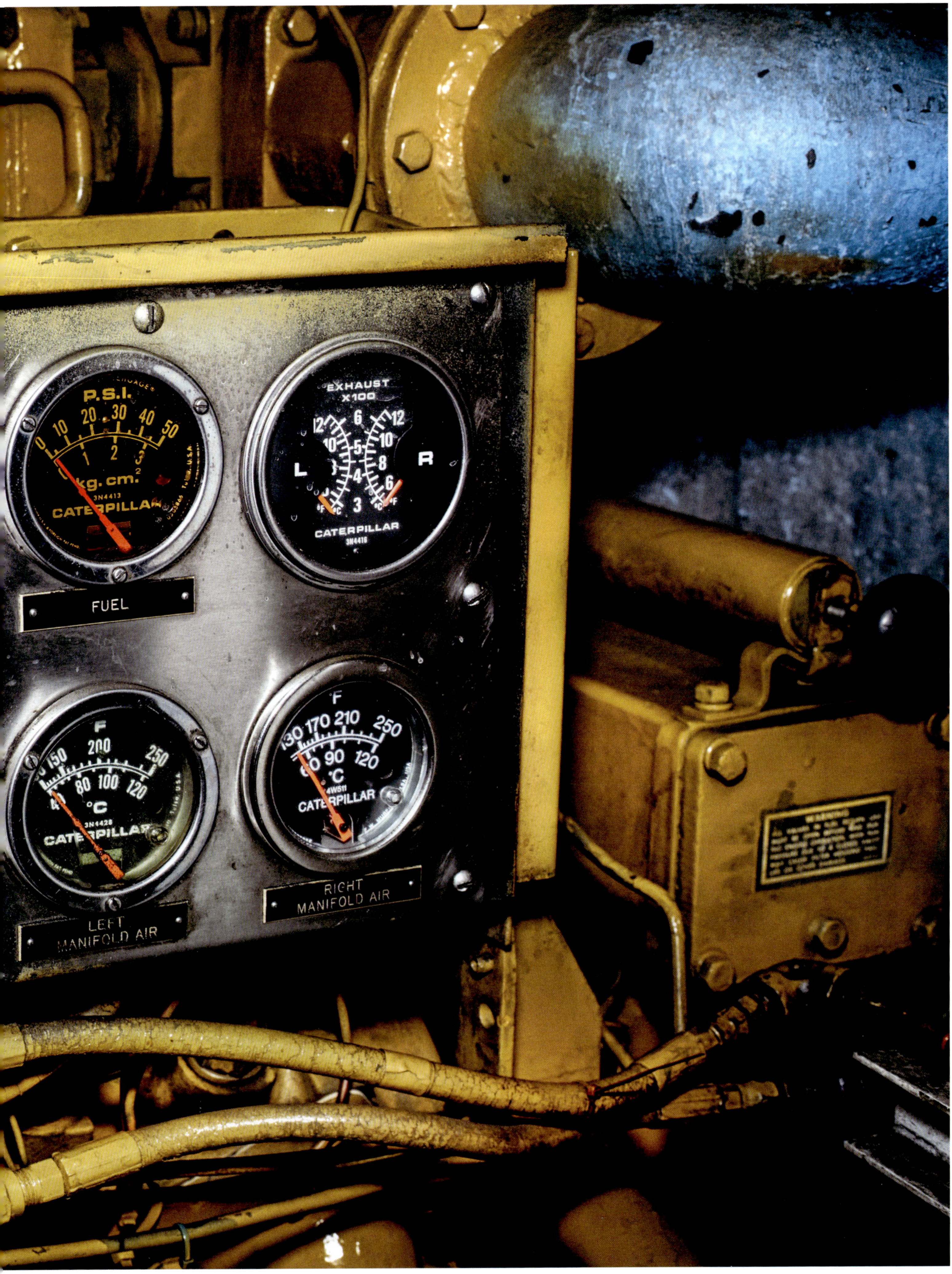
P.S.I.
kg. cm.
CATERPILLAR
FUEL
EXHAUST
X100
L
R
CATERPILLAR
CATERPILLAR
LEFT
MANIFOLD AIR
CATERPILLAR
RIGHT
MANIFOLD AIR

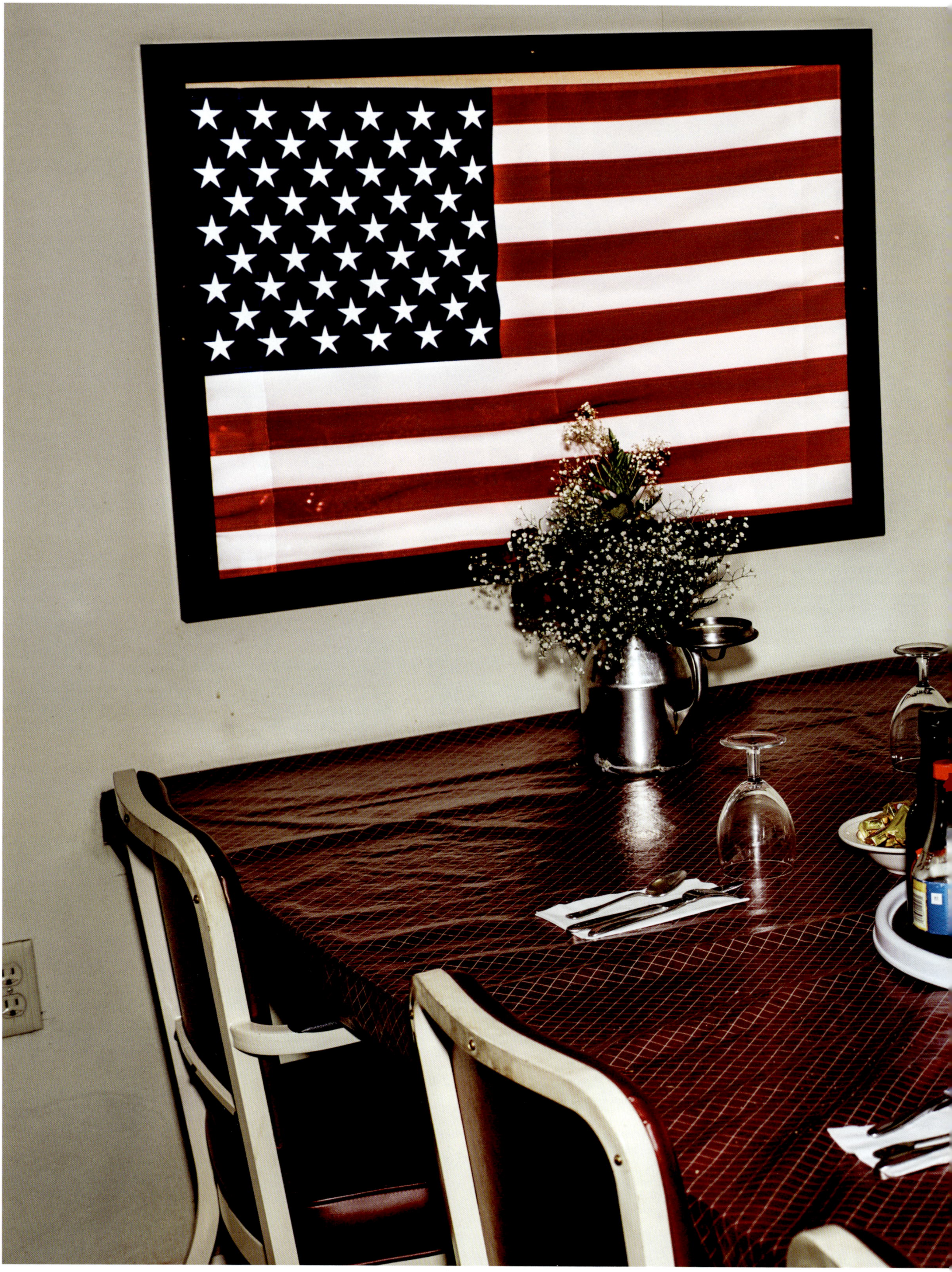

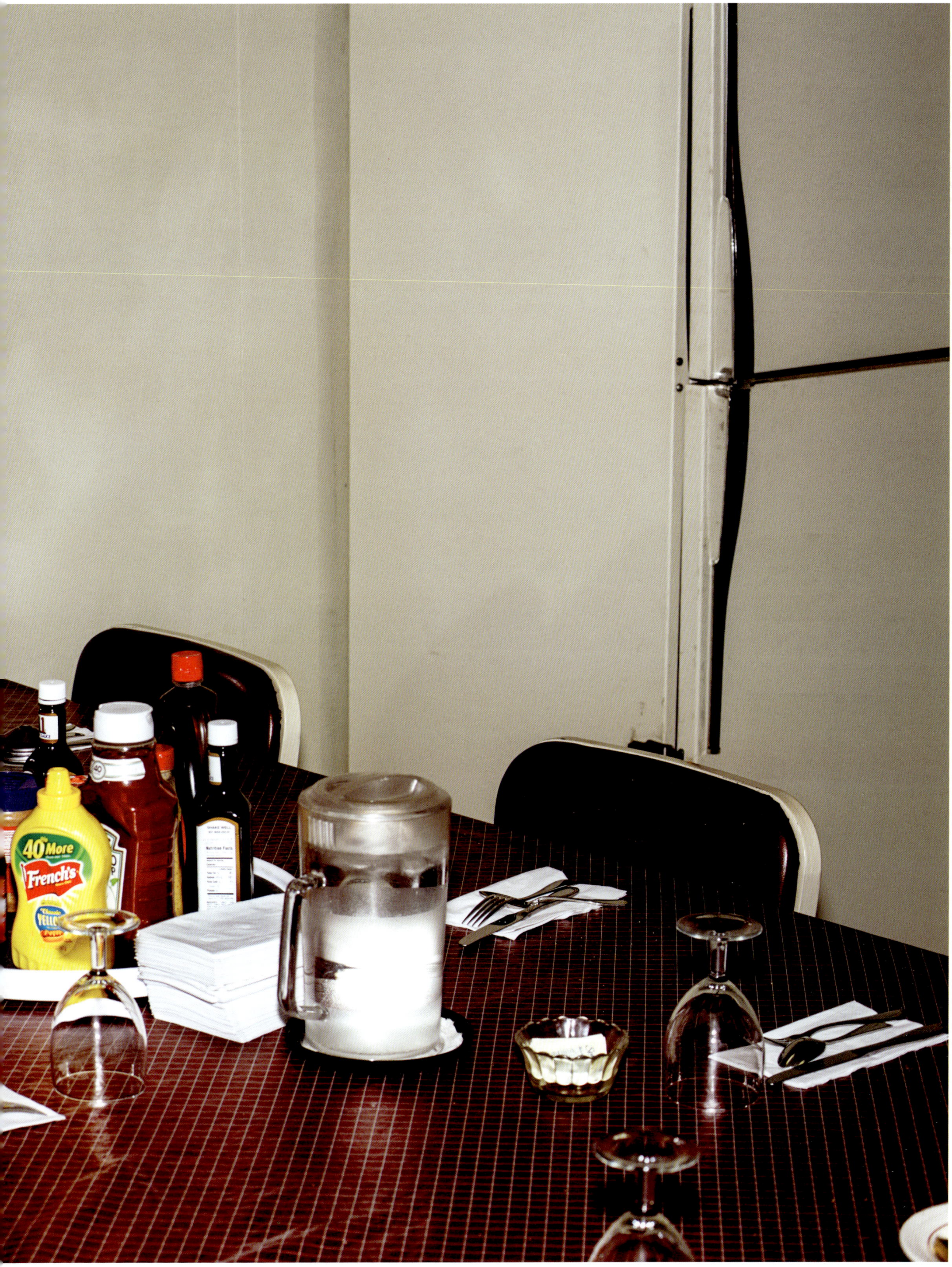
French's

IV

Lusophony Games

The Lusophony Games is a multinational, multi-sport event organised by the ACOLOP (Association of the Portuguese Speaking Olympic Committees) for athletes from Portuguese-speaking nations, or those with significant Portuguese communities.

Participating countries include: Angola, Brazil, Cape Verde, East Timor, Guinea-Bissau, Macau (Chinese SAR), Mozambique, Portugal, São Tomé and Principe, Equatorial Guinea, India and Sri Lanka.

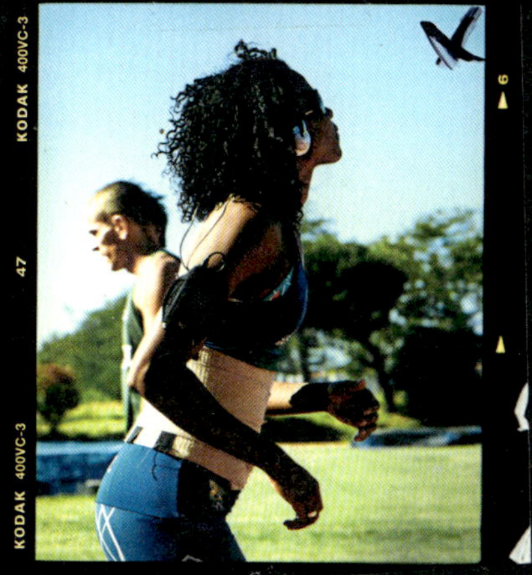
KODAK 400VC-3
47
KODAK 400VC-3

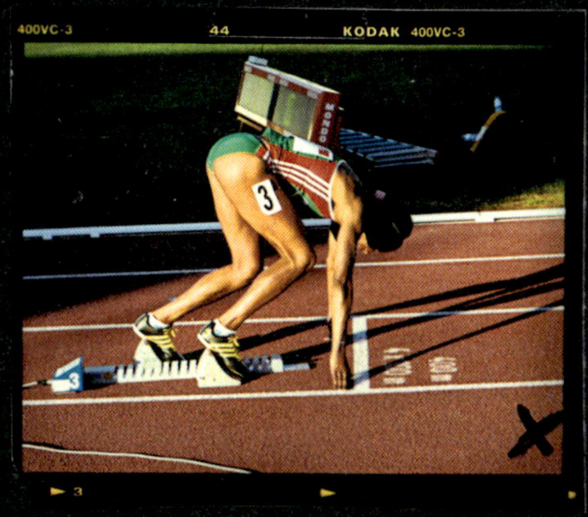
400VC-3
44
KODAK 400VC-3
3

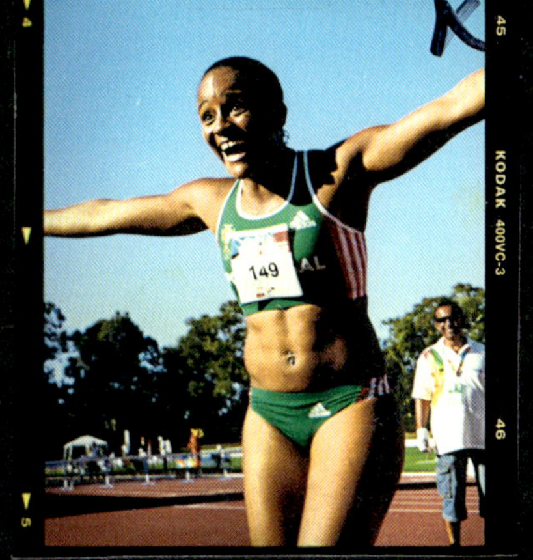
45
KODAK 400VC-3
149
46

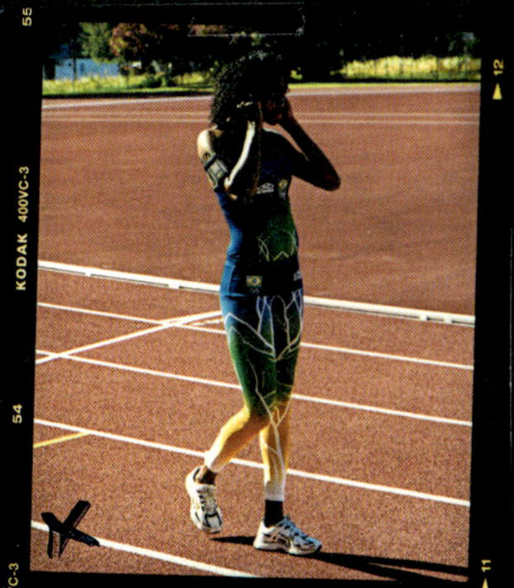
55
KODAK 400VC-3
54

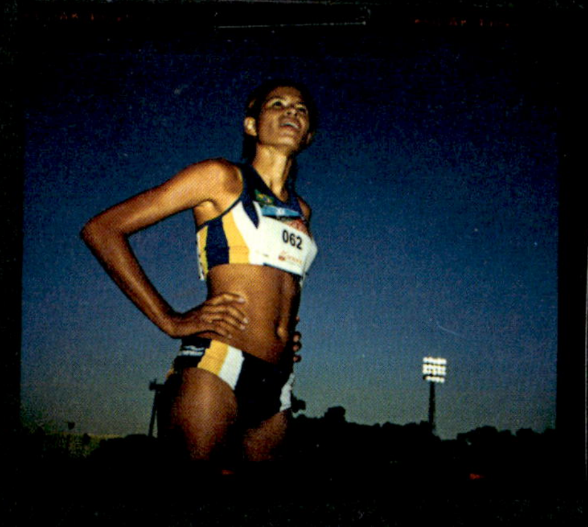
062

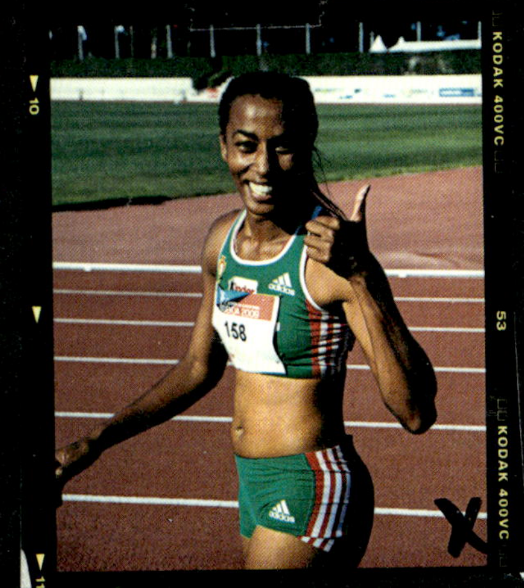
KODAK 400VC
158
53

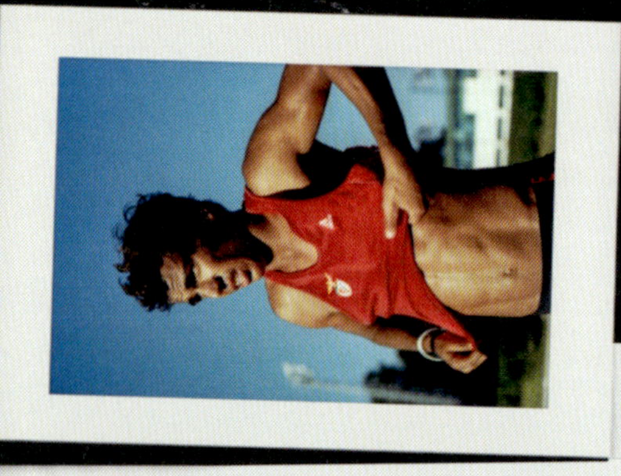

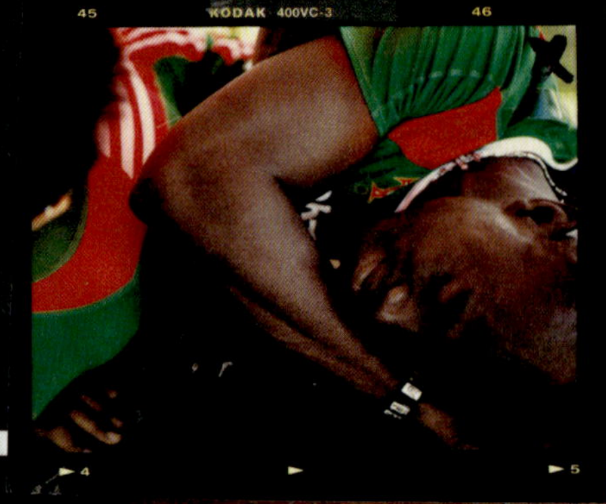
45
KODAK 400VC-3
46

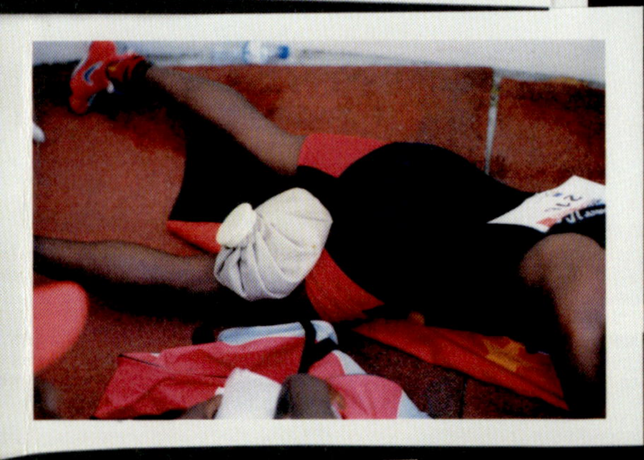

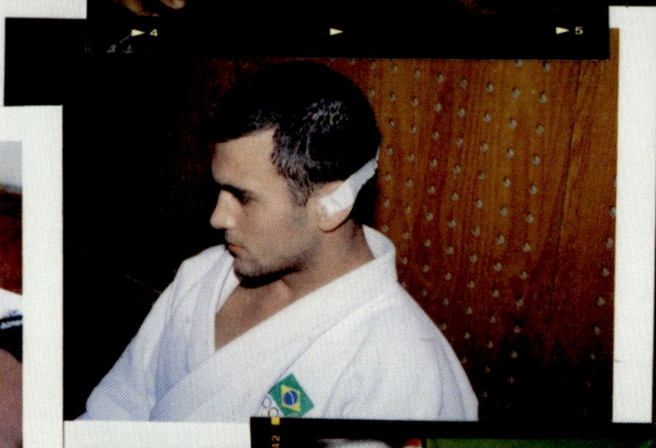

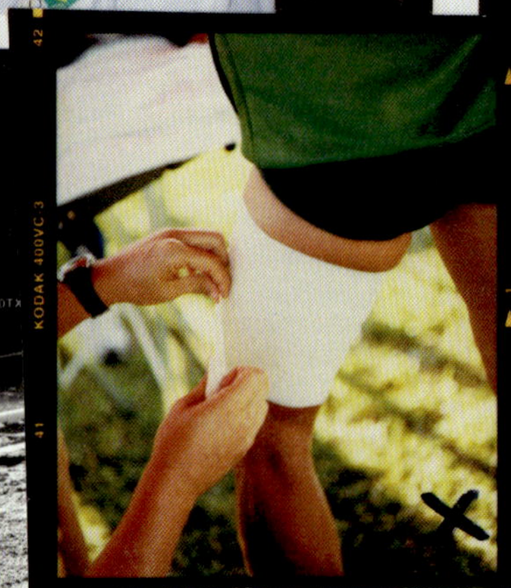
42
KODAK 400VC-3
41

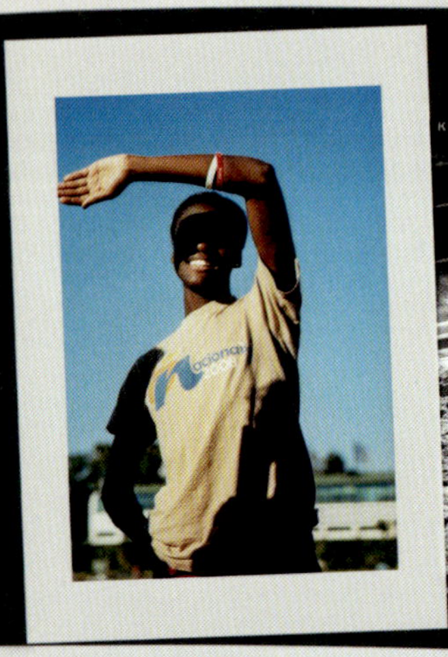

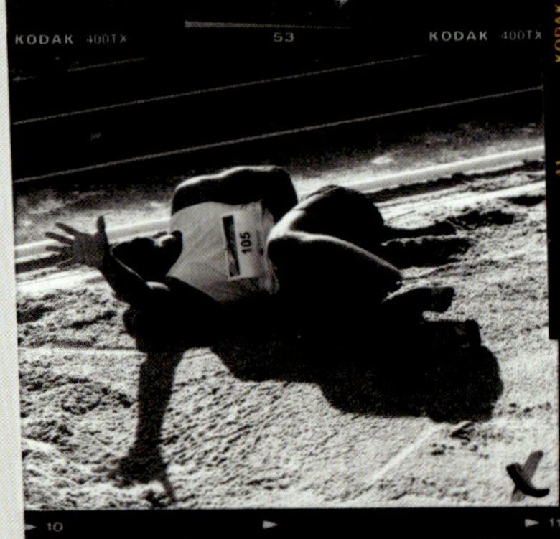
KODAK 400TX
53
KODAK 400TX
105

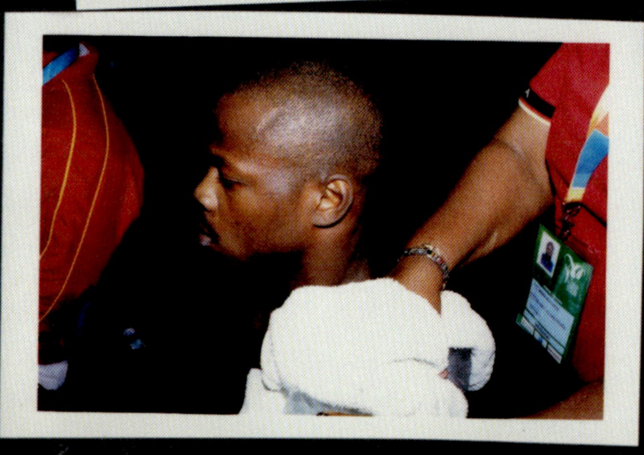

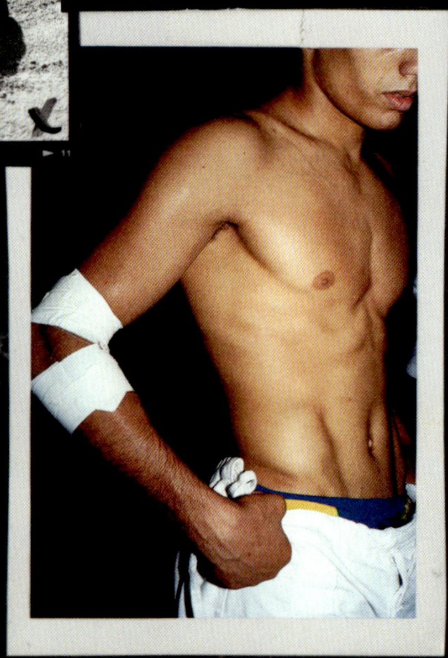

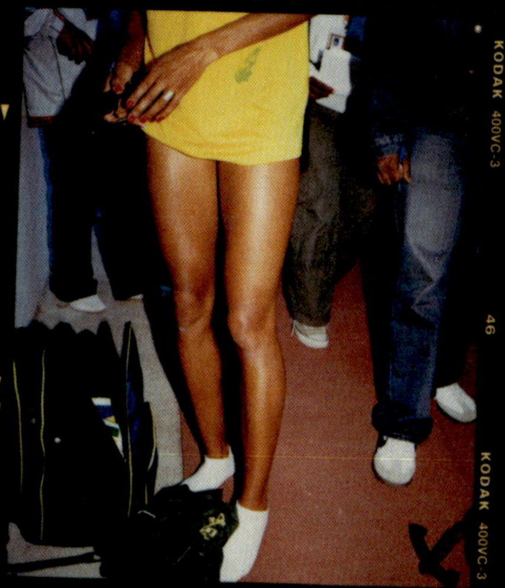
KODAK 400VC-3

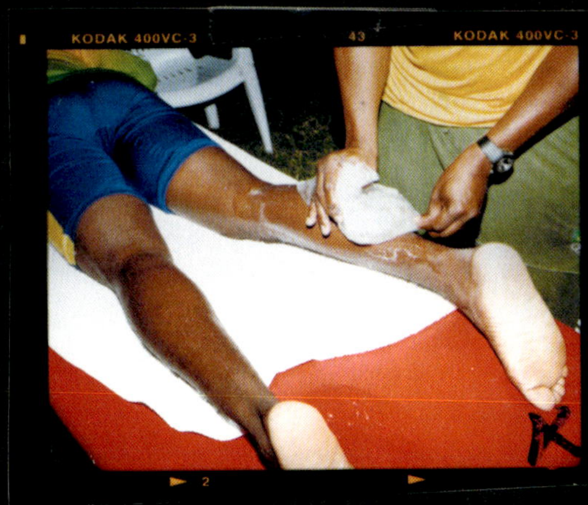
KODAK 400VC-3

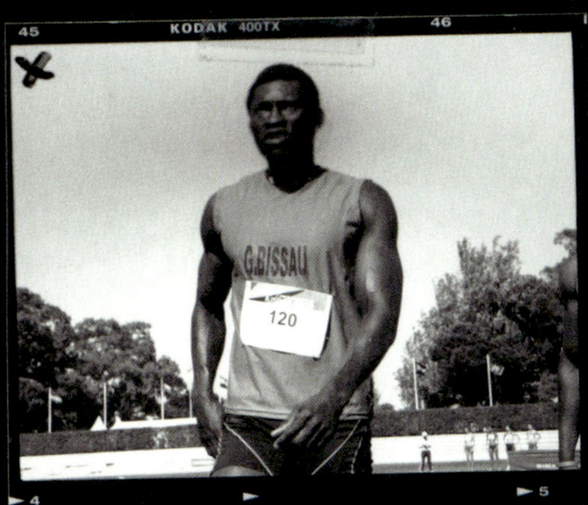
KODAK 400TX
G.BISSAU
120

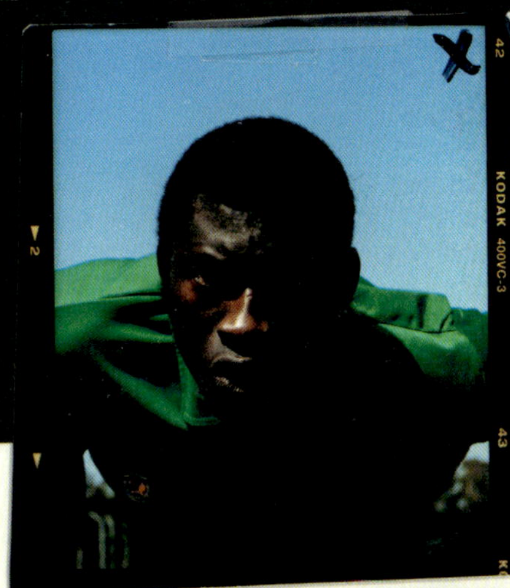
KODAK 400VC-3

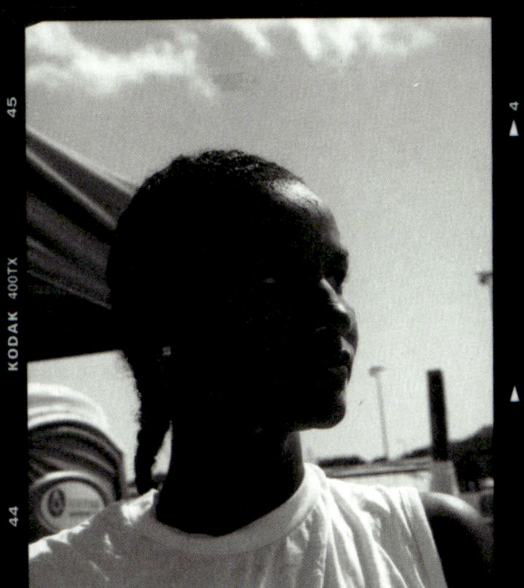
KODAK 400TX

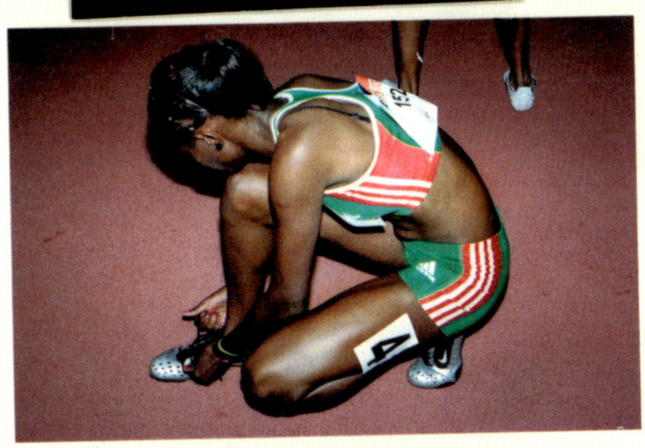

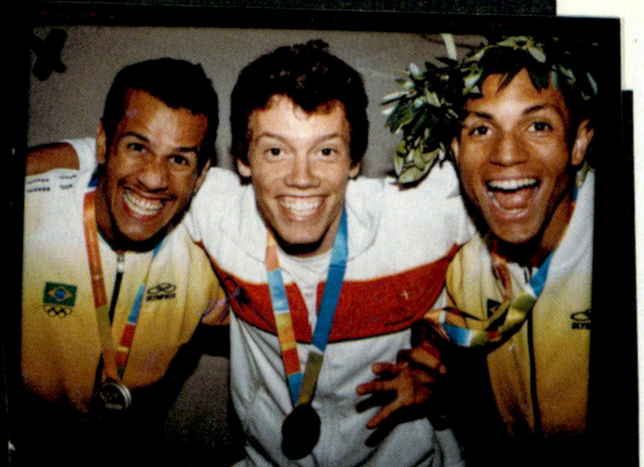

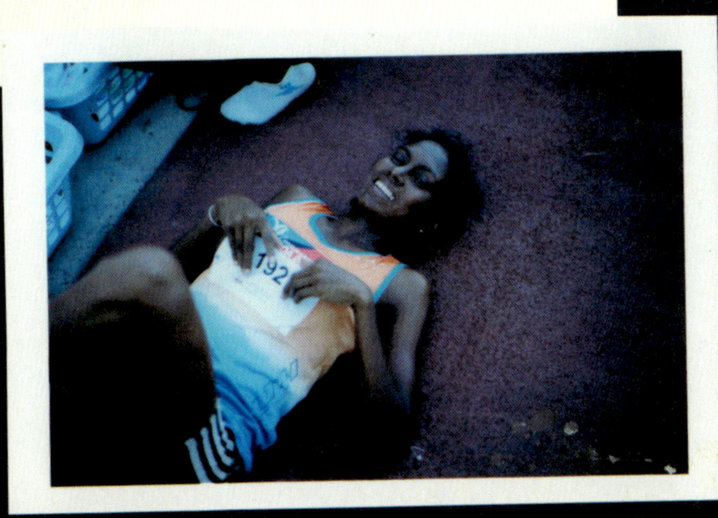
192

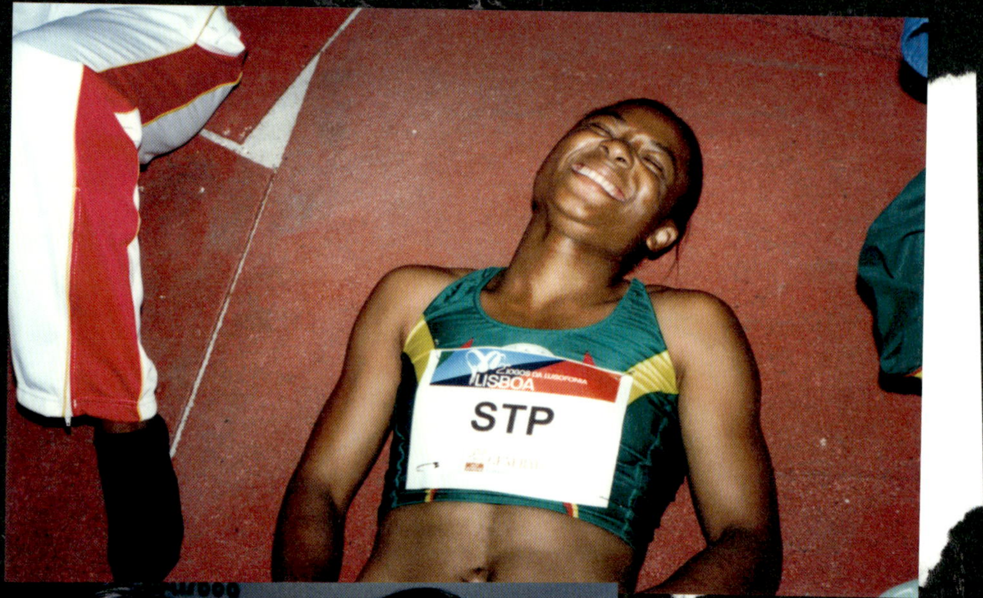
LISBOA
STP

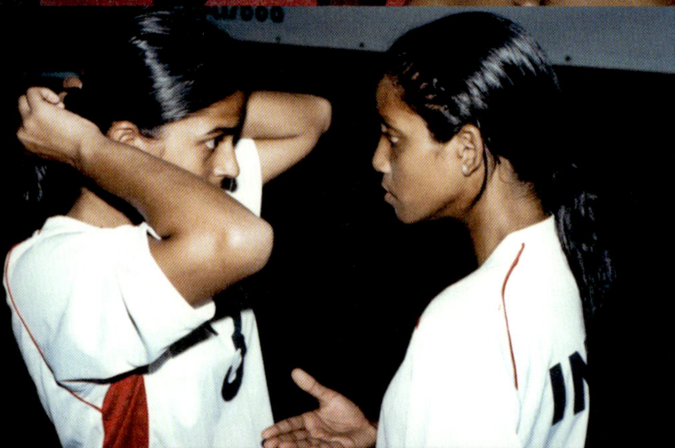

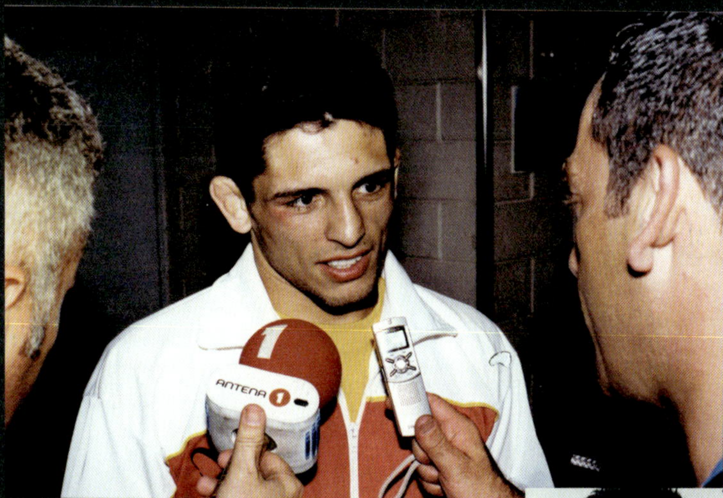
ANTENA 1

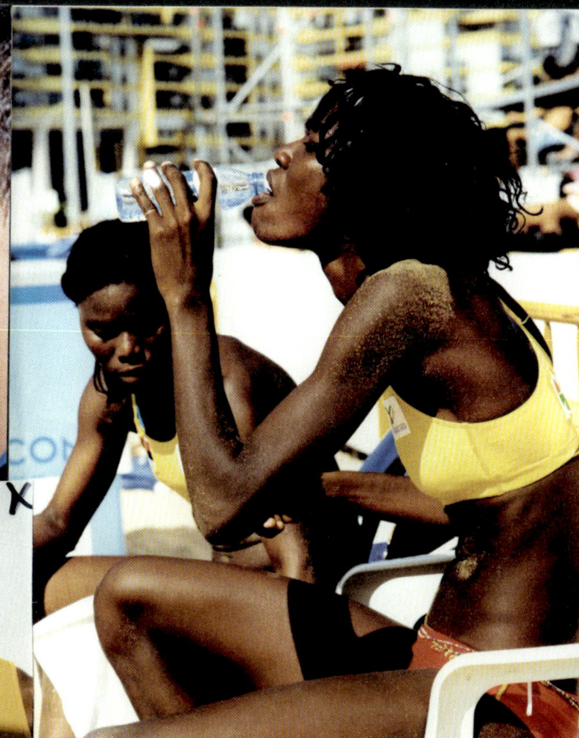

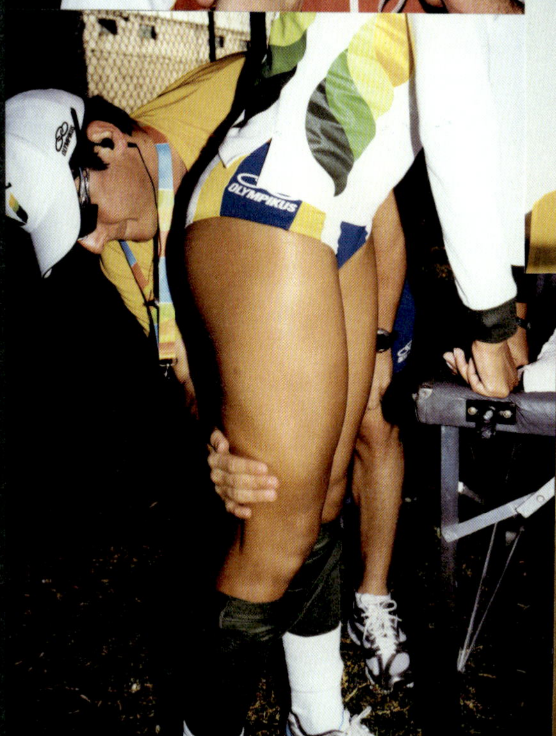
OLYMPIKUS

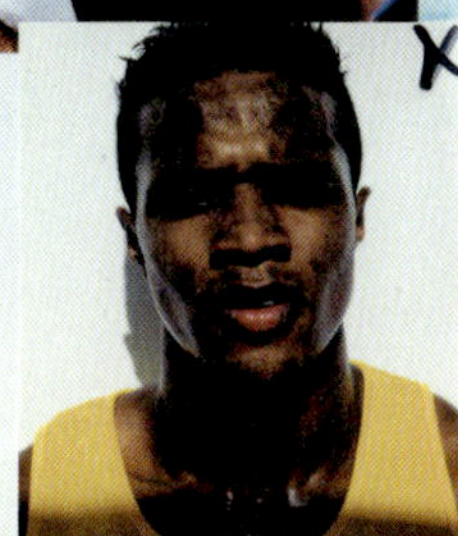

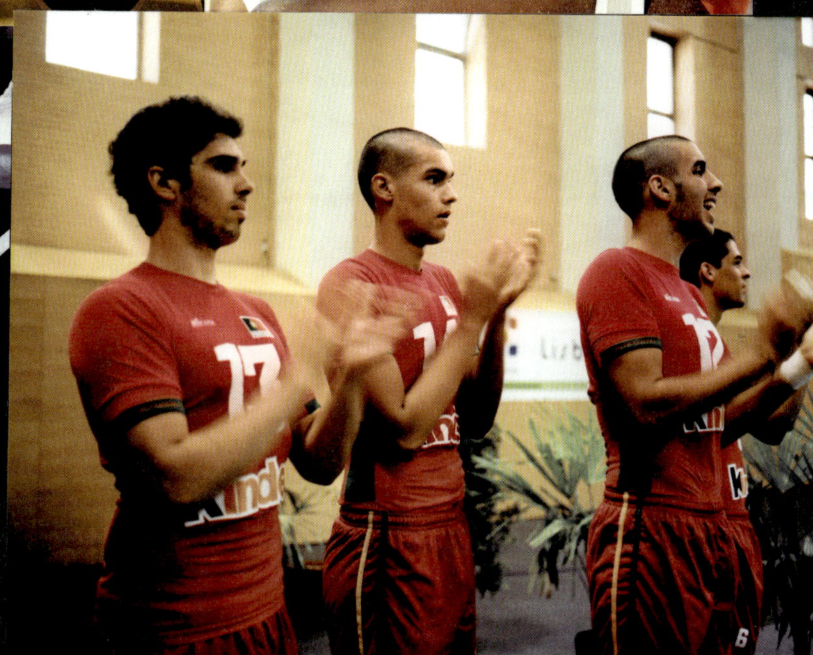
Kinder

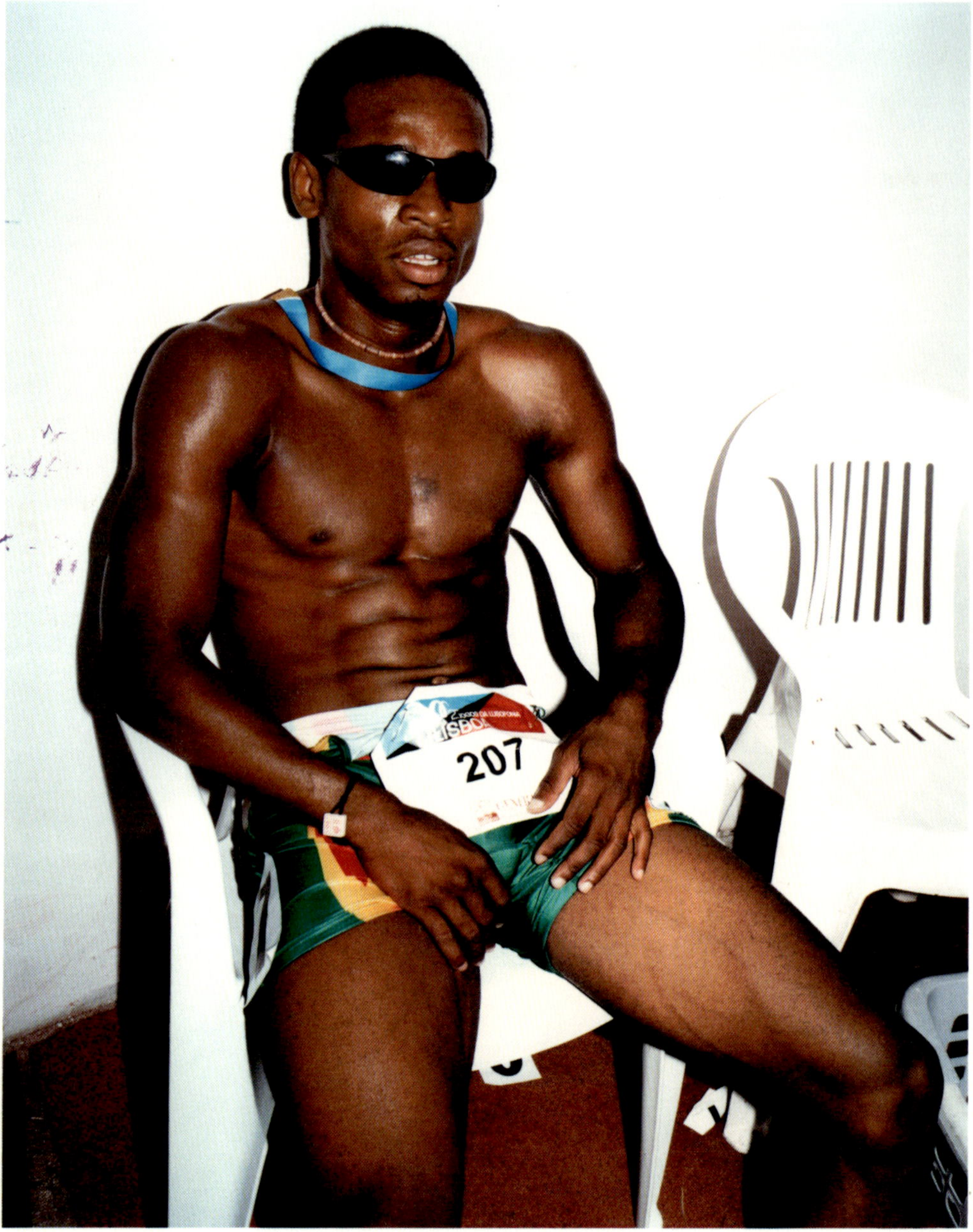
207

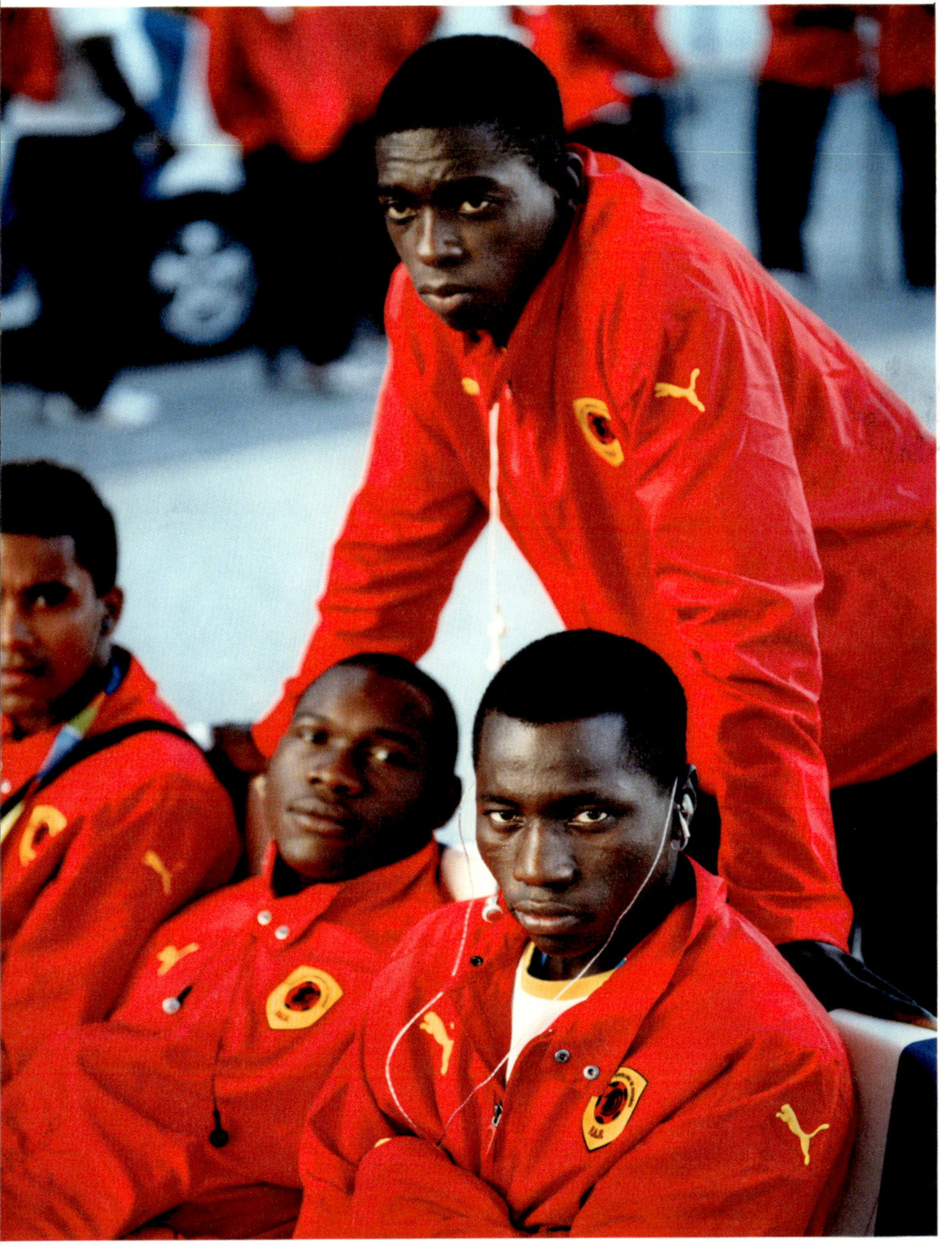

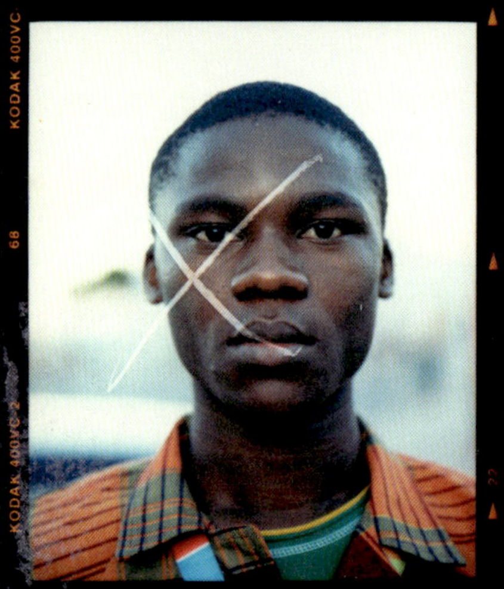
KODAK 400VC
68
KODAK 400VC-2

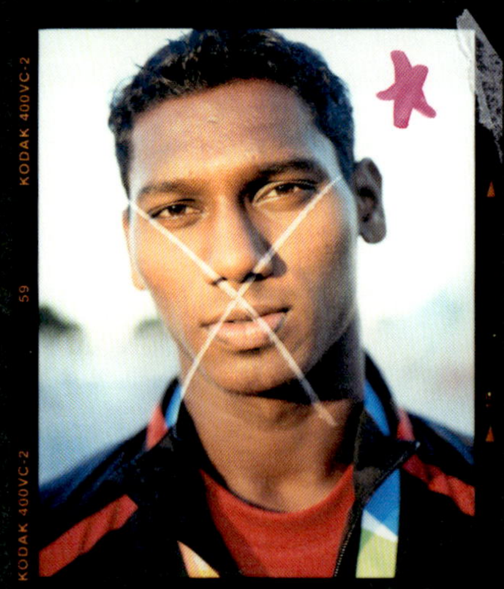
KODAK 400VC-2
59
KODAK 400VC-2

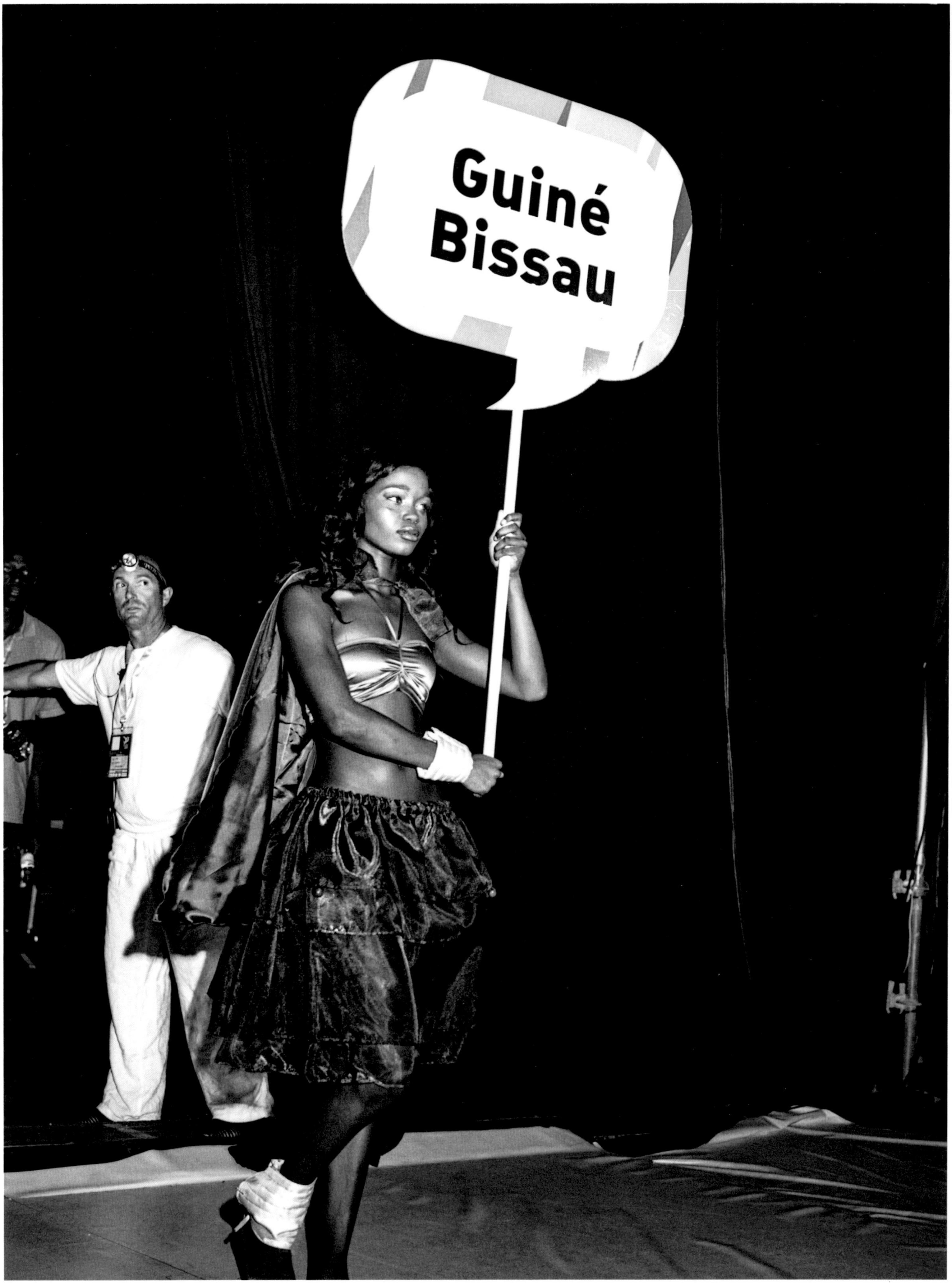
Guiné
Bissau

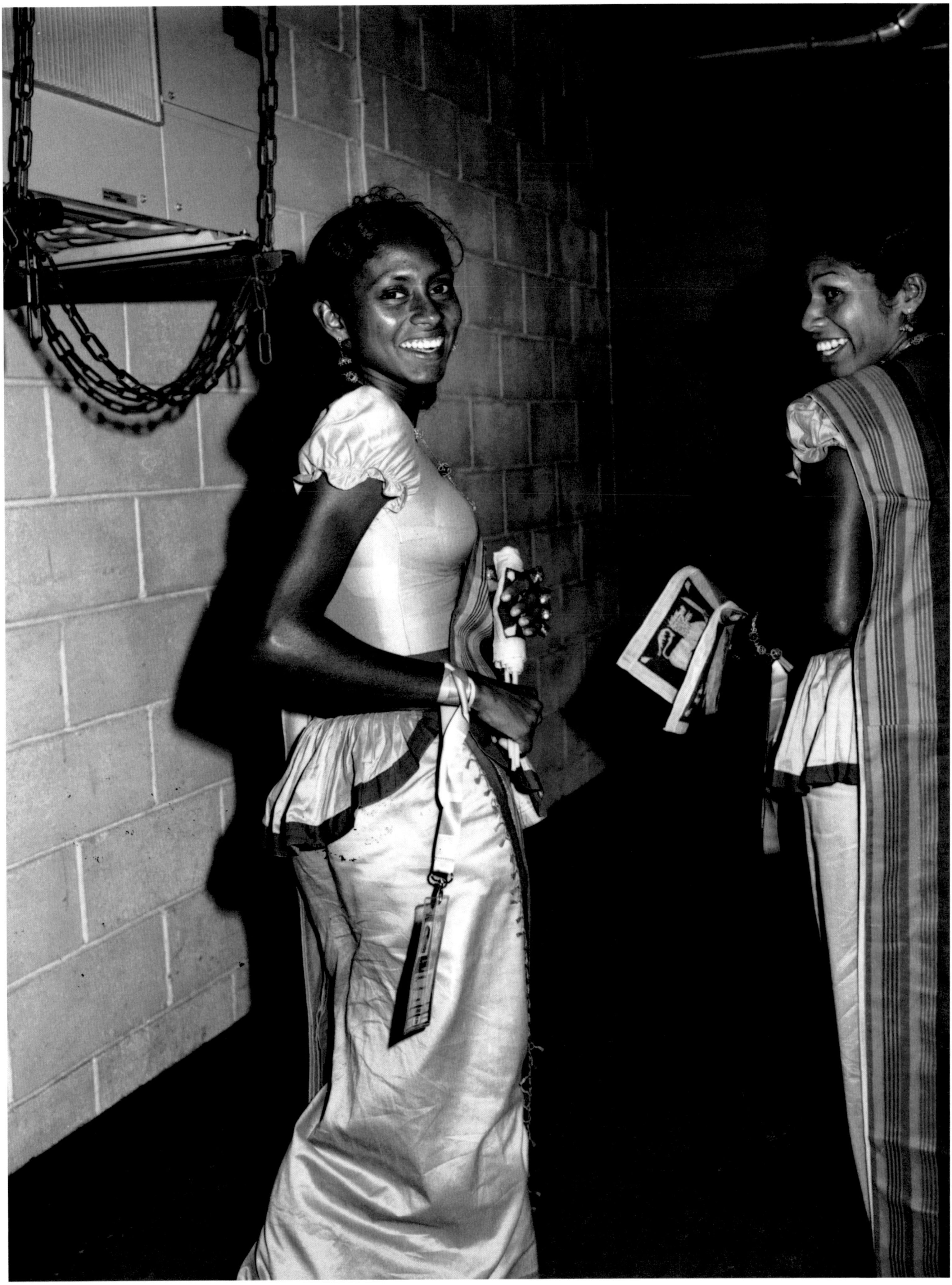

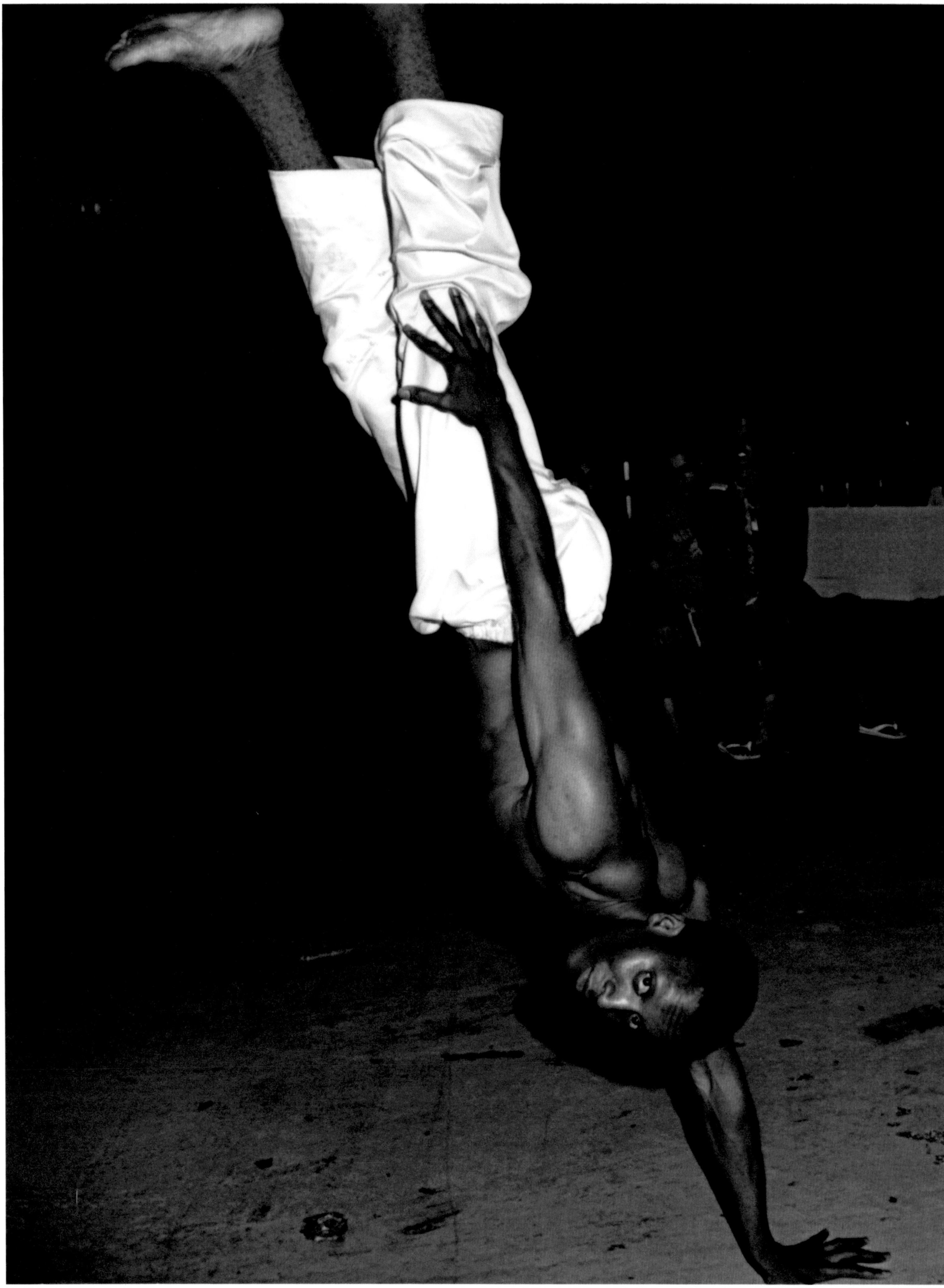

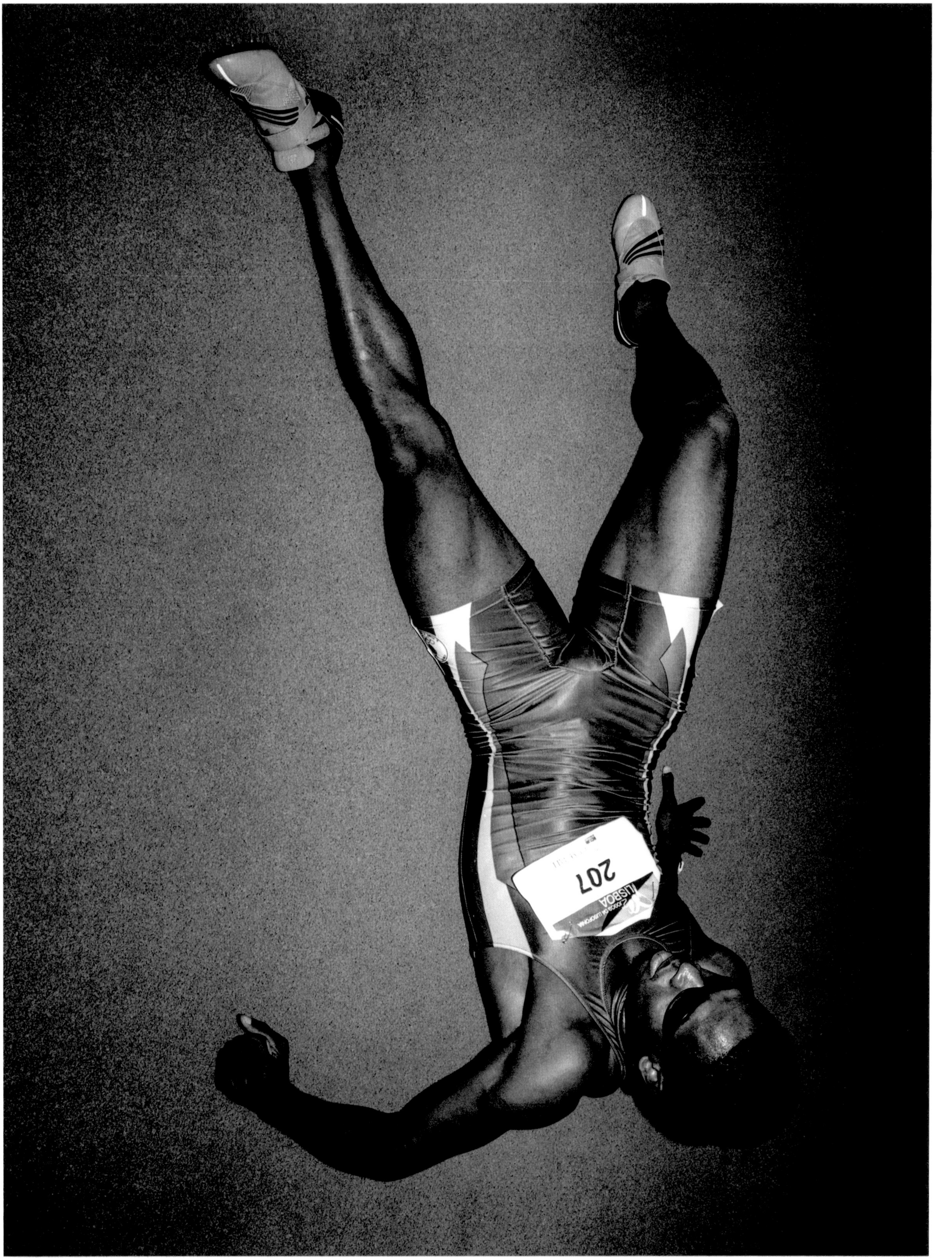
LISBOA
207

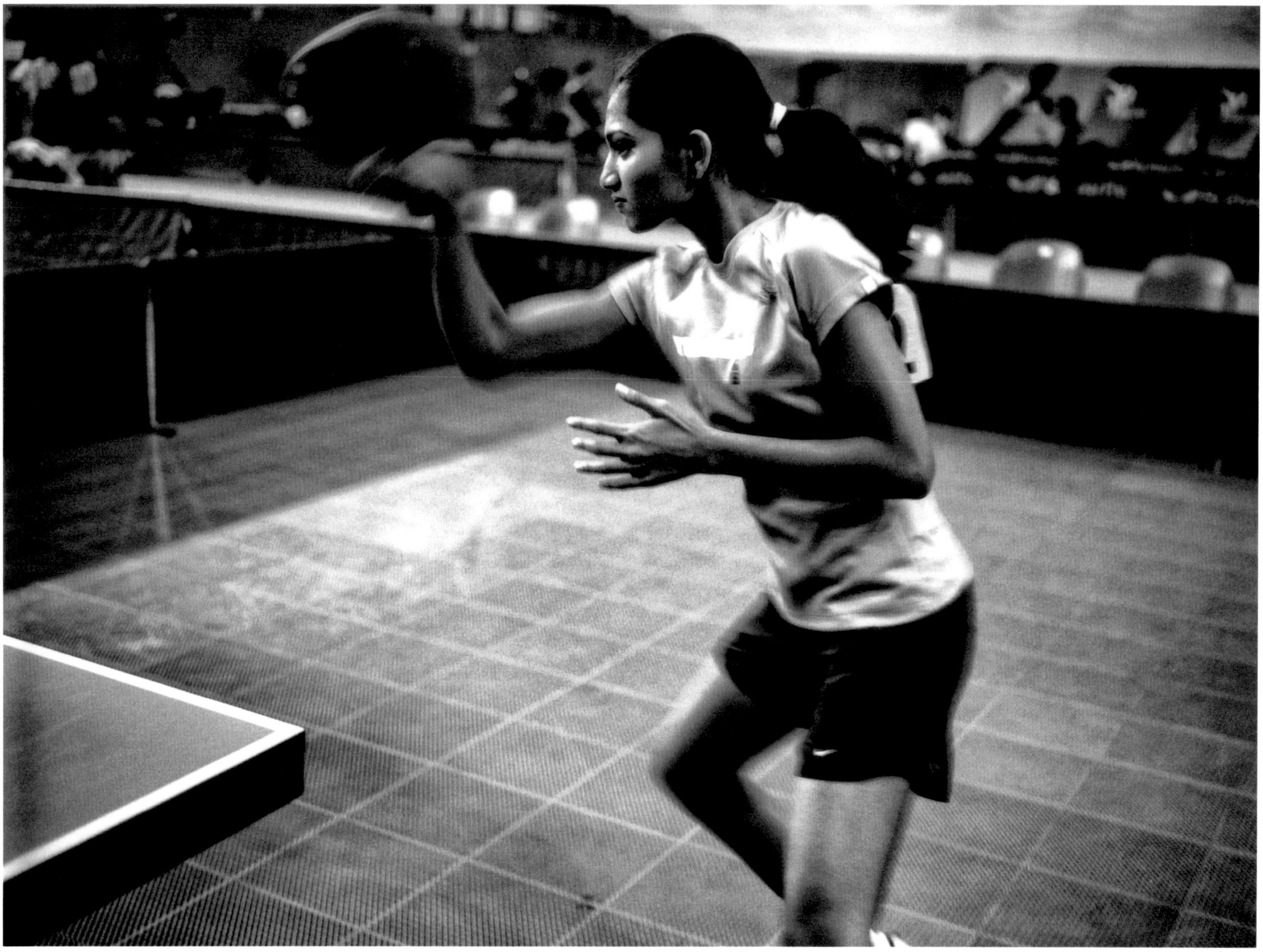

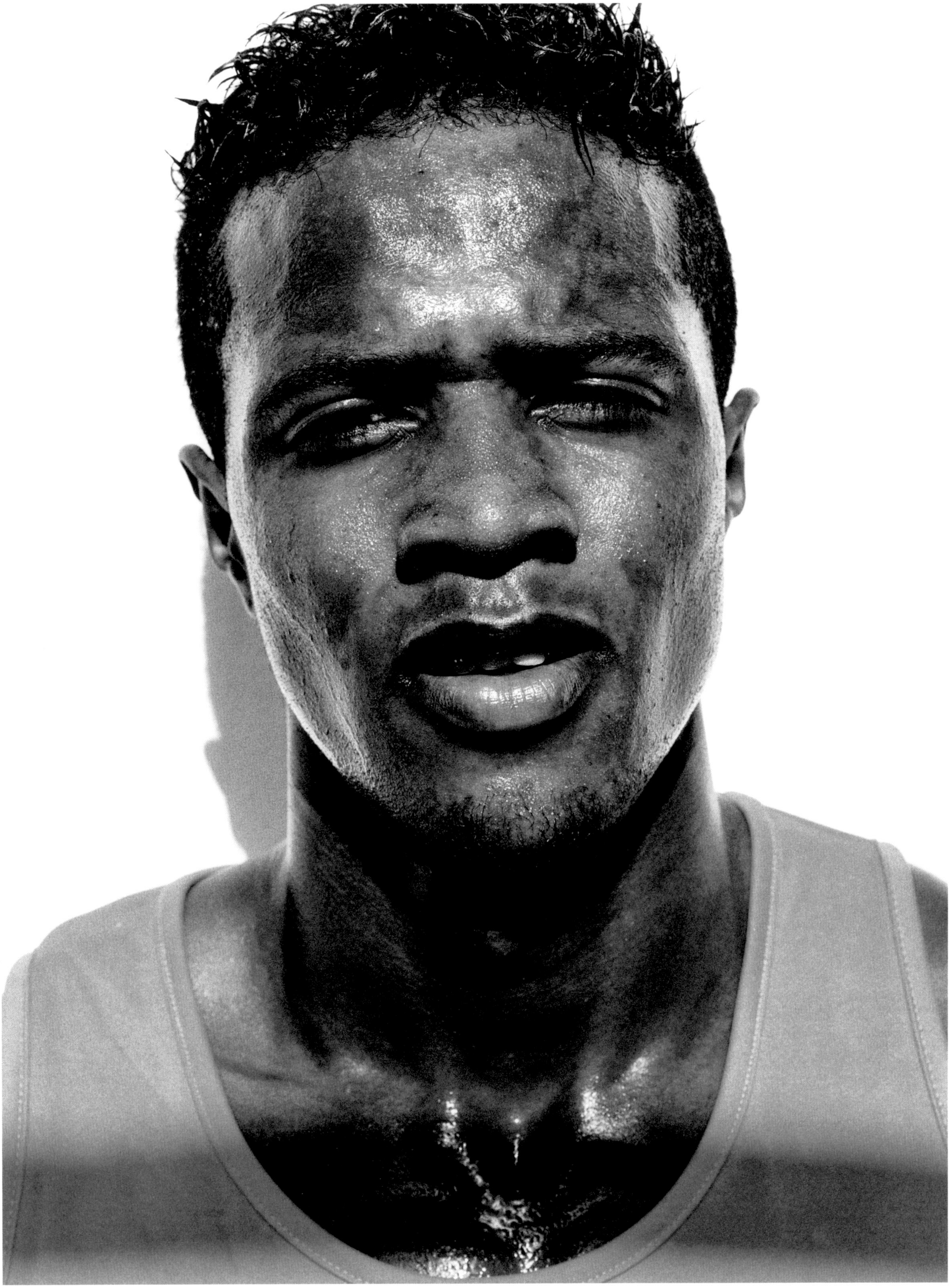

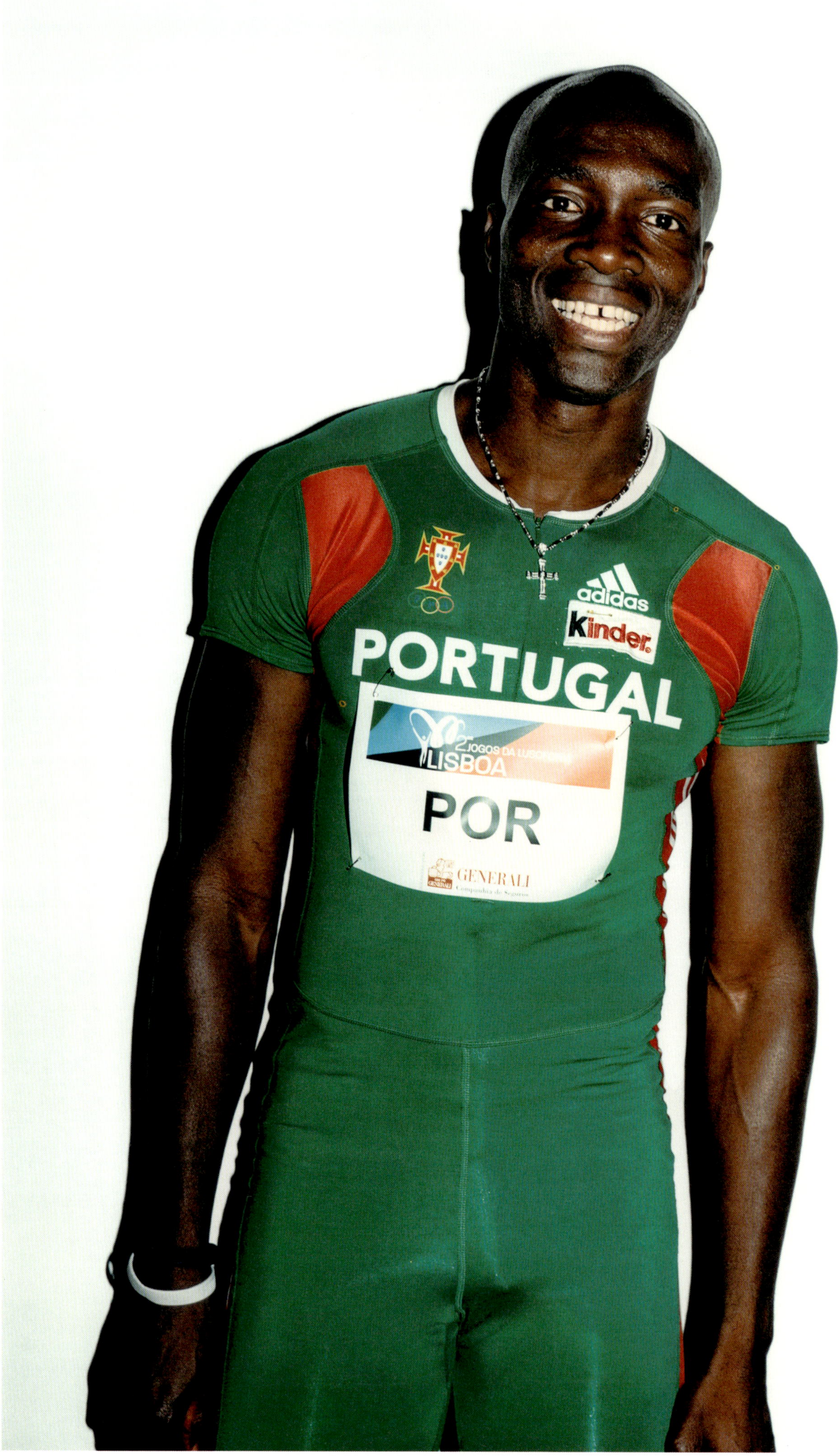
adidas
kinder
PORTUGAL
LISBOA
POR
GENERALI

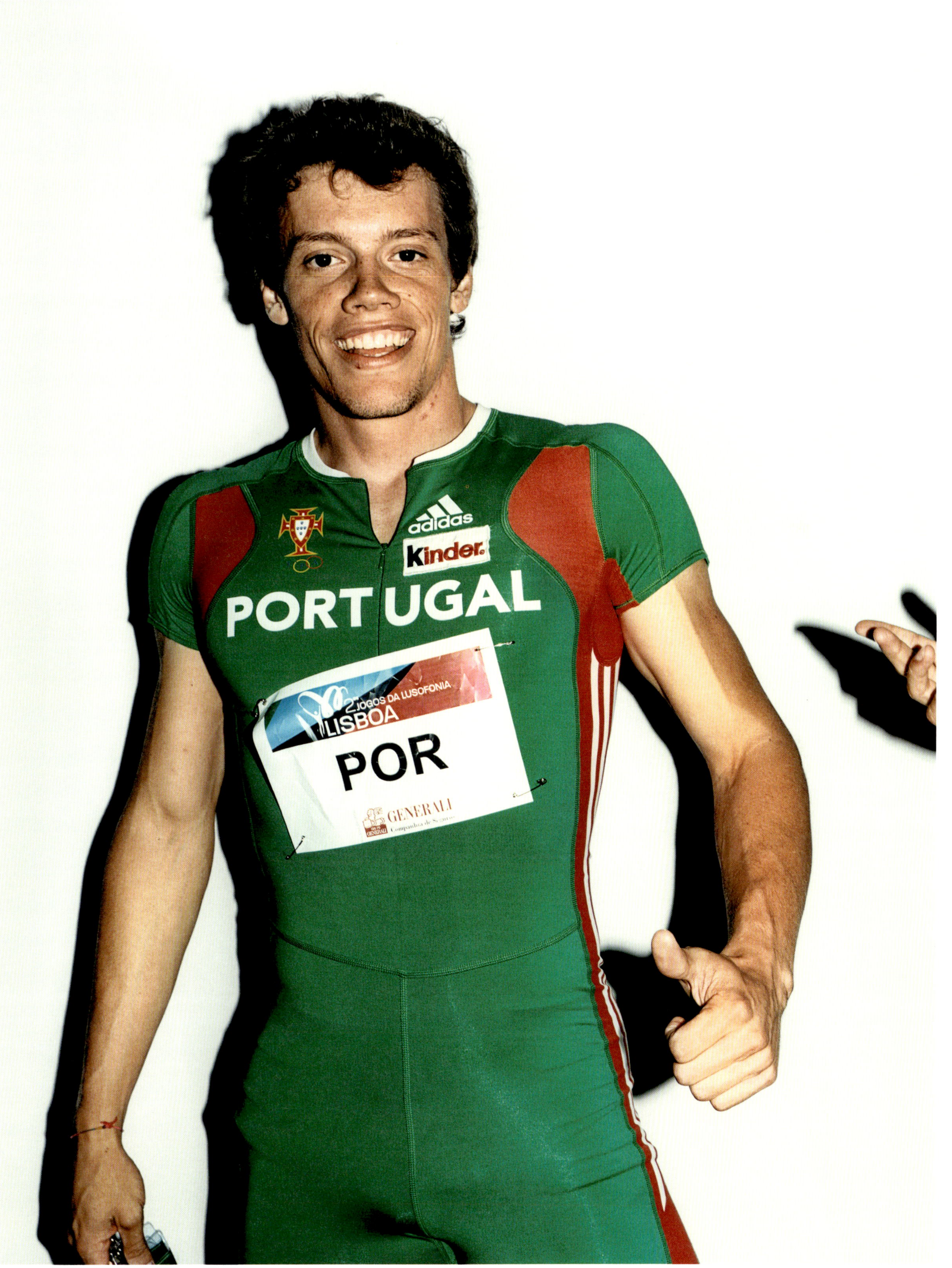
adidas
kinder
PORTUGAL
2 JOGOS DA LUSOFONIA
LISBOA
POR
GENERALI

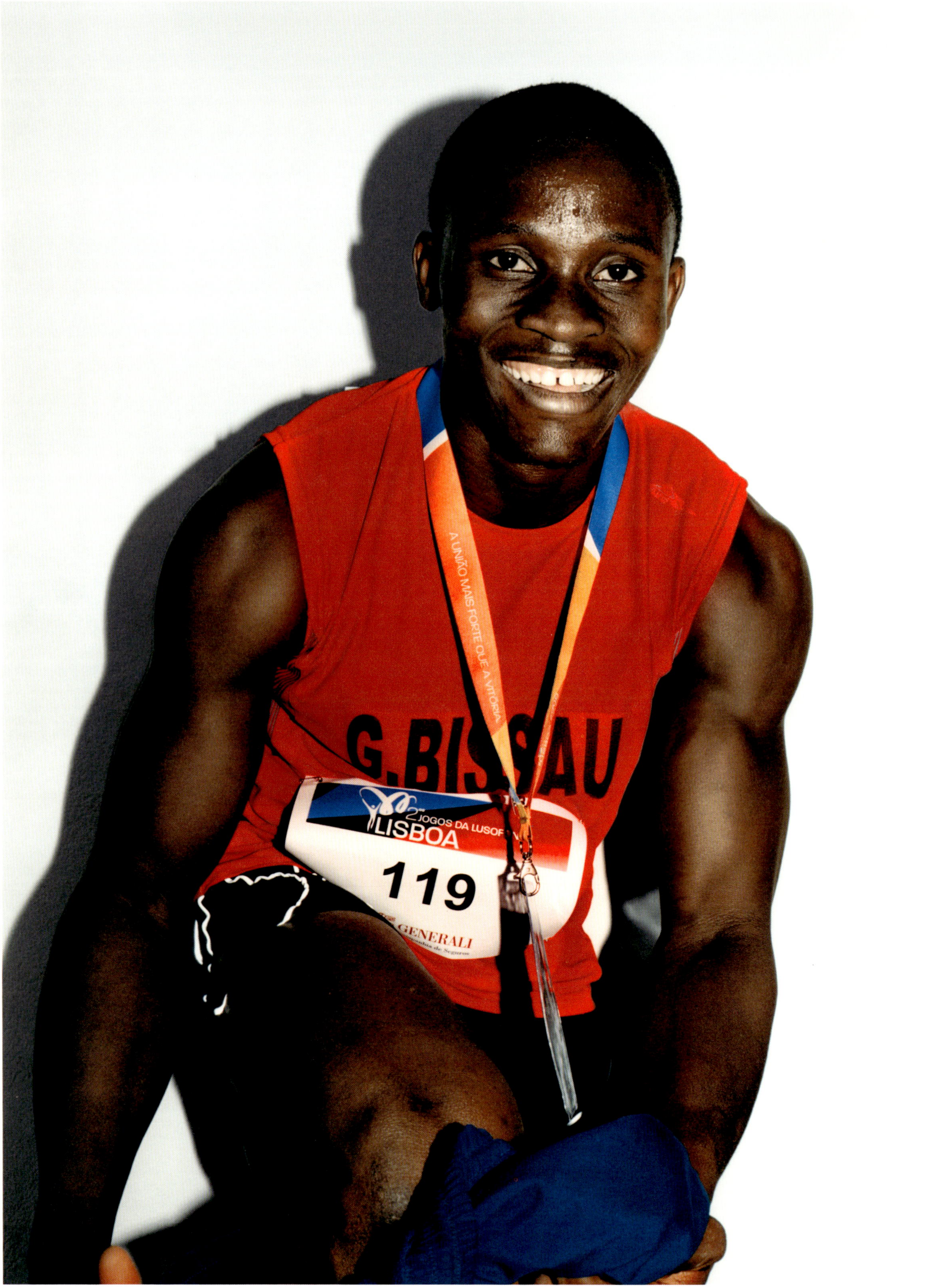
G.BISSAU
A UNIÃO MAIS FORTE QUE A VITÓRIA
LISBOA
119
GENERALI

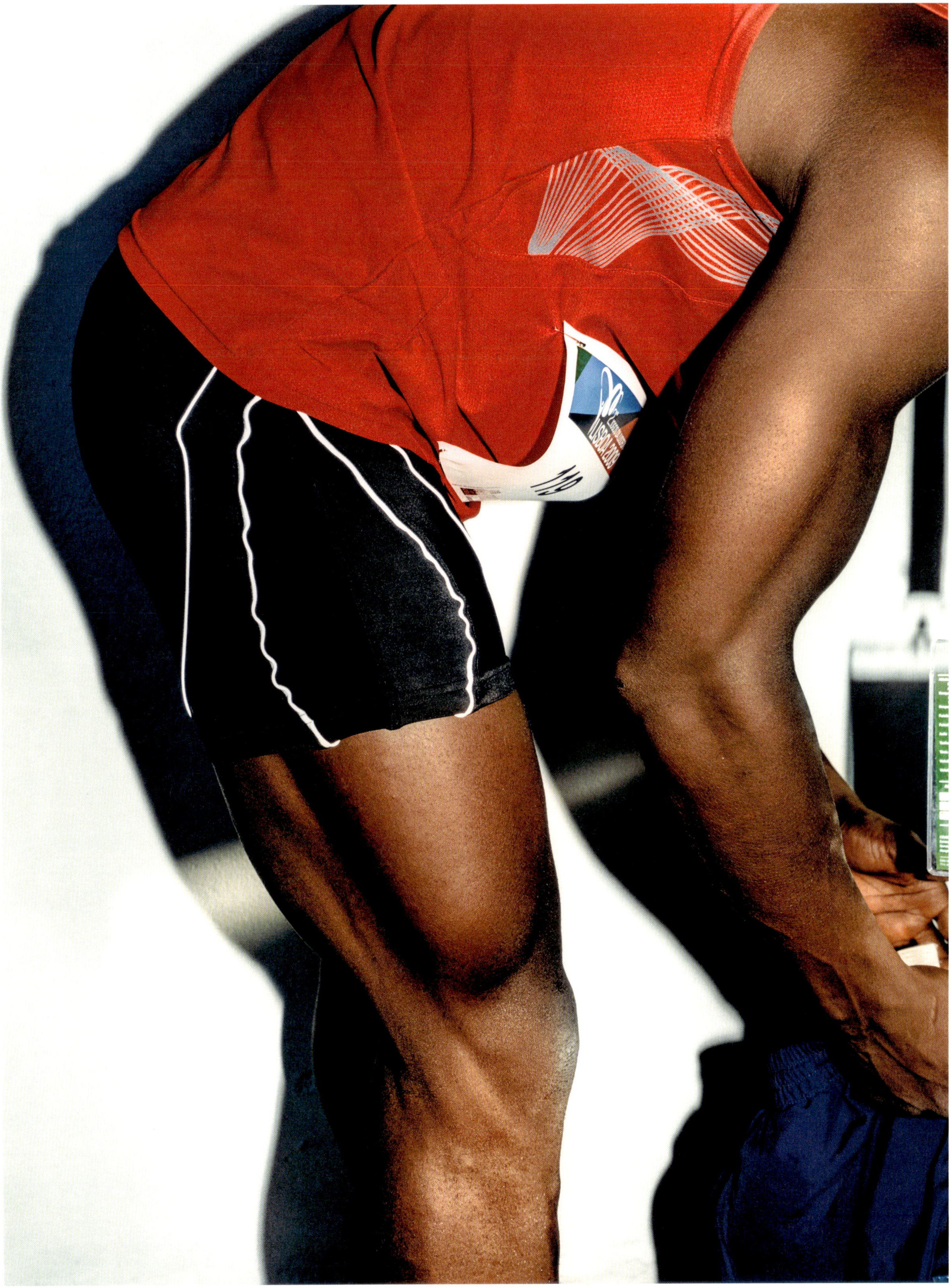
119

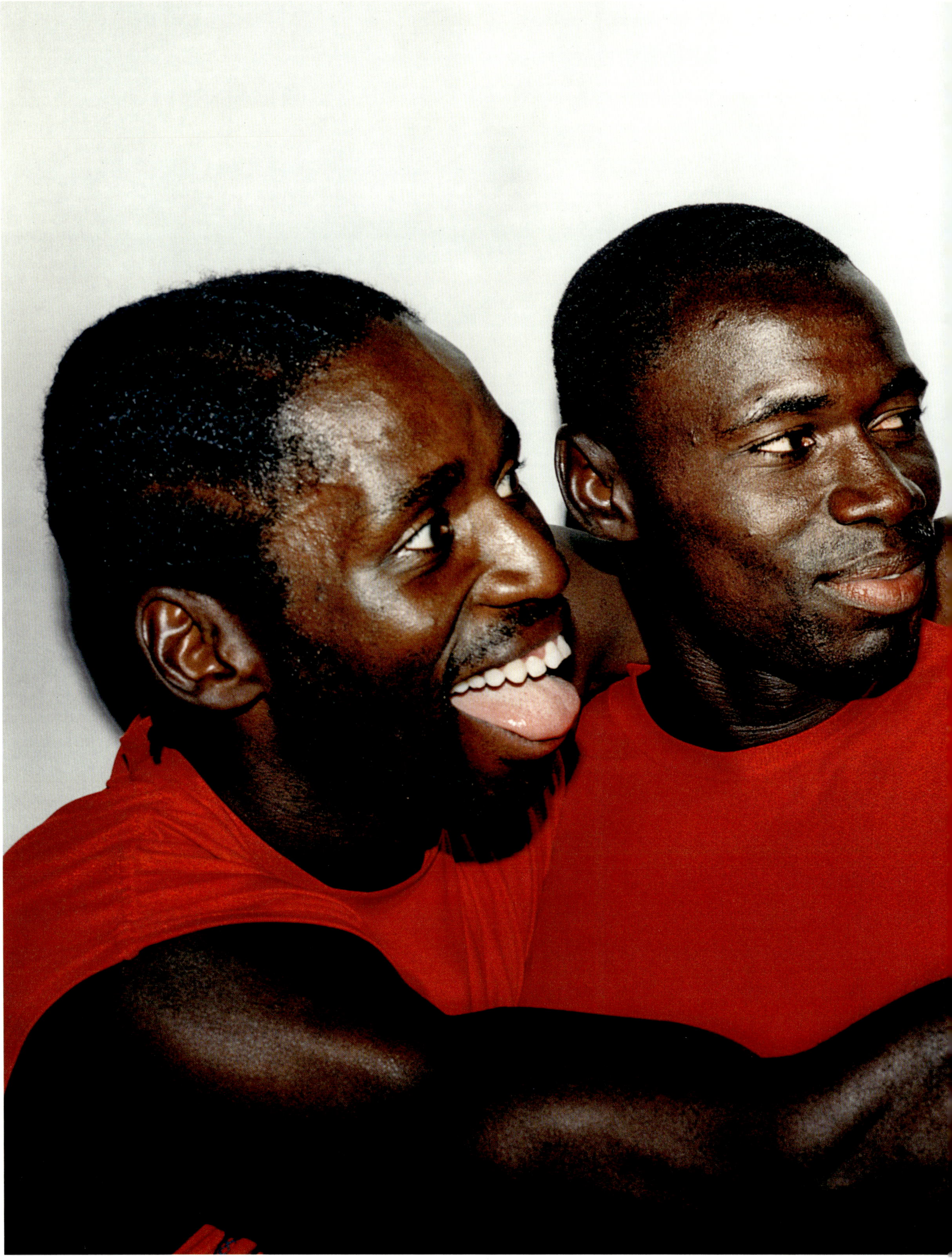

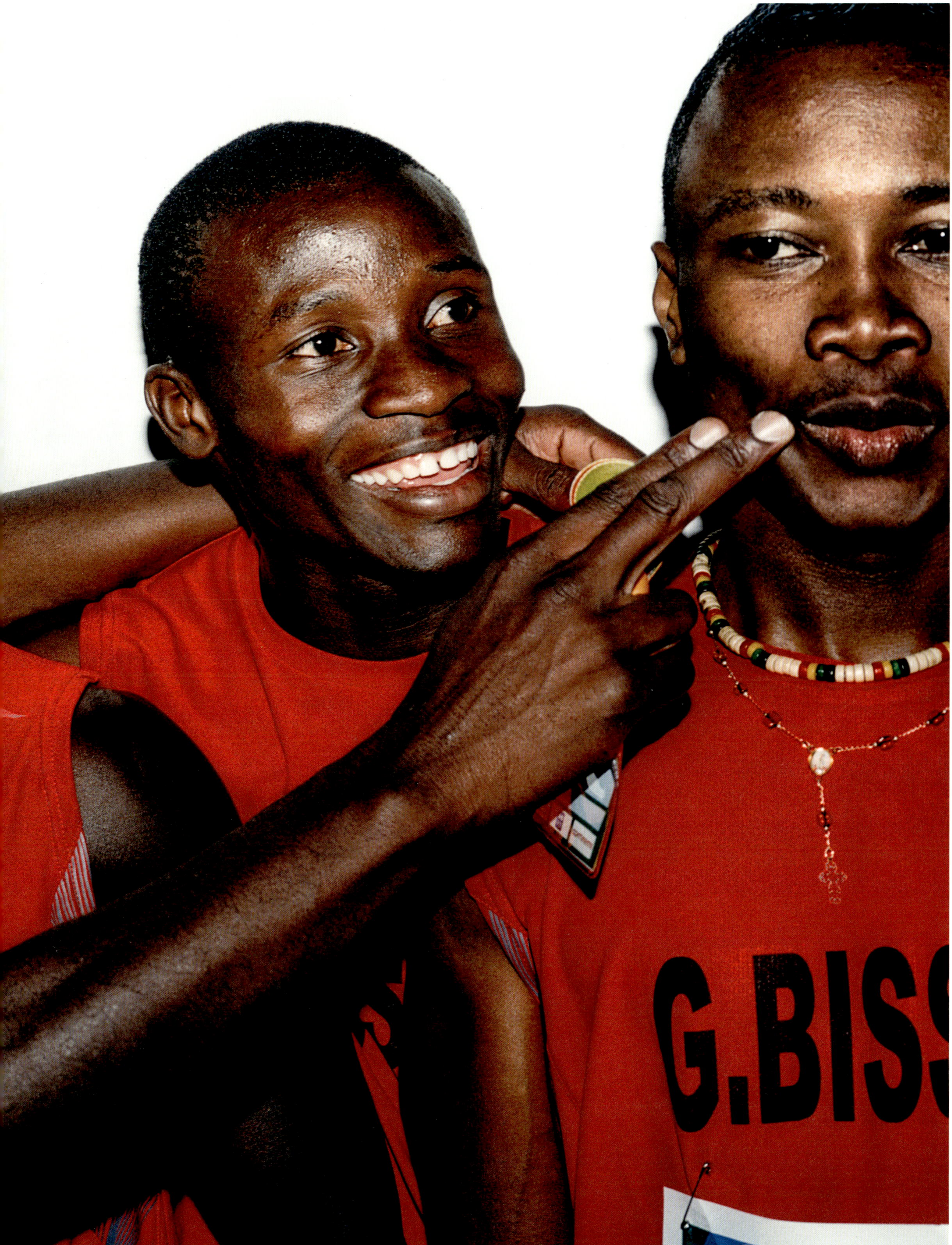
G.BISS

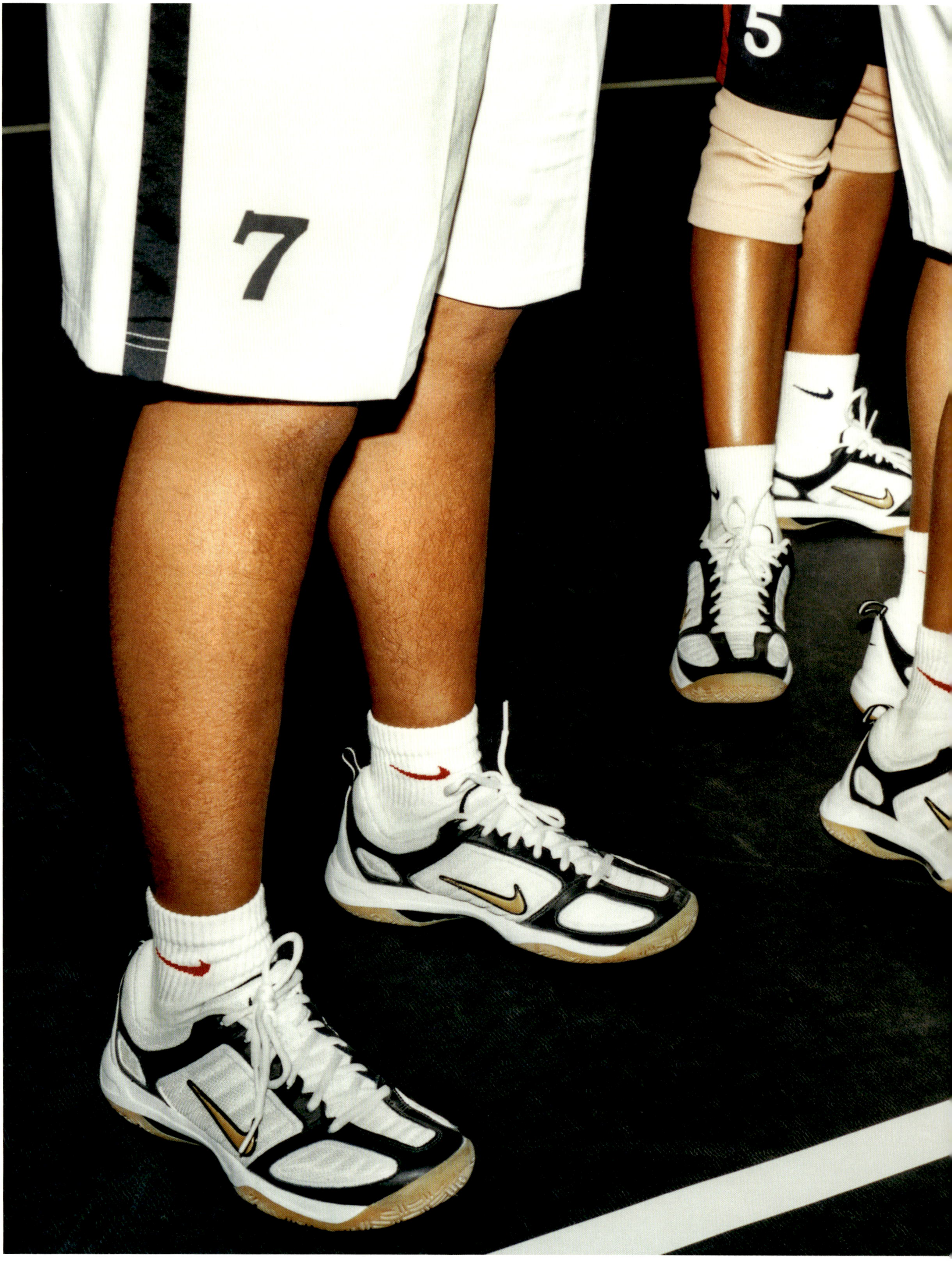
7
5

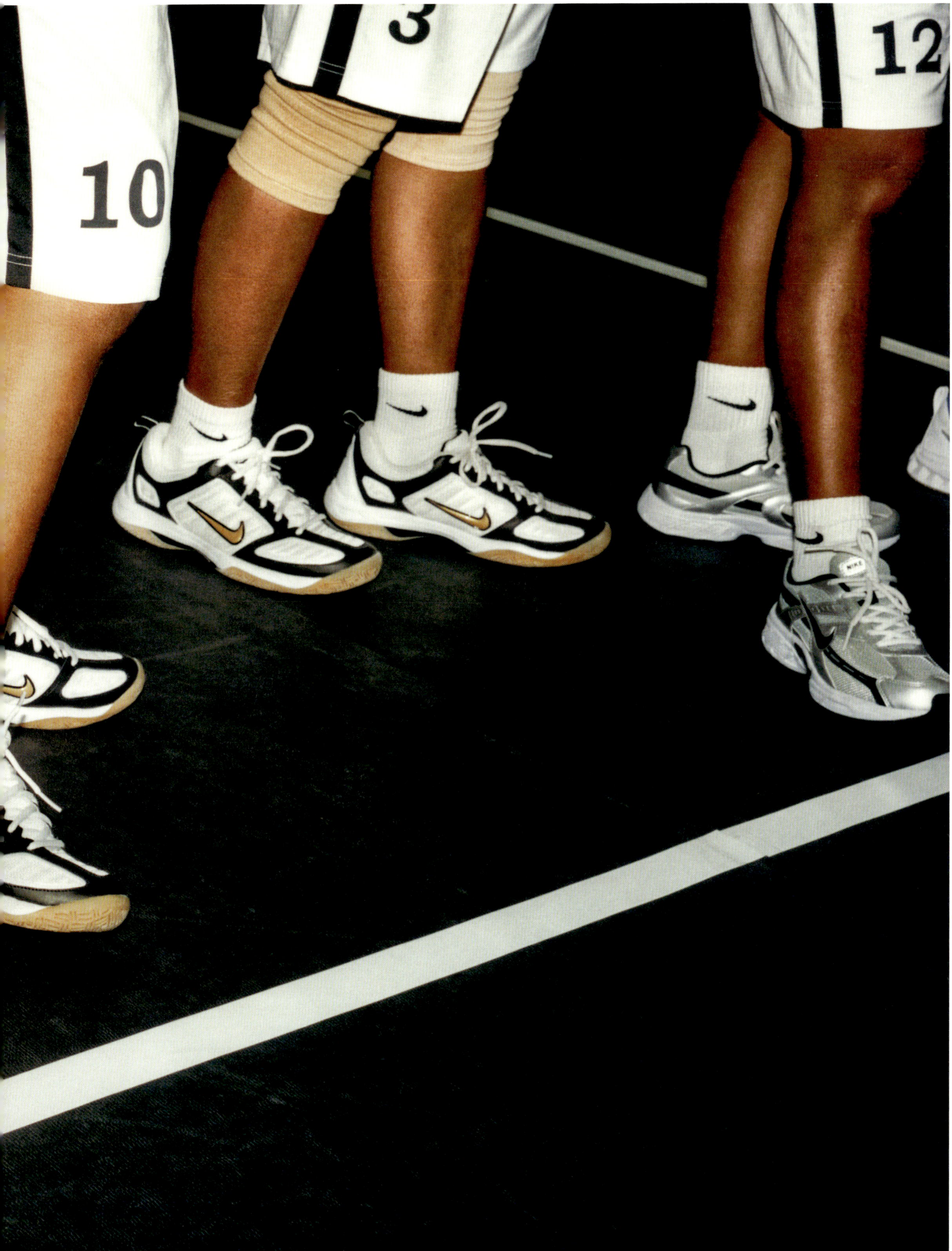
3
12
10

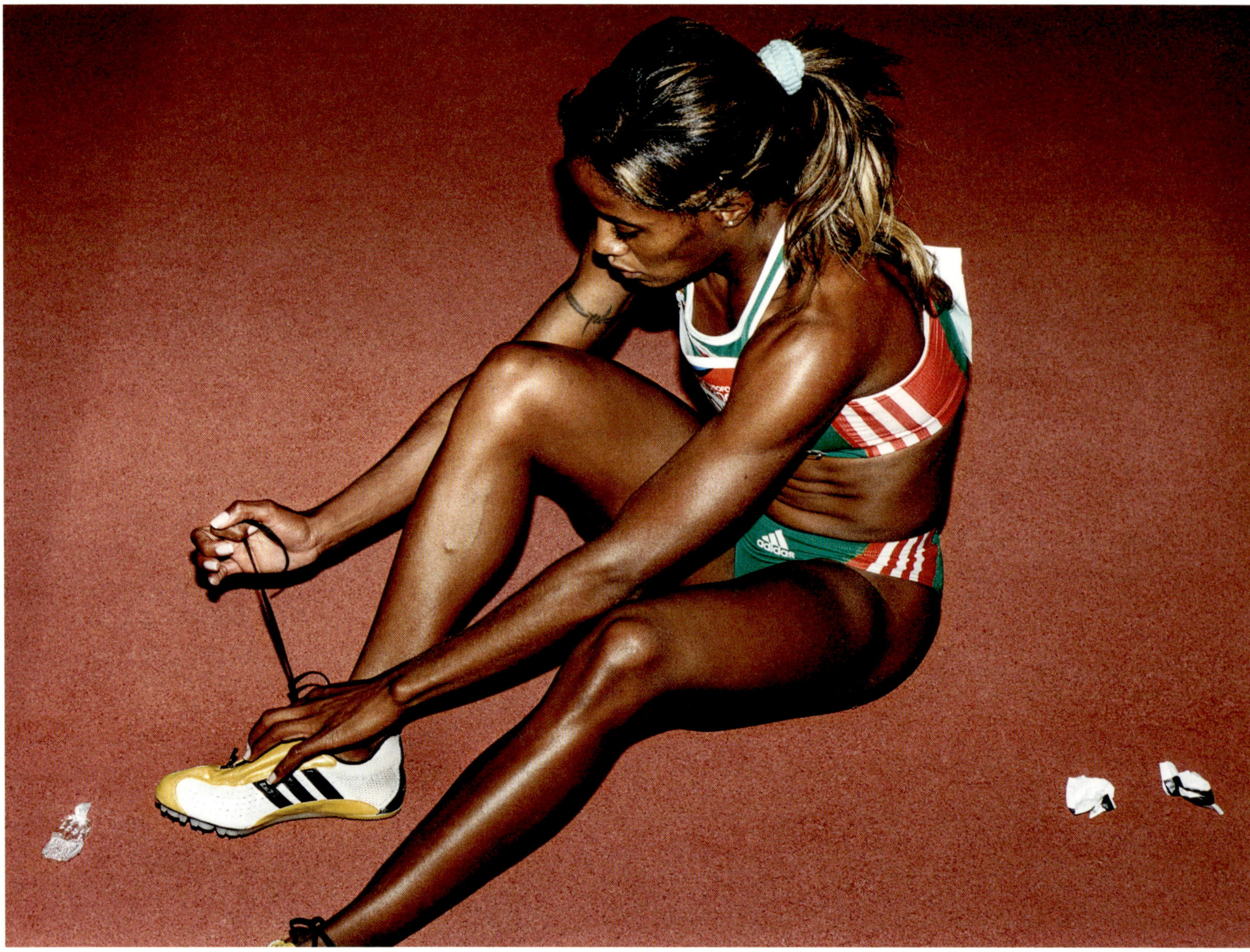
adidas

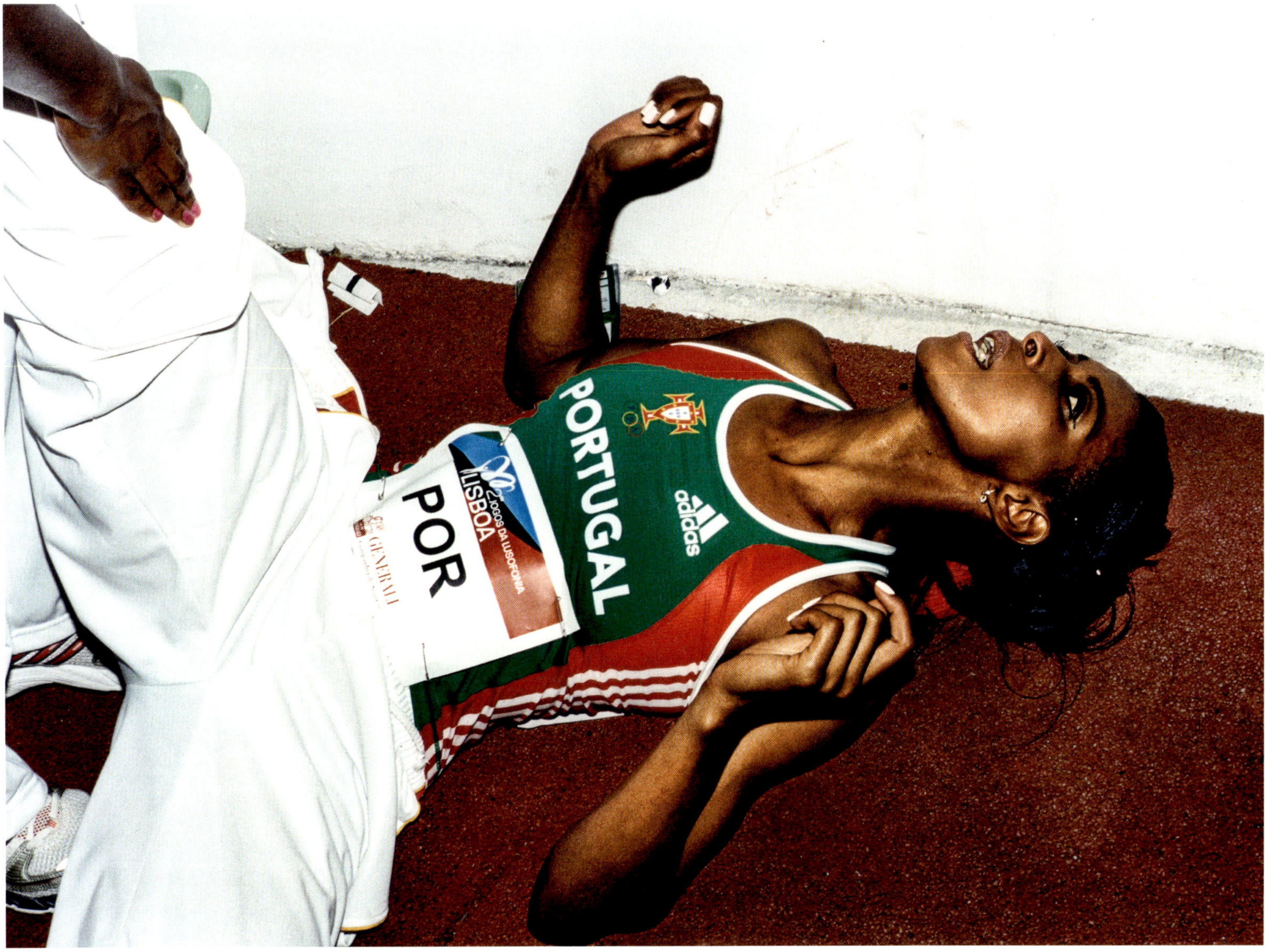
PORTUGAL
adidas
LISBOA
POR

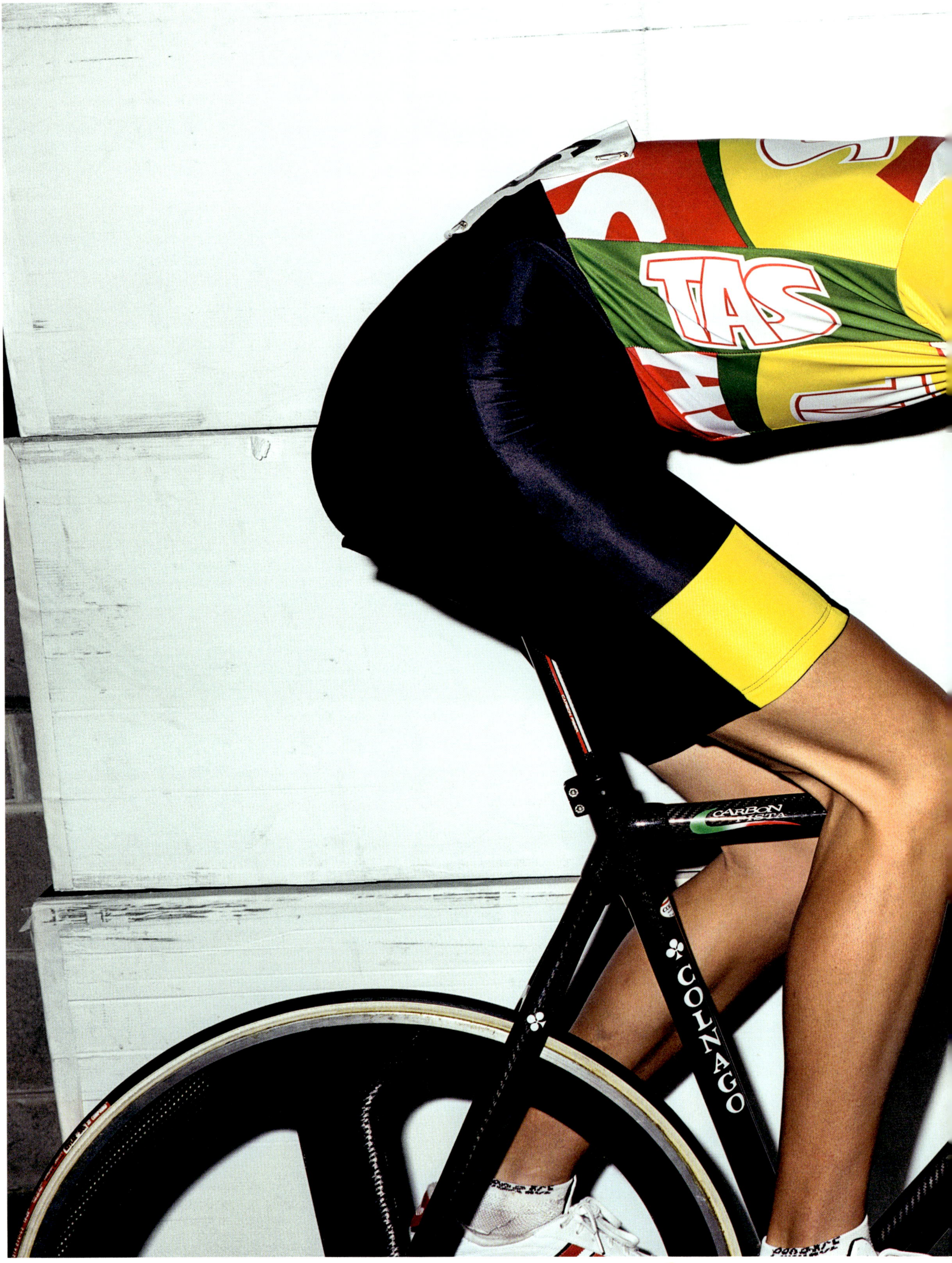
TAS
CARBON PISTA
COLNAGO

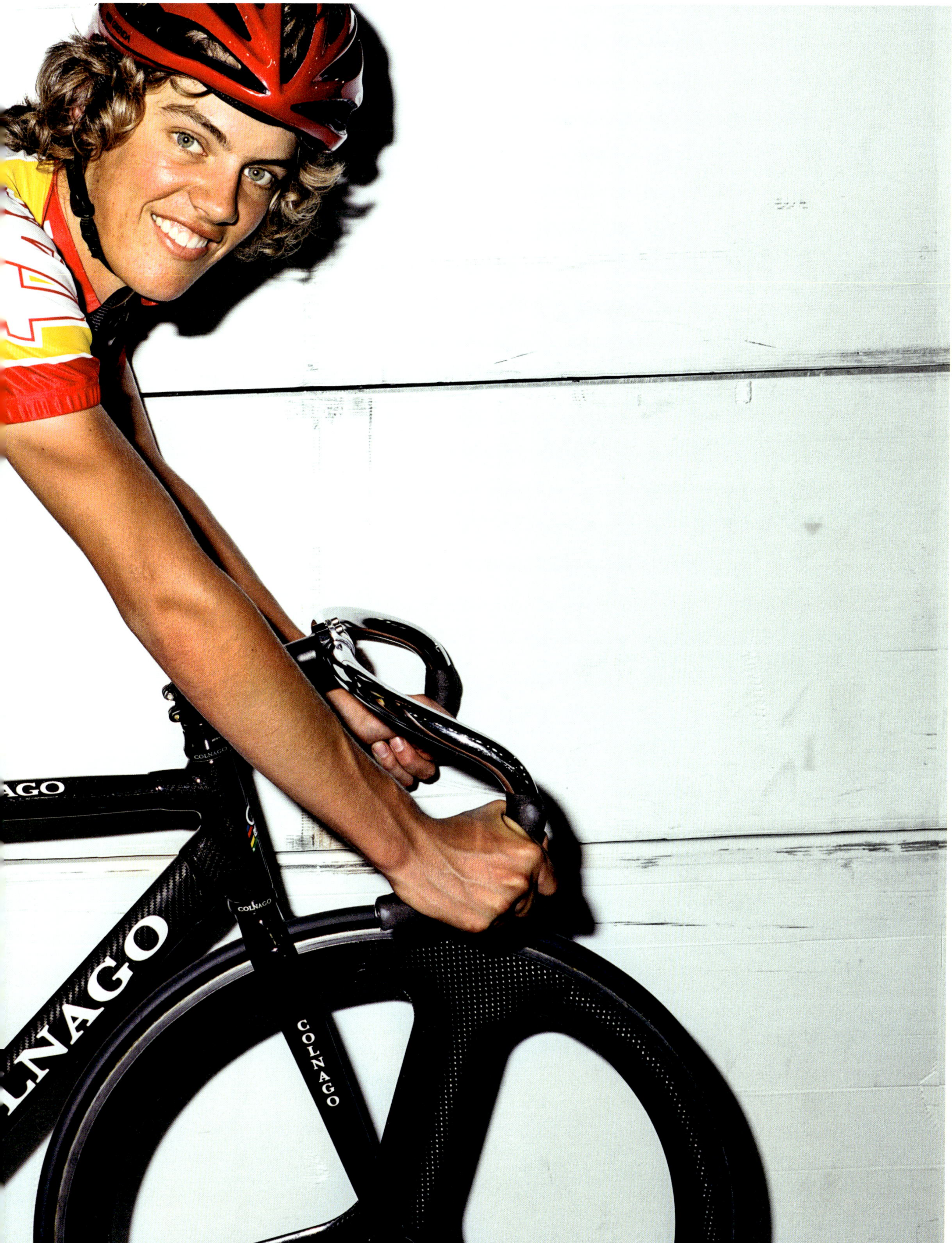
COLNAGO
COLNAGO

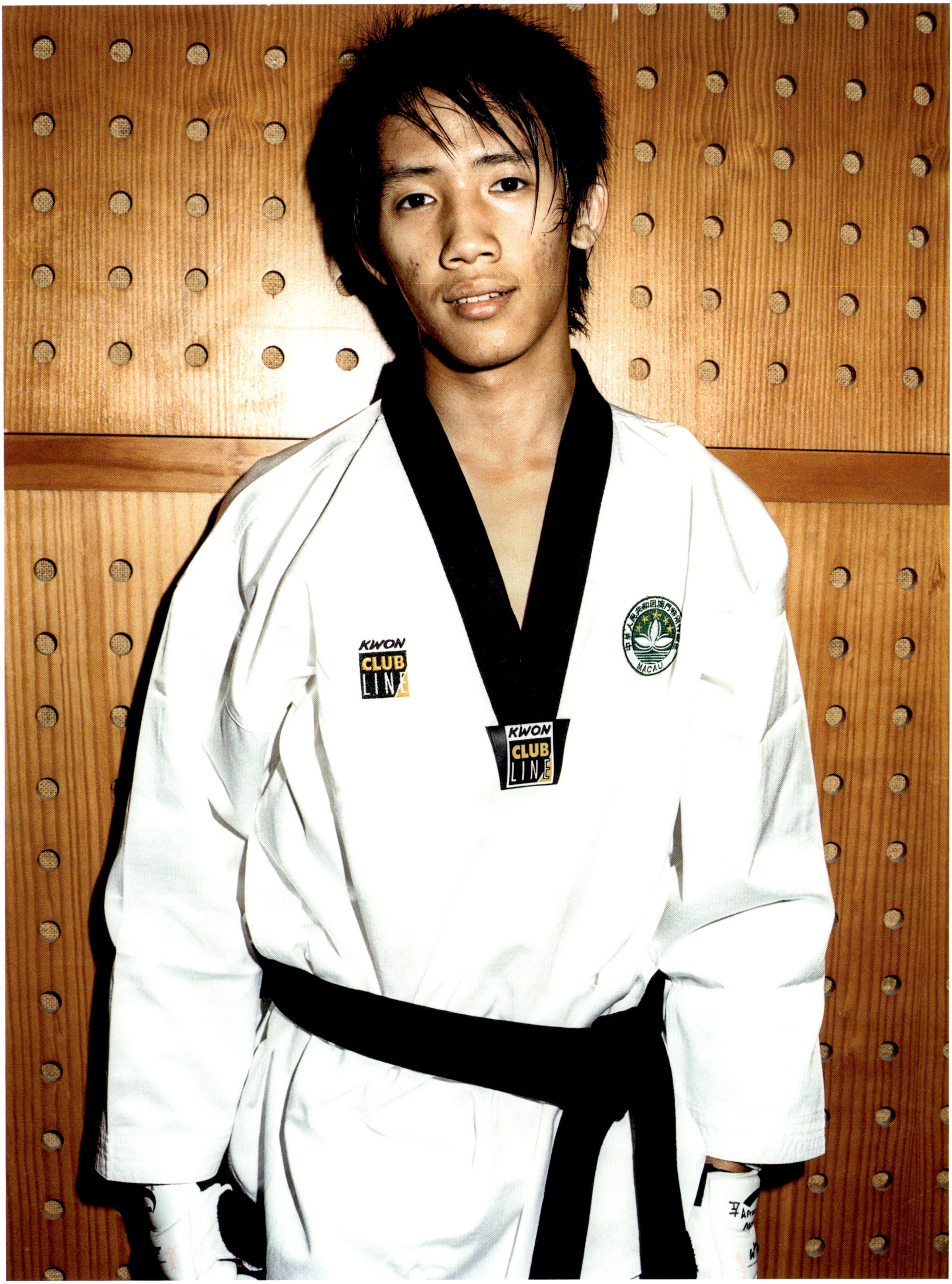
KWON
CLUB
LINE
KWON
CLUB
LINE
MACAU

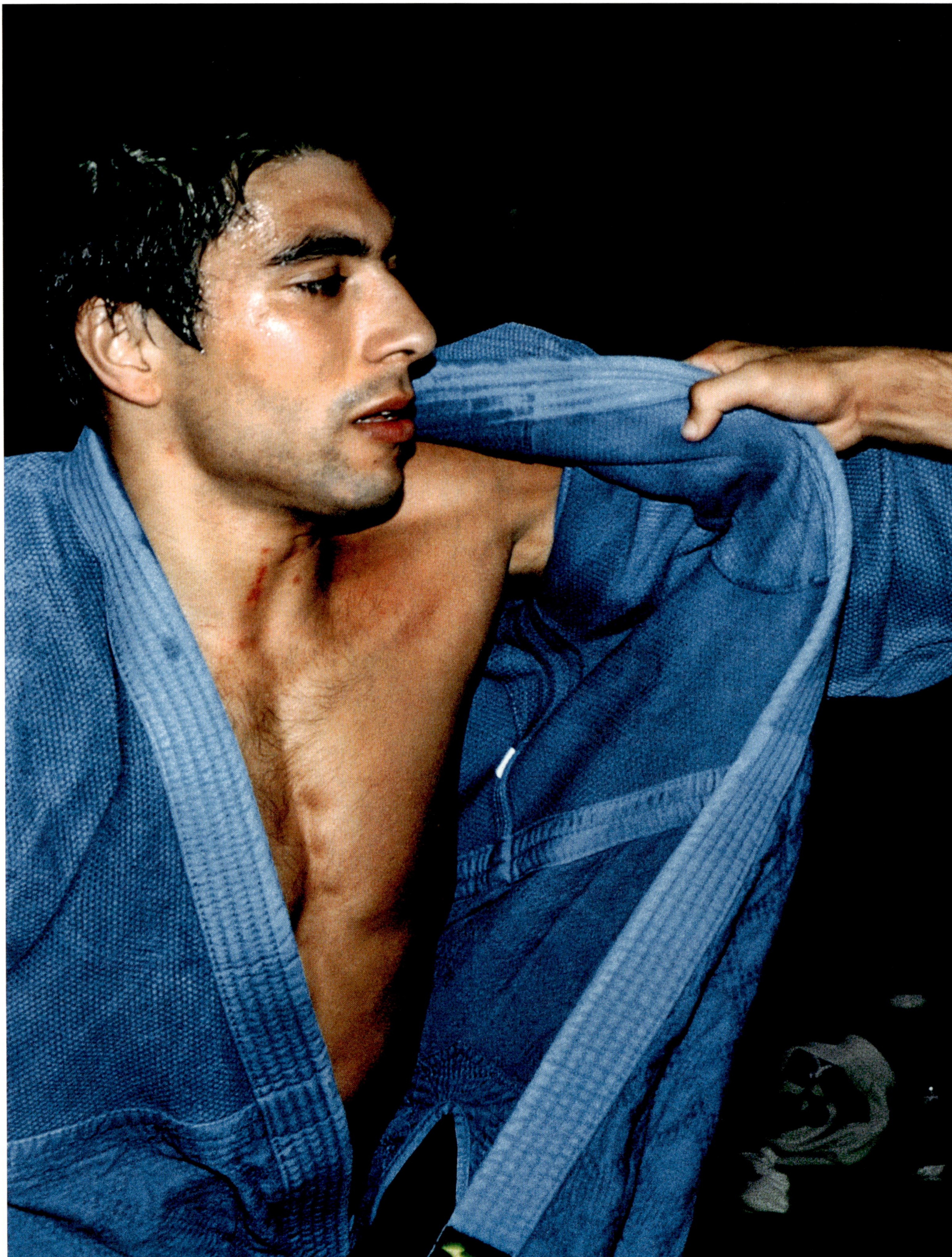

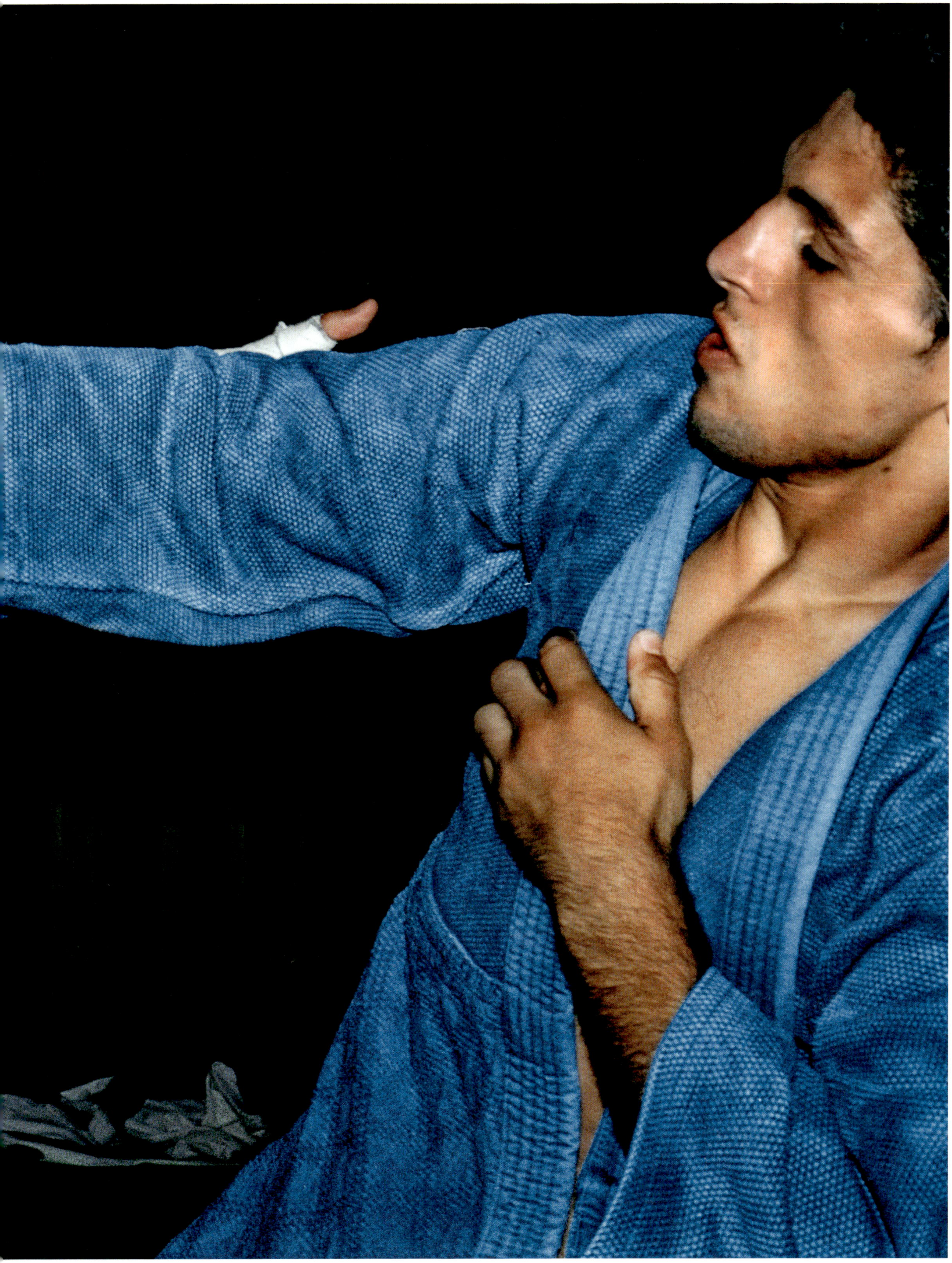

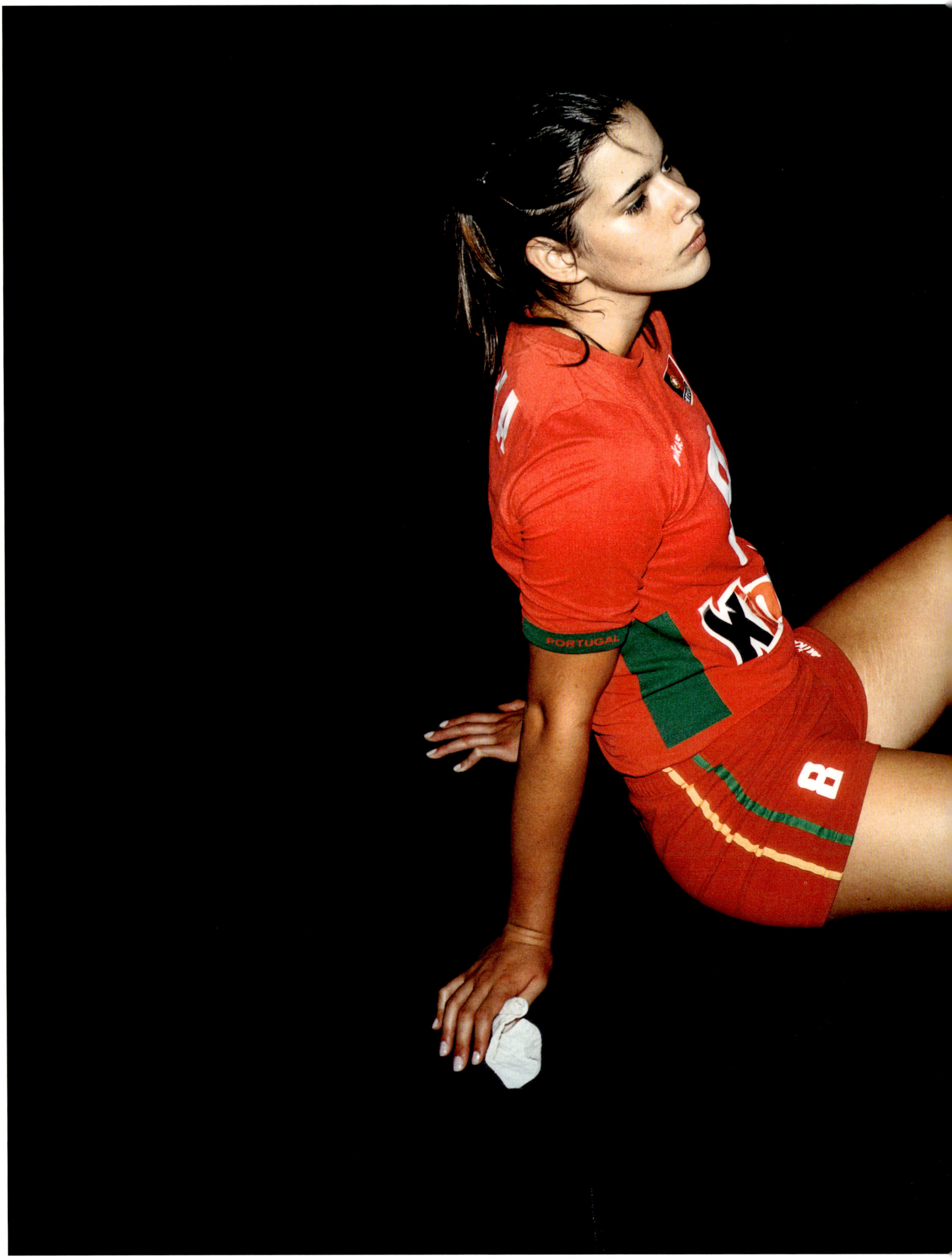
PORTUGAL
8

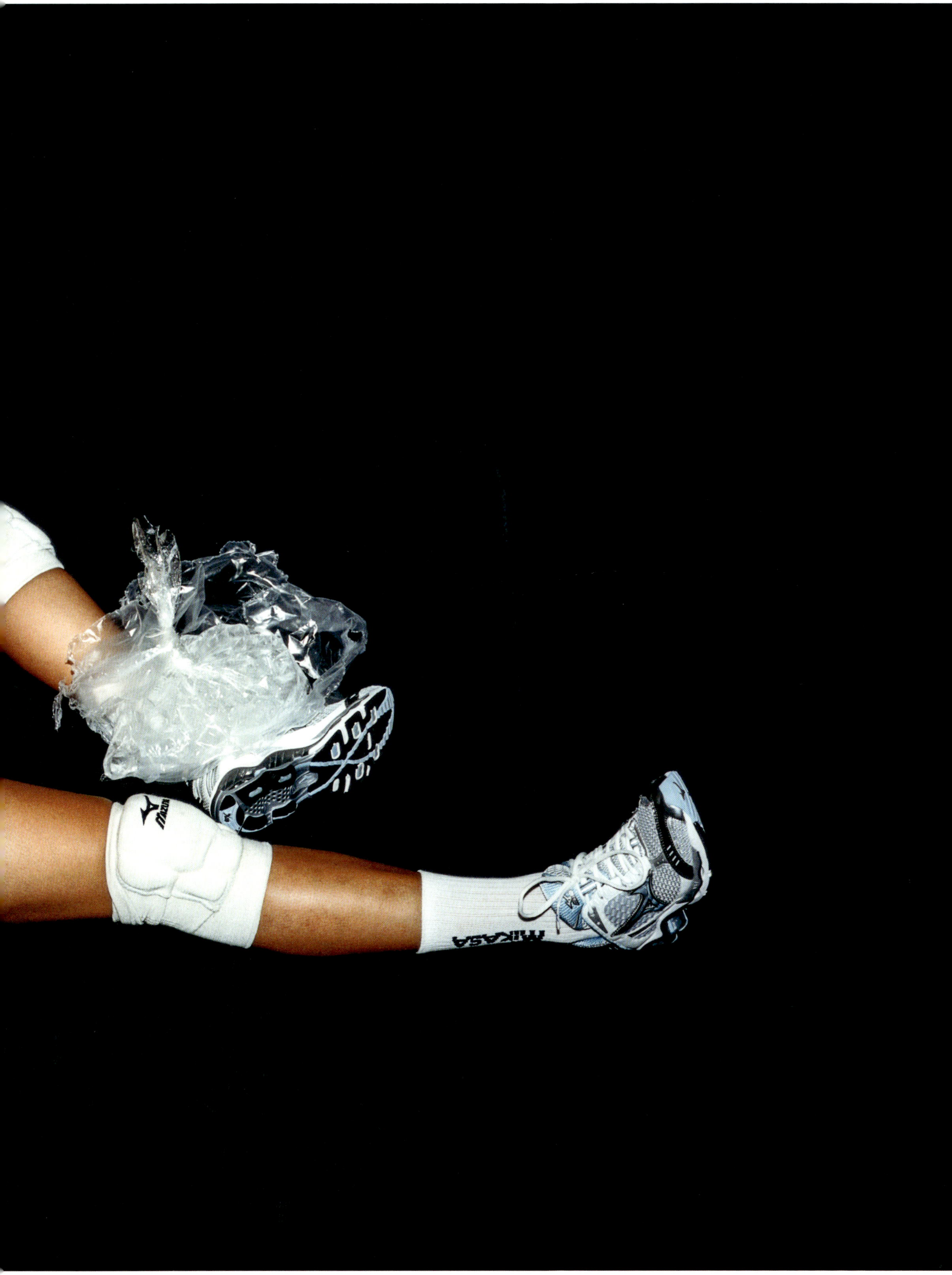
MIKASA

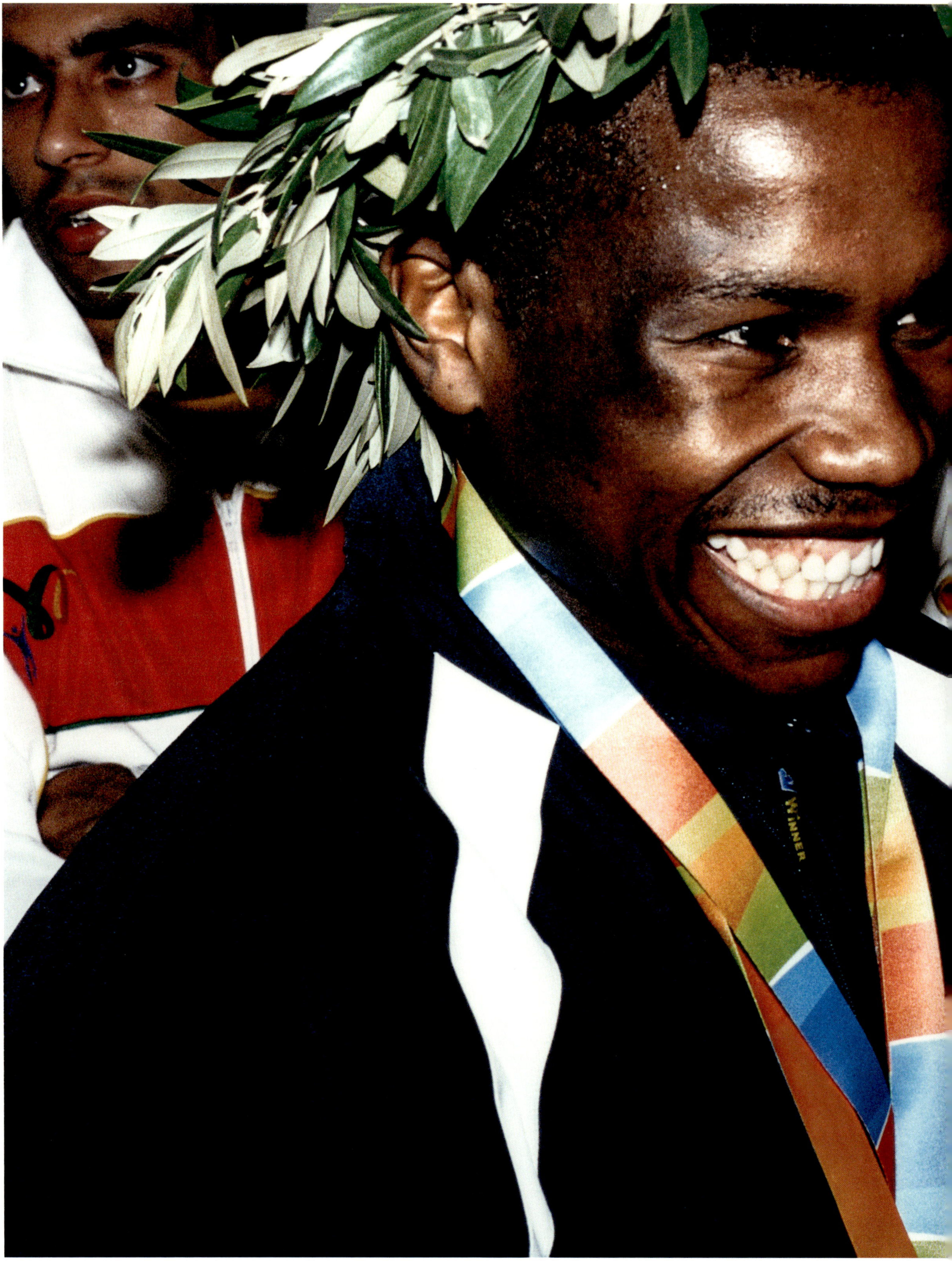
WINNER

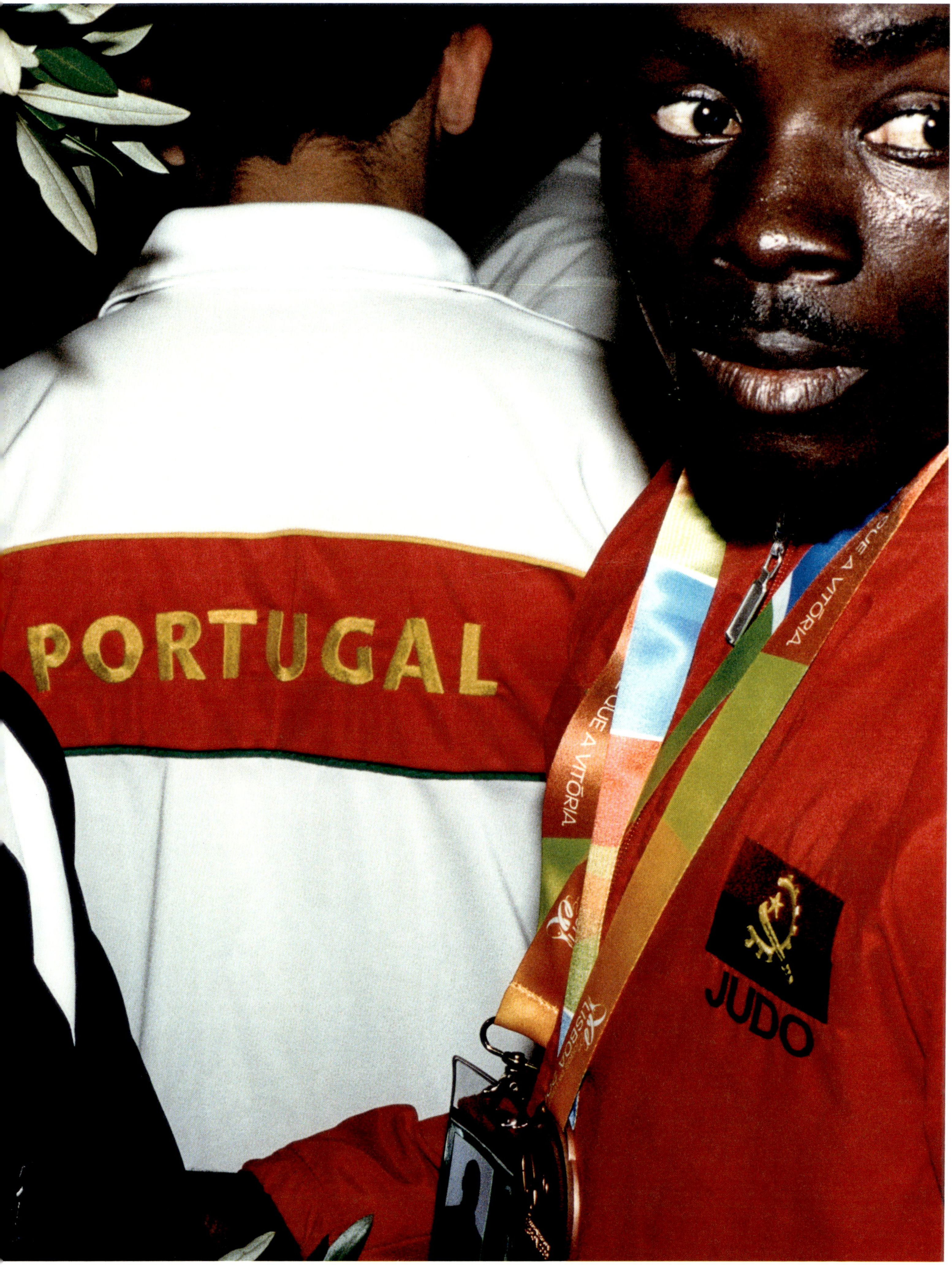
PORTUGAL
JUDO

Thank you
Margaret Balsom, Percy S. Waite, Mira Chai Hyde, Pete Guest, Bryan O'Leary, Paul Dimond, Faye Browning, Caleb Metcalfe, Andy Kyriacou, Chris Ashman, Ryan Moar, Russian Merchant Navy, crew of Paul R. Tregurtha, Pat Millin, Athletes of Lusophony Games, Tony White (RIP), Julian Broad, Stu Smith, Claudia Paladini, Glenn Wassall, Craig Shipman, Helena Whelan, Vanessa Darling, Olivier Jezequel, Katy Barker, Catherine O' Brien, Taren Cunningham

Architecture + Beauty
First published in 2021 by
GOST Books, London

info@gostbooks.com
gostbooks.com

Designed and edited by GOST:
Katie Clifford, Gemma Gerhard, Justine Hucker, Allon Kaye, Eleanor Macnair, Claudia Paladini, Ana Rocha

Printed in Italy by EBS

British Library cataloguing-in-publication data. A catalogue record of this book is available from the British Library.

ISBN 978-1-910401-67-5